Communities of Practice at the World Bank

Illustrated by the experience of the World Bank, this book explains how knowledge management, traditionally viewed as being about information systems and processes, can play a fundamental corporate role by creating a competitive edge for organizations, increasing team performance, and fostering effective, large-scale organizational change. Rich and powerful stories, told by economic development practitioners and knowledge management specialists throughout the World Bank, describe the strategies, instruments, tools, and processes at the core of one of the most important and radical reorganizations of the world's premier international development institution. Going far beyond other knowledge management titles, this book:

- shows how knowledge management can be a source of competitive advantage and team performance rather than a backroom support function;
- focuses on the role of the "software" of knowledge management, most notably the use of communities, culture, and collaboration across internal silos to create value; and
- demonstrates the role that knowledge management can play in fostering innovation and development of new business lines and strategies by global teams in diverse locations.

Written not only for knowledge management professionals but also for C-suite executives and middle managers who will see the benefits of bringing knowledge management to the core of organizational performance and competitive advantage, the book provides practical examples that can be replicated in other large global knowledge, financing, and development institutions and that will be relevant for public, private, and nonprofit organizations.

Dr. Ede Ijjasz-Vasquez is a nonresident senior fellow with the Brookings Institution and senior advisor to several financial international organizations. He retired from the World Bank in 2021, after 23 years, where he was part of the senior leadership team responsible for the sustainable development, infrastructure, and climate change portfolio. Knowledge management was the glue that delivered innovation to the 90 developing countries his team covered. Ede holds a PhD from the Massachusetts Institute of Technology, Boston, MA.

Philip Karp retired from the World Bank in 2020 after 26 years. During his career, he led the knowledge and learning agenda of one of the largest global technical practices as well as teams in the World Bank Institute, the East Asia region, and the Beijing office, where he spearheaded the World Bank's engagement with China on South-South cooperation. Phil holds a master's degree in public policy from the University of California, Berkeley.

Dr. Monika Weber-Fahr is an adjunct professor at the Hertie School of Governance (Berlin) and advises international organizations, multistakeholder partnerships, businesses, and governments on innovative approaches to cooperation and result orientation. Until 2020, Monika served as CEO and Executive Secretary of the Global Water Partnership (GWP). For over 20 years, she worked with the World Bank Group, including as Director for Knowledge, Learning, and Results for Sustainable Development.

Communities of Practice at the World Bank

Breaking Knowledge Silos to Catalyze Culture
Change and Organizational Transformation

Edited by Ede Ijjasz-Vasquez,
Philip Karp, and Monika Weber-Fahr

Routledge
Taylor & Francis Group

NEW YORK AND LONDON

Cover image: Getty

First published 2024
by Routledge
4 Park Square, Milton Park, Abingdon, Oxon OX14 4RN

and by Routledge
605 Third Avenue, New York, NY 10158

Routledge is an imprint of the Taylor & Francis Group, an informa business

British Library Cataloguing-in-Publication Data
A catalogue record for this book is available from the British Library

Library of Congress Cataloging-in-Publication Data
Names: Ijjasz-Vasquez, Ede, editor. | Weber-Fahr, Monika, editor. | Karp, Philip, editor.
Title: Communities of practice at the world bank : breaking knowledge silos to catalyze culture change and organizational transformation / edited by Ede Ijjasz-Vasquez, Monika Weber-Fahr and Philip Karp.
Description: Abingdon, Oxon ; New York, NY : Routledge, 2023.
Identifiers: LCCN 2023047574 (print) | LCCN 2023047575 (ebook) |
   ISBN 9781032057705 (hardback) | ISBN 9781032057637 (paperback) |
   ISBN 9781003199083 (ebook)
Subjects: LCSH: World Bank. | Knowledge management. | Organizational change.
Classification: LCC HG3881.5.W57 C65 2023 (print) | LCC HG3881.5.W57 (ebook) |
   DDC 332.1532—dc23/eng/20231024
LC record available at https://lccn.loc.gov/2023047574
LC ebook record available at https://lccn.loc.gov/2023047575

ISBN: 978-1-032-05770-5 (hbk)
ISBN: 978-1-032-05763-7 (pbk)
ISBN: 978-1-003-19908-3 (ebk)

DOI: 10.4324/9781003199083

Typeset in Sabon
by Apex CoVantage, LLC

This book is dedicated to the memory of James D. Wolfensohn whose "Knowledge Bank" vision launched the World Bank Group on the journey that is the impetus for this story.

Contents

About the Editors

Dr. Ede Ijjasz-Vasquez After 23 years with the World Bank, where he held senior leadership positions in sustainable development and infrastructure, Ede Ijjasz-Vasquez launched a boutique consulting company specialized in sustainability, climate adaptation, organizational change, and knowledge management. He is a nonresident senior fellow at the Brookings Institution. He recently completed coediting the book *State and Trends in Adaptation in Africa* and is working on the book *Disruptive Technologies for Sustainable Development*. During his career at the World Bank, he was responsible for a portfolio of about US$80 billion in investments and close to 800 policy and advisory reports in more than 90 countries in all developing regions of the world. At the World Bank, he was Senior Director for the Global Social, Urban, Rural, and Resilience Practice and Regional Director in Latin America, Africa, and China. Ede has been featured in several global media outlets such as CNN, *Wall Street Journal, Time, The Economist, LA Times*, and CNBC. He has been a lecturer at Tsinghua University (China) and Johns Hopkins University (US) on Sustainable Development courses.

Philip Karp retired from the World Bank in 2020 after a career in the organization spanning more than 26 years. During this time, he held a number of managerial and technical positions, mainly in the areas of knowledge and learning. From July 2014 until his retirement, he served as Lead Knowledge and Learning Specialist in the Social, Urban, Rural, and Resilience Global Practice, leading the practice's knowledge management team while also serving as Program Manager for the Tokyo Development Learning Center. Previously, he held positions in the World Bank Institute and the East Asia and Pacific Vice Presidency, including four years in the World Bank's Beijing Office, where he was responsible for leading the World Bank's engagement with China on South-South cooperation, particularly with Africa. Phil is currently engaged in research, capacity building, outreach, and advocacy work in the area of marine conservation. He holds a bachelor of arts degree in government from Clark University, Worcester, MA, and a master's in public policy degree from the University of California, Berkeley.

Dr. Monika Weber-Fahr is a development practitioner and thought leader who draws on nearly 30 years of experience with progressive leadership responsibilities in international development finance, stakeholder engagement, and management consulting. Until 2020, Monika served as CEO and Executive Secretary of the Global Water Partnership (GWP), following an assignment as COO at Sustainable Energy for All. For over 20 years, Monika worked at the World Bank Group, including as Chief Knowledge Officer for the Independent Evaluation Group and as Director for Knowledge, Learning, and Results for Sustainable Development. For the International Finance Corporation (IFC), Monika built and led the Global Business Line for Sustainable Business Advisory. In Europe, Monika worked with the Boston Consulting Group (BCG), mainly on supporting energy-sector clients. Today, Monika teaches at the Hertie School of Governance (Berlin, Germany) and advises international organizations, multistakeholder platforms, businesses, and government agencies on innovative approaches to cooperation, lateral thinking, and result orientation. She serves as a board member with the Austrian Development Bank (OeEB) and the Deltares International Advisory Board, and she is a member of the Online Educa Berlin (OEB) Global Council. She holds a PhD in business economics, a MSc in economics, and diplomas in international relations and corporate governance. Monika lives in Vienna, Austria, with her family.

Contributors

Ivan Butina is a knowledge management professional and community builder. He started building communities in high school and has never stopped since then. He brought his community-building skills to the World Bank Group, where he worked for five years on community management, communities of practice (CoP), and knowledge management. During this time, he first led a team that served the organization's 200+ communities of practice and then established the community management team that supported the 30+ CoPs in the Global Social, Urban, Rural, and Resilience Practice. Currently, Ivan is knowledge management manager with UNICEF, where he has been leading the development and implementation of the organization's first global knowledge management strategy. Besides knowledge management and communities, Ivan is passionate about leadership development. He ensured the creation of a leadership development program for UNICEF's young personnel, which he coordinates. Ivan holds a master of arts in international relations from Johns Hopkins University's School of Advanced International Studies (SAIS), Baltimore, MD.

Dean Cira is currently the Global Lead for Urban Poverty, Urban Inclusion, and Housing within the Urban, Disaster Risk, Resilience, and Land Global Practice at the World Bank. Dean has worked in over 30 countries including in Latin America, Asia, Africa, and Europe throughout his professional career. His work includes managing large and complex lending operations throughout the world, including in post-disaster contexts and in countries experiencing conflict as well as low- and middle-income countries. He has led and authored several analytical works for the World Bank focused on urban policy and urbanization and has led large Reimbursable Advisory Services engagements. Dean holds degrees in international relations and in public policy from the University of Wisconsin, Madison, WI. Prior to joining the World Bank group, Dean worked in the private and nonprofit sectors structuring complex public-private partnerships in affordable housing.

Daniel de la Morena leads the International Finance Corporation (IFC) Global Knowledge and Learning Office (GKLO), a position he has held since 2020. Earlier responsibilities included leading IFC's Operational Content and Lessons Program, establishing IFC's Asia Pacific knowledge management program—based in Vietnam—and designing and deploying IFC's social collaboration program. Daniel joined IFC in 2008 after working in knowledge management for the World Bank for five years. Daniel holds a master of science in foreign service degree from Georgetown University, Washington, DC, and a double-bachelor's degree in business administration from Spain and Germany. He has worked in the private and public sector and in countries including Vietnam, Spain, Germany, Morocco, and the United States.

Alvaro Garcia Barba is a knowledge management officer in the Global Knowledge and Learning Office at the International Finance Corporation (IFC). Alvaro has a solid professional track in designing, implementing, evaluating, and managing knowledge management and learning programs in multilateral and private organizations. Before IFC, Alvaro served at the International Monetary Fund as a projects officer, working to design knowledge transfer and learning programs for the IMF's beneficiaries and participating in high-level strategic learning interdepartmental groups. Previously, he served as the Capacity Building on Integration and Trade Program Manager at the Inter-American Development Bank. In addition to a MA in educational technology leadership from The George Washington University, Washington, DC, Alvaro holds an MSc in organizational psychology and human resources from the Universidad Autonoma de Madrid (Spain) and a MA in gamification and storytelling from the Escuela de Negocios de la Innovación y los Emprendedores (IEBS, Spain).

Francis Ghesquiere is a Practice manager at the World Bank, where he is in charge of a US$5 billion portfolio focused on urban development, risk and resilience, and land management in East Asia and the Pacific. He also coordinates the World Bank Climate Change Support team in that region. From 2012 to 2018, Francis was the Head of the Global Facility for Disaster Reduction and Recovery (GFDRR), which, under his leadership, was instrumental in rapidly expanding the resilience agenda at the World Bank. He is recognized for his leadership on several flagship initiatives, including the establishment of the Caribbean Catastrophe Risk Insurance Facility (CCRIF), the Central America Probabilistic Risk Assessment platform (CAPRA), the Understanding Risk Forum (UR), and the Averted Disaster Award (ADA). He was also key in the design of new policy instruments to help accelerate World Bank response to disasters, including the policy on emergency operations and innovative contingent financing instruments such as the Catastrophe Drawdown Option (CAT-DDO) and Contingent Emergency Response Components (CERC). He holds degrees from the Harvard School of Government, Cambridge, MA, and the University of Louvain, Belgium.

Niels Holm-Nielsen, is a Practice manager for a global technical assistance unit at the World Bank and Head of the Secretariat for the Global Facility for Disaster Reduction and Recovery. He has over 20 years of experience in international development finance from the Inter-American Development Bank and the World Bank. He has held various technical and operational positions at the World Bank covering disaster and climate risk management (DRM) work in the Middle East and North Africa, Africa, and Latin America and Caribbean regions. For the past five years, he has also been the World Bank's Global Technical Lead for Resilience and DRM, a role which focuses on supporting task teams and managers across the World Bank to achieve the highest possible technical quality of the services the World Bank offers its clients related to DRM. He holds a M.Sc. in political science from the University of Aarhus, Denmark.

Sheila Jagannathan is a lifelong learner and Head of the Open Learning Campus at the World Bank in Washington, DC. She serves as the organization's focal point on digital learning and issues at the intersection of technology use and education in emerging countries. She is a forward-thinking senior education leader with over 35 years of experience in leading capacity building, knowledge management, data, social learning, and transformation change across public and private organizations. She has been responsible for designing and implementing world-class solutions in challenging global environments, resulting in performance and productivity improvements. Sheila also provides policy advice and technical assistance to World Bank country-level capacity building programs (both government and training institutes seeking to introduce technologies in their educational systems) in East Asia, China, the Middle East and North Africa, Africa, and South Asia. She has written articles for various peer-reviewed publications and journals in technology-based learning. Her recent book *Reimagining Digital Learning for Sustainable Development: How Upskilling, Data Analytics, and Educational Technologies Close the Skills Gap* by Routledge, New York (2021) is gaining traction as a landmark in the field of digital capability building and sustainable development. She is on the advisory board and planning committees of major professional associations of learning such as the Canadian Foreign Service Institute; Global Distance Learning Network; George Mason University; E-learning Africa, an annual international conference for developing e-learning capacities in Africa; International Conference on E-learning (ICEL); and Skills Development Councils.

Steffen Soulejman Janus is a seasoned organizational change facilitator with over 20 years' experience working with private, public-sector, and academic organizations and teams around the world to help them define and achieve their goals. He has deep expertise in organizational learning, change management, knowledge management, communications, innovation, and leadership. Steffen currently works as a team leader for knowledge management and learning in the World Bank's Social Sustainability and Inclusion Global Practice on knowledge initiatives with World Bank clients and teams. Previously, he worked in different functions in the World Bank, leading teams on learning design and e-learning, knowledge management, South-South Knowledge Exchange, and organizational knowledge sharing (OKS). At the World Bank Institute, he co-developed the African Platform for Development Effectiveness (APDev) and the Global Partnership on Knowledge Sharing (GPKS). His publications on organizational change, knowledge sharing, and learning are used as reference materials by numerous organizations in the public and private sectors, the latest being "Capturing Solutions for Learning and Scaling Up." Steffen holds a bachelor of arts degree from Art Center College of Design, Pasadena, CA, and an MBA from Columbia University, New York, NY.

Jon Kher Kaw is a senior urban development specialist with the World Bank's Urban, Disaster Risk, Resilience and Land Global Practice. Since 2013, he has led numerous city engagements, investment operations, and advisory and analytical work in the South Asia, Middle East, and North Africa regions. Prior to joining the World Bank, he held various key positions at the Urban Redevelopment Authority, the national planning agency of Singapore, where he oversaw technical and policy work on urban planning and design, property and land markets, and urban resilience. He also undertook academic research and private sector work in Singapore and London. He holds a master's degree with a specialization in urbanization and real estate from Harvard University, Cambridge, MA, and a master's degree in architecture from Columbia University, New York, NY. He received his bachelor's degree from the National University of Singapore.

Shobha Kumar is a recognized international development and organizational knowledge and learning practitioner with over 30 years of experience in the international development space. Until 2018, Shobha worked at the World Bank Group as a senior knowledge and learning specialist. Key areas of contribution and passion include: 1) designing and implementing knowledge and learning (K&L) initiatives that are based on capacity development principles and grounded in practical application of K&L; 2) facilitating group processes and designing learning environments that tap into the power and potential of peer-to-peer learning; 3) converting complex ideas into simple and intuitive road maps and knowledge products that are meaningful for both an experienced practitioner and newcomers; and 4) operating at the intersection of art and science to demonstrate that, when done well, knowledge and learning can enhance development impact. While at the World Bank Group, Shobha also managed a large-scale mainstreaming initiative of results-focused knowledge exchange. She was the primary author and project lead for the World Bank Group's flagship results-focused knowledge and learning guidebook for development practitioners, *The Art of Knowledge Exchange*, which is now translated into nine different languages and adopted and adapted by different sectors in the Bank, client and partner organizations, and centers of excellence globally. This guidebook forms the foundation of the World Bank's knowledge exchange advisory services and of the design of South–South Knowledge Exchange initiatives led by the World Bank Group. Shobha holds an MS degree in curriculum design and evaluation from University of Southern California, Los Angeles, CA, and continues to consult on meaningful K&L projects.

Daniel A. Levine is Senior Country Officer in the World Bank Singapore Office. Dan is a key management team member responsible for the office's core activities, events, and strategies and facilitates the link between knowledge development, communications, and operations. Dan first began working at the World Bank in the Office of the Comptroller in 2002. He has since held a number of corporate assignments, most recently as Program Manager of the Tokyo Development Learning Center (TDLC) in Japan. In addition to program management, Dan has engaged in finance and private sector development, knowledge and portfolio management, jobs and growth, infrastructure and urban development, and, most recently, smart cities and digital development. In the private sector, Dan has worked in government affairs, private equity, and management consulting. He obtained a bachelor of science in political science from Arizona State University, Tempe, AZ, in 1998 and, as a Wolcott Fellow, obtained an MBA from George Washington University, Washington, DC, in 2002.

Dr. Elisa Liberatori Prati is the Chief Archivist of the World Bank Group (WBG) and the Director of the Knowledge and Information Services department in the Information and Technology Solutions (ITS) Vice Presidency of the World Bank. She leads the WBG Archives and Library, the Records and Information Management Program, and the Digital Publishing Program, which strengthen institutional transparency and accountability while serving the public and the WBG's decentralized work force. Elisa joined the bank in 1998 and has played a lead role in the conception and continued implementation of the strategy to open the Archives to provide access to over 70 years of the Bank's experience to both the Bank and the public. She holds a PhD in Italian literature from the University of California, Los Angeles, CA.

Barjor Mehta has spent 40+ years working on a wide range of urban-sector initiatives. He spent the first 20 years working for NGOs, consultancy firms, and academic institutions focused on slum upgrading, municipal management, regional development, and urban infrastructure projects, as well as teaching urban planning while living in Sri Lanka,

Thailand, Bhutan, and India. He has worked for the World Bank for more than 20 years involved in the design and implementation of country-wide local government programs, urban upgrading, municipal institutional development, and large urban infrastructure programs and projects while based in Washington, DC, Tanzania, India, China, and Singapore. Barjor is trained as an architect and urban planner.

Angélica Nuñez is a lead operations officer at the World Bank, working in the Sustainable Development Department in Africa East and South. She has managed several lending and advisory projects on land, housing, urban redevelopment, slum upgrading, and disaster risk management in Mexico, India, Turkey, Argentina, Bolivia, Colombia, and the Caribbean and has contributed to complex lending and guarantee operations in all regions. She has focused largely on analyzing the market distortions in the housing and land markets that can lead to unsustainable urban development and uncompetitive cities. Previous to her position in the World Bank, she was a senior associate with an advisory firm in London, UK, specializing in structured finance, infrastructure project finance, and public-private partnerships. Angélica was born in Mexico City, Mexico, and holds an MSc in economics from the London School of Economics, UK.

Pascal Saura is a senior knowledge and learning officer at the World Bank and a former deputy delegate general at the French Embassy in the United States. Overall, he has dedicated ten years to teaching literature, ten years to building leadership in the field of language and culture, and ten years to growing knowledge and learning practices. He headed professional development initiatives throughout the English-speaking network of the Alliance Française and created an online placement test which, from 2007 to 2020, connected millions of adult students with schools around the world. Within the World Bank, he served the Latin America and Caribbean region, the Water Global Practice, and the Sustainable Development Vice Presidency managed the SkillFinder project; led the virtualization of learning; and created award-winning knowledge management services. An experienced public speaker, he holds an Agrégation de Lettres modernes from the French Ministry of Education and a master's of advanced studies from Université Jean Moulin Lyon 3, France.

Horacio Terraza has more than 20 years of professional experience in the urban-environmental field, having worked both in the private sector and in multilateral development organizations. He is currently the Lead Urban Specialist for the Latin American Region of the World Bank focusing on cities, urban infrastructure, and resilience. During the previous eight years, he worked at the Inter-American Development Bank (IDB) as the Coordinator of the Emerging and Sustainable Cities Initiative (ESCI) and as the Principal Water Specialist. Previously, he worked for ten years as a senior environmental specialist at the World Bank, leading the urban environmental agenda and coordinating operations related to carbon finance in the Latin American Department. Horacio also worked in the private sector as project manager for environmental engineering companies providing treatment and final disposal of hazardous substances and basic infrastructure provision. Horacio has extensive experience in complex multisectoral projects related to urban infrastructure, urban planning, and industrial pollution. Horacio was trained as a mechanical engineer at the National University of La Plata, Argentina, and holds a master's in international economics and international relations from the Johns Hopkins University School of Advanced International Studies (SAIS), Baltimore, MD.

Rodica Tomescu-Olariu is a development practitioner, currently working as an operations officer in the Partnerships and Trust Fund team in the World Bank's Global Practice for Urban, Disaster Risk, Resilience and Land. Rodica joined the World Bank as a consultant in November 2014 and has worked as a community manager supporting several communities of practice. She developed and implemented the communication and knowledge management aspects of the Romania Reimbursable Advisory Service operation on the digital agenda and, more recently, supported the design of the capacity-building component of a Regulatory Impact Assessment project and the launch of a community of practice at the level of the public administration. Rodica is an international development specialist and diplomat by training—before joining the Bank, she was a member of the Romanian Foreign Service for ten years, representing her country in Brussels, Paris, Vienna and, most recently, in Washington, DC. She was part of the team that negotiated Romania's European Union and NATO accession and was an advisor to the Minister for Foreign Affairs. An Aspen Socrates alumna, Rodica speaks Romanian, English, French, Italian, and Spanish. She holds an MA in international relations from George Washington University, Washington, DC.

Erika Vargas is a senior operations officer focusing on the design and implementation of the information and knowledge strategy for the Global Facility for Disaster Reduction and Recovery (GFDRR). She also leads and coordinates the global knowledge agenda on resilience and disaster risk management in close collaboration with the World Bank Disaster Risk Management Global Lead. Recently, and as part of a partnership between NASA and Columbia University, Erika worked with the Chief Knowledge Officer of NASA on the conceptual and operational development of the critical knowledge notion in organizations. Before joining the World Bank in 2008, she worked as a researcher on peace and conflict resolution and on crime and violence prevention at the Center for Latin American Studies at Georgetown University, Washington, DC. Prior to this position, she worked as a diplomat at the Colombian Embassy in Washington, DC. She has earned a master's of science in information and knowledge strategy from Columbia University, New York, NY, and a master's of arts in sociology and media studies from The New School for Social Research, New York, NY.

Yianna Vovides has over 20 years of experience in higher education and international development work focusing on knowledge exchange and communications. Specifically, her work intersects three areas—education, technology, and development. Over the last two decades, she has focused her practice and academic efforts in addressing how people learn within networked learning environments. She has worked on projects that emphasize individual and group learning, institutional programs that enable systemic changes, and research that examines how new technologies support teaching and learning. Yianna has consulted with the World Bank Group since the inception of the *Art of Knowledge Exchange* efforts, collaborating on the guidebook and workshop offerings for staff and clients. She currently serves as Director of Learning Design and Research at the Center for New Designs in Learning and Scholarship (CNDLS), Georgetown University, Washington, DC. She is a professor for the Master of Arts in Learning, Design, and Technology (LDT) program and curriculum director at Georgetown University. Yianna holds her PhD in instructional design and technology from The University of Iowa, Iowa City, IA.

Kelly Widelska was the Global Head of Knowledge and Learning at the International Finance Corporation from 2012 to 2020 and led development and implementation of the organization's knowledge management strategy and programs. Prior to her career as an international civil servant, she spent 14 years in the private sector working with various teams at Ernst and Young including various roles in Europe, Middle East and Africa, and East Asia, culminating as the Global Transaction Advisory Knowledge Leader. Kelly holds a master's of science degree in information management from Sheffield University, UK.

Yan Zhang is a senior urban specialist at the World Bank, currently working in the South Asia Region as a technical lead for housing sector engagement in India and Pakistan. Yan has more than 18 years of professional experience in affordable housing policy, urban land management, municipal service delivery, and urban resilience across all regions. Yan's work has gravitated towards housing subsidy design, housing sector policy and institutional reforms, affordable housing PPPs, and rental housing. Yan has led lending operations and advisory work on urban land supply, affordable housing, slum upgrading, and rental housing in Ethiopia, Ghana, and South Africa. During her tenure in the East Asia region, Yan was based in Manila, the Philippines, where she introduced innovations and built capacities of shelter agencies, cities, and communities, with a focus on informal settlers living in hazardous areas. Yan co-led two global knowledge notes for the housing sector: *Urban Land and Housing Market Assessment Toolkit* and *Affordable Housing PPPs*. Yan holds a doctoral degree in public policy and urban planning from the Massachusetts Institute of Technology, Boston, MA. Before MIT, Yan was an urban planner in the China Academy of Urban Planning and Design.

Introduction

Ede Ijjasz-Vasquez

The World Bank is the world's largest international development finance organization. For more than seven decades, it has financed the reconstruction and development of countries worldwide, from Europe and Japan after the Second World War to emerging economies that grew from their low-income past to countries affected by conflict today. The World Bank has been recognized as having one of the most sophisticated systems and approaches for dealing with development knowledge worldwide.[1]

In 2014, the World Bank went through one of the most extensive reorganizations in its history. It went from a matrix structure that was heavily oriented towards geographic regions to a balanced matrix with globally operating sector groups. All technical specialists worldwide across the organization's 130 offices were grouped into 13 Global Practices, from health to transport to energy. The objective was to strengthen the World Bank's global nature and service delivery capacity. Like many change processes in large organizations, the transition was complex.

One of the new Global Practices was established by bringing together disparate technical teams working on cities, natural disasters, social development, and rural development. It was so diverse that initially it didn't even have a name like other Global Practices: transport, education, or environment. It was simply called Global Practice 13.

With more than 700 staff located in 70 offices around the world, this new Global Practice 13 started with a declining business outlook, mistrust among its diverse technical teams, confusion among team members on its business lines and its strategy, and clashing cultures inside the group. It was not a promising outlook.

The management team of this diverse and unnamed Global Practice decided that the group's survival was at stake. It was urgent to find new ways to leverage the knowledge and experience of every member of the team as a way to address the crisis. That knowledge would be combined and repurposed to create innovative new business lines, achieve greater productivity and efficiency, and inspire a radically different culture. This culture would productively blend anthropologists, engineers, tech wizards, urban planners, and postwar reconstruction experts, among the many technical specialists of the new Global Practice.

This book tells the journey of this Global Practice. Throughout the book, we will attempt to answer the following questions: *Why were knowledge and its management chosen as the core comparative advantage of the Practice? How was knowledge used for innovation and efficiency? What knowledge management tools were developed? Which ones worked, which ones didn't? How was a new culture around knowledge developed? And if knowledge is diffusive and, at times, intangible, how were progress and success measured?* If you have asked similar questions in your leadership role this book is for you.

DOI: 10.4324/9781003199083-1

This book is not an academic study of knowledge management tools and practices. Instead, it is a book for leaders and knowledge management practitioners. The book does not focus on knowledge management solely from the "collecting" dimensions of knowledge management, namely the processes of systematically documenting, storing, curating, communicating, and using the organization's knowledge. The book goes beyond this necessary but insufficient dimension.

The book explores two other critical dimensions of knowledge and its management that have received less attention. First, the need to break organizational silos and connect those who know with those who need to know, namely the dimensions of communities and collaboration. In this sense, it is a people-focused view of knowledge management.

Second, we discuss the knowledge management tools and experiments in the journey of our Global Practice. But we do not stop there. The book explores how knowledge management tools and communities were central to the strategy, new business lines, and growth of the Global Practice's services to clients worldwide.

The book will show how knowledge information systems are necessary but insufficient to effectively use knowledge to the core advantage of organizations and teams. Our premise is that communities of practice—groups of professionals connecting across organizational silos around innovative topics of common interest—are the most critical instrument for the successful transfer, sharing, and use of the tangible and intangible knowledge of an organization. And that they will not deliver on these goals "by themselves" but need savvy business strategies, leadership support, creativity, and grit to pull through.

You will see throughout the book's chapters that the full potential of knowledge in an organization cannot be achieved if knowledge management is seen as an ancillary support function. Instead, it must be fully integrated into all key managerial and leadership perspectives and decisions. Through practical examples, the book shows that when knowledge management is *owned* by the organization's leadership, it can be a critical tool for strategy development and implementation, innovation, efficiency, and competitiveness. Knowledge communities can also accelerate the *time to market* and the process to transform research and pilot ideas into new services and products. Clients will not only receive better services but also be able to be more involved in shaping the services they receive.

The book is organized into four sections. The first section gives an overview of knowledge and its management at the World Bank. The second section reviews the knowledge ecosystem developed by the Global Practice to accelerate innovation and strengthen its quality of services. It includes a story-by-story record of the journey taken by several of the Global Practice's communities of practice. The third section describes a selection of the many knowledge tools that the World Bank has developed to support the use of knowledge as a critical asset and the results from an independent evaluation of the World Bank and its knowledge and learning approaches. This evaluation confirms that many of the examples we present are considered "best practices" within the organization. The fourth section discusses the leadership journey and lessons learned through the transformation of what many believed to be a Global Practice destined to failure into a vibrant group with a growing portfolio of innovative services and tools.

The three chapters in the first section will give you an overview of three topics. Chapter 1 describes the history of knowledge and its management at the World Bank, the tools that have been used, and the unique knowledge ecosystem of this global organization. We then present, in Chapter 2, the story of the 2014 reorganization, its objectives, and approach.

Chapter 3 is a primer on knowledge management concepts and theoretical underpinnings. If you are a knowledge management aficionado, this chapter will be of particular interest as it connects many of the most frequently used concepts and research in the field with the practices and experiences from the World Bank that are presented later in the book. If you are a leader who doesn't have a strong interest in knowledge management theories, you may want to skip this chapter and move directly to those that discuss the practical experiences, tools, and results of the change process.

After these first three chapters, you will come to the heart of this book—the journey of a Global Practice that leveraged its knowledge by creating a very specific organizational ecosystem designed to build a sustaining comparative advantage. Chapter 4 presents an overview of the tools and structures of that knowledge ecosystem. Chapter 5 describes how the approach to work with and through communities of practice was shaped and evolved, taking a case study approach to offering a unique glimpse into the journeys of a sampling of individual communities. Each of these cases presents a specific Community of Practice, the problem it faced, the tools and the team's change of behaviors used to solve that problem, and the results that followed. The results include new business lines, new ways of delivering services, or new ways of influencing global stakeholders.

The case studies of these communities of practice illustrate what solutions were developed to different questions and challenges, including:

- How can a small team interested in a topic that was seen as fringe among the leading business lines of the organization build a vibrant business line to work with new clients? Chapter 5.1 tells the story of the Urbanscapes Community of Practice.
- How can a community of practice break silos in an organization to bring diverse—and competing—teams providing different and partial solutions to clients into a single integrated and coherent business line? Chapter 5.2 presents the journey and solutions of the Affordable Housing Community of Practice.
- How can large communities with broad areas of work spin off smaller communities to develop new business lines focused on specific innovative solutions to well-defined challenges? You will read the example of the Disaster Risk Management Community of Practice in Chapter 5.3
- Can communities of practice shorten the "time to market" for research? Most organizations struggle with the cycle from research and testing to fully fledged services or products offered to clients worldwide. Chapter 5.4 shows how the Territorial Development Community of Practice reduced the "time to market" by two-thirds.
- How can dispersed tacit knowledge, lost reports, teams operating in silos, and uncoordinated partners be brought quickly into a new coherent and growing business line? The story of the Transit-Oriented Development Community of Practice is presented in Chapter 5.5.
- Is it possible to use a community of practice to influence a global agenda? Chapter 5.6 tells how the Urban Infrastructure and Services Community of Practice was able to work with high-level diplomatic and economic bodies to raise the profile of new development topics.
- How can an internal community of practice launch a global community of innovators and practitioners efficiently? The Understanding Risk Platform achieved this goal, and Chapter 5.7 tells that story.

• Is it possible to offer a knowledge ecosystem as a client service and leverage internal knowledge management tools to create and grow new partnerships and new communities? Chapter 5.8 describes the process of doing just that when the Global Platform for Sustainable Cities was created.

Next are three additional chapters that discuss some of the foundational aspects of the knowledge ecosystem presented in this book. Chapter 6 describes the Tokyo Development Learning Center (TDLC), a platform that served as a testbed for a new way of multicountry knowledge sharing and co-creation of solutions with clients. We then share our story of bringing a communications and outreach team together with a knowledge management team. The challenges arising from differences in approaches, tools, and languages of the communications and knowledge management fields and the tensions those differences created in bringing the two teams together are part of the Chapter 7 story. Chapter 8 concludes with a review of the conscious process to change the culture of each member of the Global Practice to become a *knowledge citizen* and a communicator and how major learning and team events were used as a vehicle to undertake this process.

Later chapters present other knowledge management assets at the World Bank Group. Chapter 9 describes an innovative methodology, developed by the World Bank and embraced by the Global Practice that is the subject of this book, that guides the design and organization of results-focused knowledge exchanges across practitioners in different countries and organizations. Chapter 10 presents practical examples of supporting countries in building their own capacity to capture and share local lessons of development experience that have global relevance. This chapter shows how the World Bank knowledge management and learning tools were adapted to different countries' institutions and capacities and how the World Bank then partnered with these countries to share their experiences and solutions internationally.

In Chapter 11, we present the rapid evolution and growth of the World Bank's Open Learning Campus, a unique platform for client and staff learning. This e-learning and knowledge-sharing platform has become an invaluable tool for connecting practitioners across World Bank clients and partners and bringing them the organization's latest lessons and thinking. Chapter 12 presents the experience of the World Bank with service desks—a tool to help communities compile and curate knowledge in response to questions posed by team members and clients.

In Chapter 13, we discuss different knowledge management tools and strategies that the International Finance Corporation (IFC)—the private sector arm of the World Bank Group—has developed to mobilize "knowledge citizenry" among its staff. Finally, Chapter 14 presents the World Bank archives' role in fighting organizational amnesia. Like many large organizations, the speed of knowledge development and client services leads to teams forgetting the organization's histories and lessons of experience unless a dedicated and creative team is set to keep these alive.

Chapter 15 presents the main results of several independent evaluations of the knowledge management and learning systems of the World Bank Group. The chapter shows how many of the tools and behaviors of the Global Practice reviewed in this book were highlighted by the evaluators as good practices. The chapter also shows how difficult it is to define and measure the benefits of knowledge management tools and ecosystems.

Finally, Chapter 16 brings together the leadership lessons discussed throughout the book. This chapter also tells the story of the Global Practice leadership team's journey and its search for solutions to the challenges that put the Practice's survival in doubt. We share our choices, the failures along the way, and the continuous improvement processes we put in place to test, innovate, and deliver better services to our clients.

We are convinced that the toughest challenges in organizational change—those related to people and their behaviors—can be tackled by using tools and practices drawn from the knowledge management arena. We wanted to tell the story of how one group in the World Bank fared when using knowledge management tools and techniques to complete an organizational transformation. Will this approach work for your organization? We believe so. We saw it working in the World Bank with its myriad organizational complexities, probably not unlike other large global organizations. Even in large, complex organizations, it is possible to support intrapreneurs and scale up their ideas as new business lines. Our journey described here made a substantial difference in a short time. We believe these stories and lessons can give you pointers as you embark on your own change journeys.

Note

1 The American Productivity and Quality Centrel (APQC) annually identifies organizations whom they consider displaying excellence in knowledge management. The World Bank was recognized for excellence already in 2003.

Chapter 1

Knowledge at the World Bank

A Unique Ecosystem

Monika Weber-Fahr[1]

Products: Core Knowledge Services for Business Development, Strategy, and Consensus Building

At the heart of the World Bank's approach to business development is an in-depth and informed conversation with a client government and key stakeholders about the type and magnitude of their developmental challenges and the actions necessary to reverse, strengthen, or change current courses. An important element of this conversation is the process involved when coming to an agreement about the analysis and about priorities and choices. Only then can loan or grant services or other work even begin. The World Bank has developed a number of highly standardized knowledge products that have proven successful in supporting this dialogue, including undertaking a *Public Expenditure Review* (PER), devising a *Country Economic Memorandum*[2] (CEM), and participating in a *Systematic Country Diagnostics* (SCD). Core products like these have become an essential part of the World Bank's knowledge ecosystem; they are considered "core" in that there is a high degree of standardization, an ease with which staff from very different backgrounds interact with these products, and clarity in the clients' understanding of these products' role.

Processes: Ensuring Relevance, Quality, and Delivery of Knowledge Services

The World Bank's knowledge ecosystem includes a number of core processes that help ensure quality and delivery of knowledge services, both those associated with financing and with free-standing advisory services. Operating within a matrix organization, these processes also involve balancing local interests and the client relationship with global insight and priorities. Deploying them systematically takes institutional commitment and discipline—one of the reasons why they are often not the norm in other organizations of similar nature. First, there is a well-structured *quality assurance system,* which includes multiple formal moments for reviews allowing management to offer "stop" or "go ahead" decisions and, at different points, also involves peer review input from specialists across and beyond the organization. Second, there is an *internal budget system,* which establishes an internal market mechanism for many activities: where there is no demand, there is no product. Third, the quality and delivery of knowledge services is *managed at a portfolio level*—the internal information system with its monthly reports on progress made in the delivery of Analytical and Advisory Services (ASA) creates the opportunity for cross-departmental and cross-regional progress conversations and related consequence management. And fourth,

DOI: 10.4324/9781003199083-2

the organization has firmly *institutionalized processes to learn from its experience*: upon completion, financial services—including the attached advisory services—go through a formal internal assessment, based on verifiable information, subsequently scrutinized by specialists from the *Independent Evaluation Group* (IEG), who also sets a rating for the activity. A key aspect of these internal assessments is to identify lessons that can be applied to future projects and/or to ongoing projects in other countries, and the Independent Evaluation Group will periodically review and discuss these learnings through portfolio-based evaluations (see Chapter 15 for more on IEG and its mandate to combine ensuring accountability with the ambition to encourage learning from experience).

Box 1.1 Creating Cultural and Organizational Space for Knowledge: The Wolfensohn Reforms of 1997

The market that the World Bank serves—often called *the Development Community*—has long been dominated by purist economic thought and has not always understood the role of knowledge as a driver for social and economic development.[3] Internally, knowledge was equated with research, primarily that undertaken by the World Bank itself, and not much attention was paid to connecting clients with external sources of expertise. At a time when the World Bank saw demand for their products and services come under pressure, it took a leader of the organization to shift some of these paradigms. More than twenty-five years ago, at the annual meetings of the IMF and the World Bank in October 1996, in front of finance ministers and central bankers, the then World Bank president James D. Wolfensohn called for a new partnership for creating and sharing knowledge—"making it a major driver of development" (1996).[4] In announcing what was eventually called "the Knowledge Bank," Wolfensohn's act of leadership was to create the language and the organizational space for his teams to figure out what role to give knowledge along all major steps of the core business processes and as part of its services. Following Wolfensohn's speech, a veritable "knowledge ecosystem" was built. Its purpose—ensuring that indeed the right knowledge gets to the right person at the right time and location. Quality, extent, and day-to-day relevance as well as appreciation of the knowledge ecosystem have ebbed and flowed over the years; some specifics were added, others removed, but, by and large, seven dimensions have remained stable: products, processes, people, platforms, partners, perspectives, and approaches for how to manage the ecosystem.

People: Supporting the Bank's Knowledge Workers to Create, Share, and Use Knowledge

Anyone entering a World Bank office will immediately notice fliers posted or notes exchanged, announcing a *"Brown Bag Lunch,"* a book or study launch event, or similar opportunities open to staff to interact with new insights.[5] While anyone at any time can set up such events, many are hosted by *communities of practice* (see Chapter 5). These communities are groups of staff who share a concern or passion for a particular topic and who aim to jointly learn about the topic and from each other while also moving the engagement with the topic forward and innovating. Having existed for over 30 years, communities of practice were formalized through President Wolfensohn's organizational reforms in 1997. Today, they are one of the most critical pillars of the Bank's knowledge ecosystem, offering space to create important personal connections and to build trust among staff across all locations and organizational units. Mostly hosted and funded by technical units, they operate rather informally and all are fully open to everyone. While communities of practice have a "bottom-up" feel and function, the institutional knowledge agenda on a particular topic is shaped by *Global Leads* for a particular subject matter, a role that is discussed further in Chapter 2. The World Bank affords itself these senior positions, some five to seven per topical department, and gives them the explicit mandate to advance strategic agendas and knowledge on key development areas. Staff taking on these roles, rotating in and out regularly, are also the experts to whom others will look for answers to new challenges, for connections with outside parties, and for strategic guidance. In addition, the Bank employs a small cadre of dedicated *knowledge management specialists*—formally assigned the responsibility of making sure knowledge becomes available when, where, and for whom it will be needed. When President Wolfensohn first put forward the Knowledge Bank vision, few staff had qualifications in the new and emerging field of knowledge management and those assigned to such roles learned "on the go." Today, specialized training is available both externally and through the World Bank's own programs, as are platforms and tools for the day-to-day work, including novel AI-enabled search platforms, an internal FaceBook-type platform, and online help desk and archival functions. The World Bank also takes knowledge competencies into account when investing in staff more broadly. This begins with *recruiting a workforce that is uniquely diverse* in terms of their academic and operational background; it also involves investing in and enforcing regular *rotation from assignment to assignment* so that staff can take their knowledge to different parts of the organization and, in turn, to clients; creating opportunities *for formal and informal learning*; and including knowledge sharing among the areas of behavior to be considered during annual *performance assessments*. And even though the reality of these and many other efforts is not always what they might have set out to be originally, the intent and the associated budgets already create a unique culture, namely one where knowledge creation, sharing, and deployment have a firm and mostly respected place.

Platforms: Knowledge as a Public Good

Recognizing its role as a leader in the communities it serves, the World Bank appreciates the public good nature of many of its knowledge assets. A number of platforms serve this agenda. *World Bank Open Knowledge* is not only an online platform where all key documents pertaining to World Bank services can be found, but it also constitutes a commitment to make all aspects of creating, acquiring, sharing, adapting, and applying knowledge more accessible. Similarly, *World Bank Open Data* is a platform through which the World Bank offers free and open access to most of the global development data it collects, both data collected on a global scale for its reports but also data collected through project or program activities that may be more specific. The *World Bank's Archives* add the historical component here, allowing open access to all key documents shaping the World Bank and its operations since 1946 as well as personalized assistance in finding whatever someone may be looking for (see Chapter 14). The organization's commitment to not only openness but also accessibility—all documents and data can be downloaded for free—is both extraordinary and an invitation to clients and partners to engage on the same footing.

Partners: Investing in Client Knowledge

The World Bank understands that knowledge matters for the successful future of the projects it finances—and that turning knowledge into capacity requires an extra step, commonly called *learning*. In the context of its larger financing operations, opportunities for learning and knowledge creation tend to emerge naturally for the client teams directly involved in World Bank projects, in particular for staff in ministries and government agencies and members of NGO teams. To address their learning interests and needs more systematically and globally, the World Bank had set up, in 1955, its own learning institute, originally called *Economic Development Institute* (EDI) and later transformed into the *World Bank Institute* (WBI). With some 200+ full-time course managers and instructors, the Institute regularly offered learning and engagement opportunities to several hundred partner organizations worldwide. The concept of *South-to-South Learning* (see Chapters 9 and 10) was originally developed here and eventually became firmly embedded in many of the activities offered by the World Bank Institute, including the *Global Development Learning Network* (GDLN) that had been created to connect in-country groups of specialists with those in other countries. With the Institute's closure in 2016, some of its ambitions and accountabilities were transferred to the World Bank's *Open Learning Campus* (see Chapter 11). The Open Learning Campus today offers online opportunities to explore nuggets of knowledge through podcasts, videos, and webinars; to sign up for topical courses both facilitated and self-paced; and to connect with experts and peers around the world.

Perspectives: Shaping Insight and Opinions Through Global Thought Leadership

Organizations whose business success depends on staying on top of global research have always found ways to invest in thought leadership. Some finance or contribute to think tanks or universities, others run their own research or advocacy groups—such as McKinsey's Global Institute or BCG's Centre for Public Impact. At the World Bank, then president Robert MacNamara commissioned in 1978 the first *World Development Report*—based on the insight that his staff needed seminal research into the interconnections and complexities associated with economic growth and development to be able to master their increasingly complex assignments. He also needed a way to convince his stakeholders that expanding lending beyond infrastructure and into topical areas such as education, health, and population would have an economic impact. Still today, some 50 years onwards, many of the World Development Reports have served as agenda setters, opening up avenues for thought, innovation, and business development. Many other "flagship reports" and analytical products, produced by sector departments, country units, or by the World Bank's in-house research department, the *Development Economics Research Group* (DEC), have further contributed to the body of *thought leadership*. The DEC group—arguably the largest and most influential group of researchers in the development economics sphere[6]—is a singularly large and freely operating research and development team that also serves as a source of insight for some of the Bank's operational groups, complementing these units' own research. The quality and relevance of the research reports and analyses, both available from DEC and other parts of the World Bank, continue to be a subject of ongoing internal debate—including most recently through the March 2021 World Bank Knowledge Strategic Framework.[7] A related but separate and yet unresolved challenge in this domain is for the

World Bank to find the right balance between serving as a producer of development knowledge, through research, and serving as a knowledge broker, connecting clients with the best available solutions, whether they are developed internally or by other parties.

Managing the World Bank's Knowledge Ecosystem

With such a rich accumulation of knowledge assets and knowledge management approaches, the World Bank's choice in how to oversee and manage both may seem surprising: The organization employs no corporate-level global knowledge director or director of knowledge services, and formal accountability for the state of knowledge management in the organization has not been assigned to any one central unit or team. There is no cohesive or binding strategy that sets targets, just a strategic framework. Instead, the current setup seeks to operate on the principle of collective and distributed accountabilities; everyone involved in the knowledge agenda is expected to do their part, yet there is no "central" place to set standards or to orchestrate or oversee this work.[8] This choice exposes units and departments to the fallacy of operating in "silos" or "islands" of knowledge (about knowledge management or good knowledge practices), and it limits the potential for strategic initiatives and choices, not allowing space for achieving scale and for capitalizing on network effects from specific approaches or tools.[9] Where insights emerge on what works well and what does not, they cannot swiftly and systematically be deployed across the organization (see Chapter 15). Some steps have been taken to rationalize the way knowledge is managed and to reduce silos. This included the establishment of Global Practices to support global and cross-regional knowledge leadership and facilitate connections between staff along sectoral dimensions (see Chapter 2). However, within the Global Practices and across regional departments, separate knowledge ecosystems flourish and are tended to by separately operating knowledge management teams. Little if any effort is made to systematically promote learning among these ecosystems. Recognizing these limitations, individual knowledge management staff have taken to operating their own community—called KnowledgeMatters—to achieve some level of coordination and learning at least among themselves. From an organizational perspective, though, there has been little appetite for creating more coherence and leadership for knowledge management. Indeed, since then president Wolfensohn made knowledge "a thing" 25 years ago and successfully installed some element of authority with a global knowledge director, arrangements for leadership and governance of knowledge management within the organization have varied widely. There have been multiple models of *global* oversight; periods with no oversight followed by periods featuring a central knowledge director; periods with a knowledge and learning council composed of senior staff delegated by their departments for this role; and periods when a global knowledge director and sectoral knowledge directors cooperated. The ebb and flow of organizational models and strategic directions in this space could be taken to signal that the World Bank has not fully come to terms with its role and responsibility as a Knowledge Bank. In the meantime, though, individual departments and units have well understood the potential that knowledge management and learning tools hold in improving service delivery, driving productivity, and fostering innovation. It is one of the extraordinary features of the World Bank's knowledge ecosystem that these individuals and organizational units have been given the space and opportunity to innovate and pursue what they found worked for them and their clients. The stories of some of these initiatives form the basis for this book and its individual chapters.

Notes

1 Input to the *Products* section of this chapter was provided by Han Fraeters, Country Manager at the World Bank.

2 A Country Economic Memorandum (CEM) provides a comprehensive analysis of a country's economic developments, prospects, and policy agenda, identifying policy reforms for key economic sectors.

3 Even though one of the World Bank's first presidents, Eugene Black, in his annual meeting address in 1949 highlighted knowledge sharing as one of the most constructive contributions that Bank could make, mainstream economics picked up on the relevance of knowledge for economic growth only with the work of Paul Romer and others in the 1980s, assigning knowledge the role of a production factor relevant for long-term growth. It took until the 1990s for terms such as "the knowledge economy" to become more widely used, including in the World Development Report 1998/1999 that was titled "Knowledge for Development."

4 World Bank. 1996. Annual Meeting Address of the World Bank President, James D. Wolfensohn https://openknowledge.worldbank.org/server/api/core/bitstreams/307efc63-53e8-5cec-81a3-02f085326d81/content

5 Until the COVID-19 pandemic moved many of these events into online environments and made them accessible at a distance and over time, most could be attended only by staff present at the office at which they were held.

6 The World Bank Group ranks first in development economics in the RePEC bibliographic database, ahead of MIT, NBER, and the LSE.

7 Realizing the World Bank Group's Knowledge Potential for Effective Development Solutions: A Strategic Framework, March 2021, Figures 5 (p. 15) and 6 (p. 16). https://documents1.worldbank.org/curated/en/309981617140869469/pdf/Realizing-the-World-Bank-Group-s-Knowledge-Potential-for-Effective-Development-Solutions-A-Strategic-Framework.pdf

8 "Realizing the World Bank Group's Knowledge Potential for Effective Development Solutions: A Strategic Framework," March 2021, https://documents1.worldbank.org/curated/en/309981617140869469/pdf/Realizing-the-World-Bank-Group-s-Knowledge-Potential-for-Effective-Development-Solutions-A-Strategic-Framework.pdf

9 Only soft approaches and methods for knowledge management and learning are referenced here. In overseeing information technology relevant choices, the World Bank deploys a highly competent information technology solutions group with central oversight and accountability.

Chapter 2

The World Bank's 2014 Reorganization

A New Structure for Better Knowledge Flows

Ede Ijjasz-Vasquez, Philip Karp and Monika Weber-Fahr

The World Bank's Organizational Challenge

The challenge of balancing functional and geographical imperatives has shaped organizational reforms at the World Bank over several decades—and for good reasons. In claiming its place as the world's premier development institution, the World Bank has very much relied on its ability to get this balance right when seeking to stake out a singular approach to help its developing country clients realize their development goals. Given its global mandate, coverage, and mission, the organization takes pride in its ability to offer development solutions that draw upon lessons and experience from across the world while also being able to tailor solutions to local contexts. In delivering on this promise, a large body of staff carefully chosen from a range of professional disciplines, along with an extensive network of partnerships have been assembled and are managed carefully. No other development institution operates along such a broad range of thematic or geographical coverage or can mobilize comparable networks to tap into global knowledge and expertise.

At the same time, the World Bank's clients have high expectations, and rightly so. The clients expect multisectoral, multistakeholder development solutions with an appropriate mix of affordable financing, context-adapted knowledge, and convening of key partners and stakeholders, all of which contribute towards crafting and implementing these solutions. They rely on the World Bank to support them on evidence-based design and delivery, drawing upon all its relevant experience around the world. A unique aspect of the World Bank's support is how it extends its support beyond design of development interventions and helps clients, as necessary, during implementation. The World Bank's commitment to build a country's institutions and capacity is another aspect of its approach that makes it a partner of choice.

A Brief History of the World Bank's Organizational Structure (1997–2013)

Over the years, the World Bank has undergone several reorganizations to strike the right balance between regional and functional perspectives. Prior to 1997, the organization had a matrix structure with a very strong regional orientation. The bulk of the organization's operational staff were assigned to six large regional units with segments focused on a small group of neighboring countries, each of which had its own set of specialized teams covering the main sectoral fields (e.g., transport, education, health) in which the World Bank is involved.

This structure led to strong and frequent engagements with country clients. However, the interaction among staff working in the same sector but in different regions was more

DOI: 10.4324/9781003199083-3

difficult. While cross-regional exchange of knowledge was possible and encouraged, there were insufficient incentives and inadequate mechanisms to make this happen. The World Bank encouraged staff to rotate across regions every five years or so. This rotation helped with the transfer of knowledge and the building of global personal relations, but it was generally slow. As a result, the advice and solutions offered to clients tended to be drawn primarily, if not exclusively, from countries in the same geographic region.

A full-fledged matrix organization had been first introduced in 1997 as part of the structural reforms inspired by the then president Wolfensohn's aspiration to focus the World Bank's unique selling point of being the only organization able to offer globally informed solutions locally. Staff continued to work within regional units but were also—simultaneously—assigned to sector-focused "networks."[1]

The expectations that shaped the creation of these "networks" were multiple, including reduced fragmentation, increased information flow, better priority setting, improved quality assurance, better vetting of technical staff promotions, and improved dissemination of best practice.

However, over the course of the subsequent 15 years, a series of organizational and incentive shifts had "tilted" the balance of decision-making and staffing back in favor of the regional units, limiting the flow of information and the availability of knowledge and advice across regions. The knowledge "silos" were back. An analysis of staff time recording and a World Bank–wide staff survey in 2012 indicated that staff spent only about 0.2 percent of their time working on tasks managed by a professional network other than the one that they belonged to. Similarly, only about 0.6 percent of staff time was spent working in a geographic region other than the one the staff belonged to. Moreover, surveys showed that almost 70 percent of staff felt that they did not have time to share knowledge with their colleagues. There was a sense that a key strength of the World Bank—the ability to leverage the best possible global knowledge and expertise—was not being fully deployed.

The 2013–2014 World Bank Reorganization—A New Structure to Support Excellence in Knowledge

For an organization like the World Bank, the instinct to primarily orient its decision-making towards individual client countries is very strong. As with many other client-driven organizations, the World Bank's matrix structure has tended to "tilt" towards country or regional groupings. This tilting tends to lead to regional- or country-level knowledge silos. To address and prevent just that—so that knowledge and experience would move easily between regional and country units—newly appointed World Bank president Jim Yong Kim decided that some major organizational "surgery" would be needed.

There had been several initiatives over the years to enable easier flow of knowledge across organizational units, but they had not achieved their objective. There was a sense that unless there was a change in the organizational structure and an accompanying cultural change that recognized and rewarded knowledge work, the desired knowledge flows within the institution, and with the outside world, would not be realized.

In 2013, the World Bank embarked on an ambitious and broad-ranging organizational change path, motivated by the need to create space for the generation, curation, and flow of knowledge across the institution and with the outside world. A central change management team was established to steer the process. Several organization structure options were explored, and the pros and cons of each were discussed and debated in detail. A "Global

Practices" model was finally selected, as it was found most promising for helping address constraints and challenges posed by the earlier, "pre-2013" structure, and it had the ability to create strong incentives to generate and share cutting-edge knowledge and solutions for the benefit of clients. Box 2.1 describes the knowledge framework underpinning this new organizational structure.

In the new model, the Global Practices would be large business units responsible for a development sector (e.g., transport, energy, health) that would operate globally and to which most technical staff were assigned. They were set up with the explicit mandate to deliver high-quality services to individual clients. They were also accountable to generate and share cutting-edge knowledge and solutions for the benefit of the broader development community.

Box 2.1   Knowledge Framework Underpinning the Global Practice Model

The Global Practice model was conceived to rely on a framework that would put knowledge at the center of everything the World Bank does. The key features of the framework developed by the central change management team, in collaboration with working groups across the institution, included:

- Leadership to message and model the centrality of knowledge for all staff and all assignments and services.
- Considerable focus on *curation* of knowledge from across all regions to ensure relevance and accessibility for internal and external clients.
- Setting up of modalities within each Global Practice to tap into tacit knowledge.
- Recognizing knowledge leadership of staff at different levels in the Global Practice.
- Identification and assignment of knowledge workers with a primary role of curating and disseminating knowledge.
- Expectation set for operational staff regarding the importance of investing in "downloading" their knowledge to "knowledge curators" for wider dissemination and use.

One of the criteria for selecting the first set of Global Practice senior directors and directors was their ability to function as champions and promoters of knowledge. As the Global Practices were introduced, they were given broad latitude to adapt the Knowledge Framework to suit the specific requirements of their respective sectors.

In the new Global Practice model, region-specific sectoral teams would be assigned to countries and regional groups, yet their primary reporting line remained with the globally operating senior director of the Practice who oversaw the entire Practice staff and its portfolio of projects. The idea was to combine the client responsiveness that comes with regional orientation and delivery accountability with the ability to leverage the intellectual capacity of the entire group of professionals working in a particular sector across the institution.

The primary client relationship management function would continue to be with the country units led by a country director. They were to handle the direct in-country client relationships and then—internally to the Bank—translate the clients' strategic needs and asks into specific project or advisory engagements.

There was cautious excitement with the new structure. The World Bank's leadership felt that it would spawn excellence within the entire Global Practice community and help find solutions to the stickiest development challenges facing the world. The new structure would better ensure that each project team would be able to mobilize the intellectual power and backing of the entire corpus of staff in each sector or discipline when serving a particular country client. It would be much easier to leverage talent and expertise from across the institution, given that each Global Practice would have mapped the expertise available in the respective area and could deploy it where it was needed the most. The Global Practice model would also enable stronger links with specialized partner institutions, facilitating easier deployment of external expertise as well. Also, lessons from implementation would be easier to share across the institution, thereby providing much stronger support to country clients throughout the implementation phase of a project.

Concerns with this format for "balancing the matrix" focused on the difficulty that a Global Practice director would have in focusing on a specific country client. Would the director's global perspective make them less responsive to the needs and priorities of individual countries? Regionally operating Practice teams—operating under a regionally designated Practice manager—were introduced to mitigate this risk and ensure responsiveness of the Global Practice vis-à-vis the needs of each country client. Together with their senior director and other Practice directors, the regional managers formed Practice boards to promote globality and cross-regional skills transfer in the new structure. In a very hierarchical organization such as the World Bank, though, entrusting the regional and country orientation to middle managers rather than directors was met with some skepticism.

Implementing a New Vision for Knowledge

With 13 Global Practices set up by 2014 and endowed with newly assigned senior directors, many of whom had been recruited from outside the World Bank, the work to make the vision a reality began. The central change management team continued its work to support the new structure. Directors were given some degree of latitude in how they would go about charting the new pathways ahead. Several recognized the importance of global knowledge to drive the formulation and delivery of solutions right from the outset. However, as noted in the discussion of the World Bank knowledge ecosystem (Chapter 1), the temptation was to focus primarily on knowledge creation as opposed to identification and cataloging of knowledge and solutions already in existence, whether from internal or external sources. This would have been difficult in the absence of dedicated knowledge curators.

Part of the problem was that such systematic knowledge curation was looked upon as something to be done by dedicated knowledge management specialists rather than by operational staff. In some organizations relying on systematic curation, almost 7 percent of their staff are exclusively devoted to curation of knowledge. Moreover, the tacit knowledge derived from implementation experience had neither been codified nor curated.

Accordingly, many of the Global Practices recognized that given the rapid pace of experimentation and innovation and the dynamic and context-specific nature of solutions that needed to be found, attention would need to be given to both new knowledge *creation* and to knowledge *curation*, and the necessary skills, systems, and culture would need to be established to achieve this.

This shift represented a proposed "democratization of knowledge," where a very large proportion of staff would be engaged in knowledge production, integration, curation, and dissemination, in multiple and often unanticipated ways. The central change management team supported Global Practices in the establishment of knowledge ecosystems. The role of the Global Practice leadership was expected to be that of an enabler, helping create an ecosystem which spawned innovation and creativity, with sufficient room and scope for serendipity. Based on examples from other organizations, it was clear that Global Practices needed to instill a sense of pride in belonging to a knowledge community, and the leadership teams needed to model behaviors that emphasize the importance of knowledge.

With rapid advancements in information and communication technology and the explosion of social media platforms, World Bank professionals today are craving for more innovative ways of engaging with and of sharing and consuming knowledge. They desire better communications and knowledge-sharing tools, "state of the sector" news-sharing that covers what is happening in each development field both within the Bank and outside and multiple and more interactive formats of engagement where everyone participates in the process of knowledge generation, curation, and sharing. The change management team encouraged Global Practices to implement this vision.

Global Practice Number 13—The Social, Urban, Rural, and Resilience Global Practice (GSURR)

One of the largest groupings created by the reorganization brought together technical staff working on social development issues (ranging from social inclusion to community-driven development issues), urban development, disaster risk management, territorial development, and land. Initially referred to simply as Global Practice 13, the grouping was eventually given the title of Global Practice for Social, Urban, Rural, and Resilience and the acronym GSURR.

Right at the outset, the GSURR leadership team recognized the power of the Global Practice structure in terms of ensuring globality of the knowledge and solutions they would be able to offer to clients. However, their specific challenge was that the GSURR Global Practice brought together, under one umbrella, groups of staff from several thematic sectors that had not previously worked together closely.

Indeed, a key challenge of the new Global Practice was to integrate more than 700 staff located in more than 70 developing country offices globally into a seamlessly operating team with a shared vision and sense of purpose.

The urban, disaster risk management, and land teams were composed mainly of planners and engineers who focused heavily on technical solutions and on hard infrastructure, while the social development teams were made up of sociologists, anthropologists, and economists, focusing much more on people, behaviors, processes, and institutions. Each group brought a strong culture and sense of belonging to their technical disciplines.

The logic behind bringing these rather different groups together had been the desire to offer integrated, "spatially situated" solutions for clients, covering both urban and rural spaces and paying particular attention to resilience and social inclusion. For example, cities are not only about infrastructure, finance, and spatial development, but they are also—fundamentally—about urban residents.

With the new spatially oriented mandate, a first step was to set out generating and consolidating knowledge that would bridge the various sectors and themes covered by the

Global Practice. In other words, the strategic focus on new knowledge creation became an instrument to achieve the new mandate to deliver integrated solutions In fact, GSURR management took the strategic decision that only by putting knowledge and knowledge management at the heart of its business development and reorganization efforts could such a diverse group of people be led to become and operate as a team and connect with each other and their clients in ways conducive to deliver high-quality and innovative solutions.

This strategic decision included three core elements. First, the GSURR leadership team paid special attention to creating a culture wherein development, capture, curation, and sharing of knowledge would be seen as "everyone's business" rather than the responsibility of a few knowledge management specialists.

Second, rather than mandating specific knowledge strategies or structures, a knowledge ecosystem was created that centered around communities of practice wherein all staff were expected to engage in production, integration, curation, and dissemination of knowledge.

Third, staff were introduced to new and innovative modalities for capture and sharing of knowledge. These included the use of collaboration platforms; TED Talk or "Ignite" style presentations; use of gamification; communication via contemporary, attractive formats; and multiple and more interactive modes of engagement where everyone participates in the process of knowledge generation, curation, and sharing. Tools for knowledge sharing—such as the *Art of Knowledge Exchange*—were systematically promoted through messages as well as through deployment (see Chapter 9).

The strategic focus on knowledge creation and knowledge management put the GSURR Practice at the forefront of what the World Bank's senior management had envisaged when creating the Global Practice structure—namely a contemporary vision of knowledge management wherein knowledge becomes a part of the "DNA" of everyone who works at the World Bank. The various approaches utilized to pursue this vision are explored in subsequent chapters of this book.

Note

1 A Network was an aggregation of sectors with strong connection among them. For example, the Sustainable Development Network included at the time environment, social development, agriculture and rural development, urban development, and water. The World Bank set up four such Networks for professional mapping of staff.

Chapter 3

A Primer on Knowledge
Useful Concepts and Theoretical Underpinning

Monika Weber-Fahr

Introduction

Successfully deploying knowledge management and learning approaches to support organizational behavior and delivery involves focusing on the role of individuals and teams—as they come together over time in communities of practice that bring together staff, their clients, and counterparts for building on, sharing, and eventually leveraging their experiences and motivations for service improvements. Throughout the experiences described in this book a number of common threads emerge, including the insight that organizational change can (only) be successful if leadership teams find new and strong ways to mobilize and connect staff as well as their counterparts in ways that allow for building new relationships, discovering new shared interests, and connecting with each other in safe spaces. This work needs to be done by staff themselves and is largely self-driven—the details of individual steps are too minute and too personal to be "mandated from the top." The relationships between people—how they work together, coordinate with each other, think ahead, and take care of each other—are what make a (new) organizational chart or strategic direction come to life and shape how different parts of an organization interact.

The performance journey described in this book is shaped by and centered around *collaborative communities of practice* (CoPs) that are cross-cutting and connected (see also Chapter 5). As an instrument of learning and knowledge management, communities of practice were first described by Etienne Wenger and John Lave in "Situated Learning" (1991); at the time, they spoke of groups of people who "share a concern or passion for something they do and learn how to do it better as they interact regularly."[1] The concept was further refined by Wenger in *Communities of Practice: Learning, Meaning, and Identity* (1998).[2] Much research has since gone into showing that communities of practice—linked loosely together across time, space, and organizational boundaries—can solve problems faster than individuals or specific teams. Across the experiences described in the coming chapters, communities of practice emerge as the glue connecting the many tools and approaches deployed. Different approaches to communities of practice will be featured, all of them having invested in their longer-term evolution from loosely connected teams that informally share knowledge and support connections among individuals to globally coordinating centers of technical excellence that influence the development, testing, and scaling up of solutions to complex development challenges.

DOI: 10.4324/9781003199083-4

Box 3.1   Communities of Practice: Key Features

Communities of practice are central to creating a new culture, continuous innovation processes, and linkage of knowledge flows with better services to clients for a more competitive and effective organization. They do this by drawing on collective knowledge, experimenting and sharing experiences rapidly in real time, and identifying and adopting best practices better than any other mechanism deployed to achieve performance improvements today. Communities of practice leverage knowledge that resides in people and in the interactions they have with each other, following often unspoken and unreflected "protocols"—a dimension of knowledge called "intangible" or "tacit" knowledge. Intangible knowledge is best shared through partaking in others' routines, allowing us to reflectively observe, and through collaboration, throughout which tacit knowledge and its applications can be discerned. In contrast, "tangible" or explicit knowledge is knowledge that can be codified and shared through books, films, websites, or other media, "codified" by a person who writes, codes, or visualizes a particular insight.

Conceptual Underpinnings: How to Effectively Engage Staff With the Knowledge Ecosystem

The behavioral change domain offers a useful set of conceptual approaches for designing activities in a way that would bring the highest likelihood for effectively engaging staff with a new knowledge ecosystem. It would be naive to assume that staff in any organization would simply "go ahead" and adjust their behaviors and priorities insofar as knowledge creation, curation, sharing, and using are concerned—just because there may be newly minted expectations or mandates. Introducing a new knowledge ecosystem does require staff to adopt new ways to learn and collect knowledge from each other and to collaborate in delivering new and improved services to their clients. How to initiate the behavior change necessary? How to model and continuously nurture such behavior change? In looking for answers to these questions, the behavioral change wheel and the EAST model of nudge theory offer helpful insights.

1. *The behavioral change wheel:* Originally developed by Susan Mitchie et al. in 2011, this model identifies three key elements shaping whether or not and how individuals undertake and maintain change. These three elements are *motivation, capability*, and *opportunity*. The model helps understand why—across various initiatives launched—success relied not only on giving teams financial resources/time support to invest in "skill transfer" (capability) but also on creating motivation and on creating specific moments of opportunity for staff and counterparts to *act on* and *use* the knowledge identified.
2. *The EAST model:* Popularized through the 2008 book *Nudge: Improving Decisions About Health, Wealth, and Happiness* (Richard Thaler, Cass Sunstein), the concept of "nudge" or "nudging" calls for the use of positive reinforcement and indirect suggestions

as ways to influence behavior and decision-making of groups or individuals. The EAST model was developed by David Halpern and the UK Cabinet Office's *Behavioral Insights Team* in 2012. The model summarizes the collective experience in nudging in four simple, practical features of successful behavior change interventions. Effective interventions should be *easy, attractive, social, and timely*—four attributes that are easier said than designed into engagement approaches but, when taken seriously, can truly give rise to a deep shift towards user-centricity and, as a consequence, changed behaviors.

Conceptual Underpinnings: How to Design Effective Tools for Knowledge Management and Learning

Knowledge management and learning are broad areas of research and application that offer useful concepts to consider when building long-lasting and evolving communities of practice as instruments of change. Knowledge, in the words of Steve Denning, the World Bank's first program director for knowledge management and one of the preeminent thinkers in the field, is not just an explicit tangible 'thing,' like information, but information combined with experience, context, interpretation, and reflection. Denning argues that knowledge involves the full person, integrating the elements of both thinking and feeling. In his view and in light of this definition, knowledge itself cannot be "managed"—instead, the processes applied to making it available to others require managing. Knowledge management is a systematic process designed to connect people with one another and with the information and knowledge they need to achieve results, through the identification, capture, validation, and transfer of knowledge. Carla O'Dell, co-founder of the American Productivity & Quality Center (APQC), a key promoter of the understanding and practice about knowledge management, expands the definition by emphasizing the aspect of value creation. She describes knowledge management as the effort to "help people share and act on information in order to improve organizational performance."[3] Knowledge, in her view, is one of the few organizational assets that tend to grow when being shared. It knows no boundaries, and while often embedded in people or groups, it is essentially fluid. The elements of knowledge management initiatives that focus on people are, thus, key instruments for supporting or even initiating—successful organizational change. Four specific concepts emerge as relevant: the dynamic knowledge trajectory, the knowledge workflow, knowledge "stickiness," and adult learning theories.

1. *The dynamic knowledge trajectory*: This model understands knowledge to be one step on a dynamic path that leads from data to information, knowledge, wisdom, and choice/action. In terms of cognitive processing, this path is driven by contextualizing, on the one hand, and personalization, on the other. The concept of "contextualization" explains how information can mean one thing or another depending on the setting in which it is either generated, presented, or applied. The concept of "personalization" explains why knowledge is best understood when presented by people we know, respect, relate to in some way, or with whom we can associate. "Personalization" is the driver behind the increased use of techniques such as *storytelling* in the knowledge and learning space. The path that leads from data to knowledge and the moment of making a choice or taking action is dynamic and moves along as information is organized into knowledge residing with people. Only then—when taken up by individuals or groups—can knowledge translate into choices or action. New experiences are made, and they feed into the information base, creating new knowledge and leading to further actions.

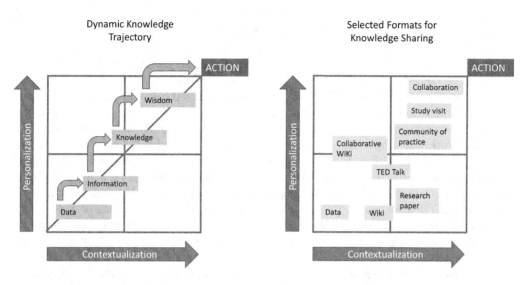

Figure 3.1 The Dynamic Knowledge Trajectory

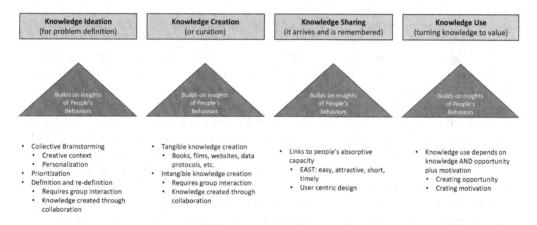

Figure 3.2 Four Steps for Knowledge Management Through a People-Lens

2. *The knowledge management workflow*: The knowledge management workflow described here (adapted from Carla O'Dell) assumes that there are four main steps associated with knowledge management that need to be actively supported so that knowledge can not only emerge but also flow and be used: Knowledge Ideation/Problem Definition; Knowledge Creation (and Curation); Knowledge Sharing; and Knowledge Replication, Using and Turning Knowledge to Value. The way they are conceptualized here, these four steps have an action orientation, defined with the individuals in mind that need to take specific action steps. To this end, the conceptualization may differ from other categorizations used in parts of the literature.

3. *Knowledge stickiness and the human attention span*: Knowledge loss—the other side of "stickiness"—is one of the key challenges for organizations today. In order to

lead to action, knowledge must reside in people, and, to this end, the concept of *knowledge stickiness* is mostly about extending the time throughout which knowledge remains with a particular person, remaining accessible within or for the organization. *Knowledge stickiness* is also relevant at the organizational level, an important concept to consider when looking to have an individual's knowledge transferred to and "stuck" with particular platforms or other individuals. The feasibility of extending the time knowledge remains with a particular person is often underestimated by learning and knowledge management professionals. Nearly a century ago, early research into learning effectiveness found that most kinds of knowledge will be entirely forgotten within one to two months of acquisition, a phenomenon called the *forgetting curve*. Designing "sticky" formats for knowledge sharing, therefore, becomes important—applying learning methods such as repeating, reusing, and associating and creating opportunities for retrieval. Across the chapters of this book, formats to create "knowledge stickiness" will be discussed, including work done by the *Art of Knowledge Exchange* (Chapter 9) and the re-tooled World Bank's Archives (Chapter 14).

4. *Adult learning theories*: Most organizations tend to neatly separate teams and mandates dedicated to knowledge management from those dedicated to (staff) learning: The former often resides either with information technology departments or in strategy, research, or front office units, while the latter typically "lands" with human resource departments. The people-centered view of knowledge management taken here, however, calls for a close integration of the two fields, if only because adult learning theories applied by learning teams include key concepts important to be deployed by good knowledge management. Professionals in the learning field—*instructional designers*—seek to construct ways for people to interact with knowledge in ways that make a difference to their lives, inspire, change mindsets, and drive performance. While mostly focusing on "course settings," the principles of *andragogy* (different from pedagogy or "how people learn"), developed originally by Alexander Knapp in 1833 and popularized by Malcolm Knowles since the 1950s, can be usefully applied to any knowledge-sharing setting. These principles include elements such as motivation (adults must *want* to learn and need to know why), practicality, relevance-in-time, learning-by-doing, problem-solving, informality of setting, un-learning, and socialization. The learning field has obviously developed since Knowles, but key elements of his principles continue to find themselves in evolving practices such as experiential learning, e-learning, gamification, or transformational learning and influence the design of knowledge curation and sharing interventions.

Conceptual Underpinnings: Understanding and Taking Decisions in Complex Systems

Key Dimensions of Operating in Complex Systems: The Cynefin Framework, Cognitive Bias, and the Learning Organization—Most of the world's key development challenges have become more and more complex over the last years, as speed and interdependencies of key evolutions have grown, expanding detail and accelerating in time through scale and network effects. Leading, managing, and delivering the right decisions has consequently also become more complex, including for policymakers and development practitioners. Operating in complex environments—whether these are social systems or organizations—requires particular skills and ways of working, and many of them are well-integrated in good learning and knowledge management practices.

- *The Cynefin Framework is a tool to make decisions in complex environments*: Developed by David Snowden as a "sense-making device" in 1999 when he worked for IBM, the Cynefin Framework is largely a tool to aid in decision-making. The framework considers five distinguishable contexts—simple/obvious/clear, complicated, complex, chaotic, and disorder—and it suggests different formats for decision-making for each of the contexts. For example, where a context is complicated, actions to take include sensing, analyzing, and responding based on good practice and requiring expert knowledge. However, where the context is chaotic, actions include acting, sensing, and responding based on novel practices. The word *cynefin* is drawn from the Welsh language where it refers to the *familiar* or *acquainted;* Snowden uses it to describe the role of the framework—offering a known or understood location or space for decision-making. The Cynefin categories are a useful first step when solving a problem, helping to understand what kind of knowledge needs to be mobilized—and the types of people to involve, ranging from practitioners to experts and facilitators.
- *Cognitive bias as a "byproduct" of having to operate in overly complex environments*: While research into cognitive bias has evolved over the past 15 years or so, the relevance for development professionals has been elevated when the World Bank picked up the topic for its *2015 World Bank Development Report on Mind, Society, and Behavior*. The third chapter of this flagship report explores the biases potentially influencing development professionals' decisions and choices, in particular—while submitting that most cognitive biases are the result of having to maneuver through increasingly complex environments. Some of the most well-known biases discussed include the simplification bias, the confirmation bias, the sunk cost bias, and contextual biases. As the report points out, "good people can make bad decisions," and for most organizations, it is vital to put measures in place to prevent or limit biased decision-making. Methods for "de-biasing" are common practice for learning and knowledge management practitioners, and many of the interventions and initiatives described in some of this book's chapters can assist in de-biasing.
- *Operating in complex environments at the organizational level: The Learning Organization*. Peter Senge's 1990 seminal book *The Fifth Discipline: The Art and Practice of the Learning Organization* has changed how organizational change scholars look at cause-effect thinking in addressing complexity. Senge proposed various steps to help move from a reactive events-based or transactional approach to longer-term "pattern" thinking that would allow organizations and their staff to understand systemic structures behind these patterns. In his view, creating "learning organizations" is the only way to introduce system-relevant techniques as described in "Fifth Discipline" thinking. The concepts underlying the Fifth Discipline can help understand the work of the World Bank teams in organizational learning and culture change.

Conceptual Underpinnings: Shaping Solutions Requires Understanding Replicability

Moving From Knowledge to Solutions: Understanding Replicability—Beyond *knowing* all there is to know in addressing a particular challenge, finding, developing, and delivering a solution that can address the challenge in a particular country, time, institutional, and political setting requires an *understanding of replicability*; why did a particular policy or technological intervention work and under what circumstances can it be replicated elsewhere, or even scaled up, or where and how does it need to be adapted? Much neglected in the knowledge management or learning domains, the notion of delivering solutions involves careful analysis as much as the courage to act in environments of imperfect information. In the context of the World Bank, the replicability and scalability of projects, programs, or policies is considered based on a thorough process of documenting, sharing, and analysis as well as consultation (see Chapter 5.4). Key characteristics of replicability include responding to specific and well-defined development challenges; a record of successful implementation in one or more instances, with demonstrable positive impacts; and "un-packable" elements that can be analyzed and adjusted where necessary when moving to replication or upscaling in other geographic, social, or sectorial contexts. *Solutioning* then requires identifying the potential for replicability, that is, carefully considering where success has been achieved and "unpacking" key elements and drivers to determine the elements that made them work, including institutional arrangements, modalities for stakeholder engagement, technical approaches, incentive structures, and so on.

Co-Creation: Innovation Beyond Boundaries—From a knowledge management perspective, co-creation is the process that sometimes is described with the shorthand "$1 + 1 = 3$". Two or more parties, jointly agreeing on a problem to solve or challenge to face, embark together on a creative journey and find approaches and answers that are beyond their own original perspectives. Co-creation, in the *business world*, took hold when companies invited their customers and suppliers "in the kitchen" of designing processes and products, removing barriers between departments and industries. Prominent examples include *Anheuser-Busch, BMW, and Ikea* and tools include specific facilitation techniques as well as spaces such as specifically designed co-creation labs. Achieving such progress is also possible in development cooperation, and this book will describe co-creation approaches used between World Bank teams as well as country government teams and within organizational units belonging to both; the main instruments used are carefully designed and highly facilitated *collaborative* communities of practice as well as modalities such as *technical deep dives* (see Chapters 5 and 6).

Notes

1 Lave, J., and E. Wenger. 1991. *Situated Learning: Legitimate Peripheral Participation*. Cambridge: Cambridge University Press. https://doi.org/10.1017/CBO9780511815355.
2 Wenger, E. 1998. *Communities of practice: Learning, meaning and identity*. Cambridge, UK: Cambridge University Press. ISBN 0521430178hbk;05216636pbk
3 Carla O'Dell and Cindy Hubert. 2011. *The New Edge in Knowledge. APQC.* Hoboken, NJ: John Wiley & Sons.

Chapter 4

Transforming the Knowledge Ecosystem

Philip Karp[1]

Organizational Context

As noted in Chapter 1, one of the surprising characteristics of the overall World Bank knowledge ecosystem has been the absence of any strong (centralized) governance structure or prescribed blueprint for the knowledge ecosystems of individual business units. This was very much the case at the time of the reorganization that resulted in the creation of GSURR. Rather than seeing this as a constraint, the management of the new Global Practice saw it as an opportunity for innovation. The newly appointed senior director of the Practice was a strong proponent and recognized champion of knowledge and saw it as a vehicle for addressing some of the challenges which the Practice faced. Principal among these challenges was the composition of the Practice itself. As noted in Chapter 2, GSURR inherited nearly 700 staff located around the world and comprising an amalgam of groups of staff from several thematic sectors that had not previously worked together closely or, in several cases, at all. This included four distinct groupings covering urban development, disaster risk management, social development, and land administration. The challenge faced by GSURR management was to integrate this large number of staff into a seamlessly operating team with a shared vision and sense of purpose—despite being dispersed across the world and representing diverse professional disciplines and business sectors that had not historically worked together or seen eye to eye. The urban, disaster risk management, and land teams were composed mainly of planners and engineers who focused heavily on technical solutions and on hard infrastructure, while the social development teams were made up of sociologists, anthropologists, and economists, focusing much more on people, behaviors, processes, and institutions. And as if the challenge, alone, of getting these groups to work together was not enough, the GSURR senior management team set itself a goal of seeking synergies across the groups such that the whole would be greater than the sum of the parts and would result in creation of new business lines and an expanded portfolio of projects and client engagements.

In thinking about how to address this challenge, the management team had a number of key questions to consider, most notably the following:

1. How can we create a new joint identity for the practice?
2. How can we leverage the diversity of staff across countries and professional disciplines?
3. How can we create a culture of good knowledge citizenship?
4. How can we connect and integrate a highly decentralized team?
5. How can we identify new business lines that would capitalize on synergies?

DOI: 10.4324/9781003199083-5

Creating a Joint Identity

GSURR management chose the theme of "building sustainable communities" as a unifying identity for the Global Practice. This theme was intended to capture the spatial dimension of the Practice, spanning both rural and urban settings; the social dimension, associated with communities; and the resilience dimension, reflected in the focus on sustainability. In addition, the use of the term "communities" signaled the Practice's focus on the "connecting" (as opposed to "collecting") dimension of knowledge management (see Introduction). Subsequent chapters will explore, in detail, the role of communities of practice in promoting flow of knowledge and in shaping the global practice's work programs. It is sufficient to note here that communities of practice were at the heart of the Practice's knowledge management strategy and knowledge ecosystem. The identity of a sustainable communities team was reinforced through communications to staff from GSURR senior management and through the *Sustainable Communities Blog,* an external communications platform that included both written and video blogs and emphasized the multisectoral nature of the practice's programs and activities (see Chapter 7).

Recognizing Value in Professional Diversity

One of the characteristics that set GSURR apart from some of the other Global Practices was the professional diversity of its staff. As previously noted, the Practice's 700 staff spanned several thematic sectors and represented diverse professional disciplines including planners, engineers, economists, sociologists, and anthropologists. While this diversity posed a challenge, in terms of getting different groups to work together, GSURR management saw it as an opportunity to forge new business lines shaped by synergies across teams. The resilience dimension, in particular, proved to be a good basis for cross-sector collaboration and new products as business lines emerged around resilient infrastructure, resilient cities, resilient transport, resilient schools, etc. Another unifying dimension was that of social inclusion, again melding inclusion with spatial and infrastructure parameters.

A key element of the GSURR knowledge ecosystem, which also set it apart, was its reliance on knowledge management professionals. A notable failing of a number of knowledge management initiatives elsewhere in the World Bank was the assumption that technical staff with training as economists, engineers, or one of the other predominant technical disciplines among World Bank staff could magically be transformed into knowledge management specialists and could do so on top of their regular duties. This resulted in knowledge management programs and approaches that were far from cutting edge, giving the discipline a less than stellar image within the institution.

In contrast, the senior leadership of GSURR recognized the value of having a group of knowledge management specialists as part of the practice. They recruited a lead knowledge management and learning specialist with strong operational experience to spearhead knowledge management within the practice. And contrary to the norm in the World Bank wherein knowledge management staff were merely expected to implement strategies and initiatives developed by management, GSURR made this specialist part of the Practice's management and technical leadership team, putting him in a position to help shape strategy upstream and to be fully aware of implementation downstream. Whereas other Practices might have one or at most two knowledge management specialists as part of their staff, GSURR assembled a team of five, in addition to the lead specialist/team leader.

Yet, it was emphasized that knowledge management was not an isolated or standalone function to be undertaken solely by this team of specialists. Rather, the mantra of the Practice was that *knowledge is everybody's business*, with staff expected to incorporate good practice knowledge into their work and to document findings and lessons to inform future projects. The knowledge management team was there to facilitate these processes and to help with curation, but all staff were expected to be part of and contribute to the knowledge ecosystem.

Early on, the knowledge management team was assigned the role of organizing the first Practice-wide Forum, an ambitious event that brought the Practice's staff from around the world together at three locations for a "follow the sun" program of team-building and knowledge-sharing activities. This event and its role in creating a culture of knowledge citizenry is described in Chapter 8. Its success and innovative elements helped to establish the Practice's knowledge management team as a valuable asset and to demonstrate the role it could play in fostering innovation. Moreover, the event provided a platform to introduce a number of innovative knowledge management formats and approaches that became hallmarks of GSURR knowledge programs.

The use of specialized knowledge management staff extended to the GSURR communities of practice as well. As discussed in Chapter 5, the practice engaged a specialized consultant to coordinate the community of practice network as well as a team of community managers, bringing the specialized skills and experience needed for this important role. In large part due to the work of this team, GSURR's knowledge communities became recognized as "best practice" across the World Bank and helped to revive the reputation of this modality after the mixed record of previous community of practice initiatives in the institution.

Thirty Minutes on Thursdays—Integrating Staff in a Global Organization

Another challenge facing GSURR management was how to effectively integrate decentralized staff into the Practice's knowledge ecosystem and culture. The World Bank employs approximately 10,000 staff located in 130+ offices around the world. A large cadre of these staff are recruited and spend much of their careers at World Bank headquarters in Washington, DC, with occasional stints of three to four years in one of the institution's country offices, usually in a developing country. These staff typically have stellar academic credentials, international experience, and strong technical expertise. They hold most of the managerial positions within the organization and heavily influence its policies and procedures. However, an even larger cadre of staff are recruited locally in developing countries for positions in that country's World Bank office. These staff also have strong academic credentials as well as practical experience. Many have held senior-level positions in government and, hence, have strong networks and connections with local counterparts in the institutions that are implementing agencies for World Bank projects. They are very good at figuring out how to get things done in the country and at managing client relationships. What they often lack, however, is the global perspective that comes from work in and exposure to solutions from other countries. As World Bank clients increasingly demand cutting-edge technical knowledge and solutions from around the world, a key challenge faced by the organization is how to effectively integrate country-office based staff, particularly those recruited locally, into its knowledge ecosystem. This challenge is exacerbated by the fact that, like many other global organizations, the World Bank's structure has been overly headquarter-centric, revolving around its office in Washington, DC, particularly when it comes to knowledge development and dissemination.

GSURR was no different. Priding itself as a learning and knowledge organization that depends on a highly informed, globally mobile staff poses unique challenges—how to ensure staff located across the globe have access to the same knowledge as that available to Washington-based staff? Should new knowledge be created centrally and disseminated outwards from headquarters to field staff? What is the role of country office–based staff in generating knowledge drawn from their daily contact with the 189 member governments? What is the best way for staff based in country offices to learn from each other without having to go through or involve headquarters?

These were among the challenges and questions faced by management of GSURR when it set out to develop a knowledge ecosystem for the Global Practice. To help come up with ideas and hopefully a solution, the management team turned to one of its lead technical specialists, the Co-Global Lead for City Planning, Finance, and Management. This staff member was uniquely placed to think through how to incorporate country office staff into the Practice's knowledge work. After first spending nine years at World Bank headquarters, he had embarked on a series of successive assignments in World Bank country offices, first in Tanzania, then in India, then in Beijing, and finally in Singapore from where he continued to work on projects in China.

While working in the four country offices, he experienced, firsthand, the frustration felt by many of his local colleagues when interesting-sounding knowledge sharing and learning events or activities were announced, only to find that these were taking place at a time that was in the middle of the night in the office where they were located. Nor was he placated by the stock offer, from headquarters, to provide a recording of the event, as this couldn't replace the opportunity to participate in the discussions or share the valuable experience and solutions that were being derived from projects in the countries where he was working.

Canvassing colleagues based in country offices across Sub-Saharan Africa, the Middle East and North Africa, Eastern Europe and Central Asia, South Asia, and the East Asia and Pacific regions, it became clear that many of them shared similar frustrations. Besides the inconvenient times at which headquarters-organized knowledge events were being scheduled, the other most cited concerns were that the format of sessions didn't work because the headquarters presenters and folks in the room with the presenters occupied the bulk of the time allotted, leaving little, if any, time for questions or comments from staff connecting from country offices. Moreover, the country office–based staff noted that while the sessions tended to cover professionally interesting topics, they often weren't really of concern or applicable to the country or the projects the field-based staff were working on.

What they needed was a new knowledge-sharing platform that was geared primarily to country office staff and that skipped formalities such as lengthy opening remarks from senior management and rambling comments from designated discussants, instead emphasizing opportunity for practical discussions between and among peers. Moreover, these exchanges needed to take place during time slots that were convenient for staff outside of Washington.

The consultations made it clear that a decentralized—country office to country office—knowledge-exchange platform (with a distinct identity, predictable schedule, and technical support) with content driven by field-based staff, in a short less-than-an-hour format, more like a chat over tea/coffee among peers during their working hours was what country office–based staff were looking for.

Thursdays seemed like the ideal day in any week to organize such events—the first three days of the week are always hectic and quite a few staff follow the World Bank's alternative work schedule (AWS), which enables them to take every other Friday off work if they work more than nine hours a day for the rest of the week. In an ideal world, a chat over coffee shouldn't take more than 30 minutes. That's how *Thirty Minutes on Thursdays* was born. That didn't mean staff couldn't or wouldn't organize such sessions on any other day of the week or that they'd stick to a hard 30-minute format. After all, staff at the World Bank are not known for their brevity.

The aim was to connect as many country offices as possible during their working hours. A sweet spot was identified that would allow offices across East and South Asia, Middle East and North Africa, all of Africa as well as in Europe and Central Asia to connect at a time convenient to them. That spot was towards the end of the day in Tokyo and Sydney; late afternoon in Beijing, Hanoi, Manila, Jakarta, and Yangon; mid-afternoon in Dhaka, Kathmandu, New Delhi, Colombo, Islamabad, Almaty, Ankara, and Tbilisi and mid- or early morning in Rabat, Cairo, Paris, Nairobi, Dar es Salaam, Pretoria, Accra, and Abuja. The Tokyo Development Learning Center (see Chapter 6) was enlisted to help with organization and to manage videoconference connections between the participating country offices.

The *Thirty Minutes on Thursdays* sessions kicked off in the summer of 2016 with a presentation from Hanoi (on an ongoing project in the city of Danang). This was followed over the subsequent months with presentations from Islamabad (historic inner-city rehabilitation in Lahore), Kampala (performance grants for local governments), West Bank and Gaza (solid waste management in fragile states), Jakarta (national slum upgrading program and OneMap for land management), New Delhi (new city development and land pooling), Nairobi (national urban program), Singapore (transit-oriented development and urban placemaking), and Rabat (program for results operation for the city of Casablanca).

Events were generally well-attended. Each session attracted around 25 to 30 individuals from 4 to 6 country offices. As planned, each session jumped straight to a presentation which lasted between 15 to 25 minutes followed by questions and answers for another 15 minutes or so. Sessions rarely lasted more than an hour, which was welcomed by all. Unfortunately, however, after about 10 sessions, the series fizzled out.

In reflecting on why, the team made the following observations: There's a limit to what personal peer-to-peer relationships can achieve. The easiest way to organize the sessions was through personal networks and relationships. While this informal networking may have been a good starting point, it proved not to be an effective way to curate the program and sustain it over time. What was needed was for regional managers to encourage and reward their staff for participating, but this went against the informal, bottom-up nature of the initiative.

Furthermore, operating the initiative from outside of the established setup for GSURR's global knowledge programs proved to be a mistake. Each World Bank Global Practice includes a global unit that functions out of Washington, DC, and is expected to be the curator and often the creator of new technical knowledge. GSURR was no different. In bypassing this unit when setting up the *Thirty Minutes on Thursdays* initiative, the organizers not only missed out on the potential support that this unit could have provided but also failed to institutionalize it.

Recognizing this, responsibility for country office–staff focused knowledge exchanges shifted to the various GSURR communities of practice, nearly all of which included country office staff among their members. In this way the initiative was mainstreamed into the overall knowledge management ecosystem of the Practice.

Leveraging Peer-to-Peer Knowledge Exchange

Another key element of the GSURR knowledge ecosystem was attention to South-South and peer-peer/practitioner-practitioner knowledge exchange. The GSURR knowledge team believed strongly that such exchanges are among the most effective ways of sharing, replicating, adapting, and scaling up successful solutions to development challenges and/or to avoiding repetition of unsuccessful approaches. Practitioner exchanges are particularly effective for sharing "how to" or tacit knowledge about solutions, as these "tips and tricks" tend to not be fully codified or recorded in written descriptions or case studies. Practitioner exchange as a modality for capacity building represented something of a departure from more traditional approaches such as technical assistance or deployment of expert advisors, whereby external experts (usually academics or consultants) are relied on to share successful solutions with which they are familiar only through research and may, therefore, lack a complete understanding of the full range of factors that underlie the successful implementation elsewhere or the pitfalls to be avoided.

While peer-peer exchange can be very effective, it was recognized that good design was extremely important. Particularly in the case of exchange modalities such as study tours, poor design can lead to monumental waste of resources, giving these exchanges a bad name. As described in detail in Chapter 9, the GSURR knowledge team recognized this reality and embraced an existing program that had been developed by the World Bank Institute to train staff on design of results-focused knowledge exchange.

The team also recognized that good peer-peer knowledge exchange requires knowledge providers who have adequately documented and are able to effectively communicate the successful solutions that have been adopted by their countries or organizations. The challenge is that these solutions often reside in technical agencies and departments whose staff are not trained in skills such as communication and knowledge exchange. This, in fact, is why the process of sharing these successes has often fallen on academics or consultants rather than on the practitioners themselves. Again, GSURR embraced an existing program focused on building client capacity for knowledge sharing, leveraging client engagements that had already been initiated with knowledge provider institutions in GSURR sectors and countries of interest. This is described in Chapter 10.

Perhaps the most notable element of the GSURR knowledge team's innovations in the realm of peer-peer knowledge exchange was the introduction of multicountry knowledge-sharing modalities and platforms. Like other groups across the World Bank, GSURR teams did organize a number of bilateral knowledge exchanges, often in the form of study tours, but the GSURR knowledge team recognized that an even more powerful modality for knowledge sharing involved bringing together groups of practitioners from multiple countries that are facing common challenges. GSURR's urban team already had some experience with this modality through a program known as Metro Lab, which brought together a peer group of practitioners from cities wanting to learn how to better manage their cities on a metropolitan area–wide scale.

As described in Chapter 6, GSURR built on the Metro Lab experience to introduce a new modality for multicountry exchange, known as technical deep dives (TDDs). These became another hallmark of GSURR's knowledge ecosystem and were utilized in several programs and locations. In similar fashion, GSURR worked with several client cities to help them to establish themselves as "knowledge hubs," focused both on sharing their experiences and learning from others. The most notable of these was the city of Medellín, Colombia.

As described in more detail in Chapter 10, GSURR partnered with the city's International Cooperation and Investment Agency to organize a series of events that brought delegations from other cities to Medellín for a weeklong, immersive program of knowledge sharing, site visits, action planning, and co-creation of solutions.

Giving Prominence to Knowledge Management

How did GSURR management accomplish building knowledge citizenry in such a coherent and long-term consistent way? Early on, management team had decided to create space within the leadership group for the department's knowledge and learning team leader. This was both a signal to the rest of the department ("Knowledge matters to Management") and it created space for the leadership group to be involved in building and supporting the various dimensions of the Practice's knowledge ecosystem, allowing for it to be designed and built in an integrated, self-reinforcing fashion.

Indeed, whereas knowledge management initiatives elsewhere often are implemented in an ad hoc and/or uncoordinated fashion, knowledge and learning became an important part of the DNA of GSURR, with the various parts of the knowledge ecosystem closely coordinated and supporting one another. Hence, GSURR communities of practice took leadership in design of TDLC technical deep dives focused on topics within their purview; communities of practice also were enlisted to develop the content, by way of knowledge and learning sessions, for Practice-wide forums; counterparts from Medellín were invited to TDLC technical deeps dives both to serve as resource experts but also to observe how these programs are run in view of the organization of similar programs in their city; TDLC handled logistical arrangements for the *Thirty Minutes on Thursdays* sessions (see Chapter 6); and presenters at knowledge and learning events were given coaching on messaging and presentation skills, helping to reinforce the importance of good design and good communication skills. In addition, as discussed in Chapter 7, the coordination/integration of knowledge management and communications was another important element of the overall GSURR knowledge ecosystem.

Shortcomings and Lessons Learned

While the GSURR knowledge ecosystem was recognized across the World Bank for its innovation and success, it was not without shortcomings, several of which stemmed from corporate-level weaknesses. The foremost of these was the lack of an adequate information technology platform to support knowledge management, particularly online collaboration. The World Bank has a robust information technology system to support communications and online access to business systems by its globally distributed staff. However, when it comes to tools for online collaboration, particularly for communities of practice, the institution was seriously lacking at the time. In large part due to concerns about information security, the World Bank's central information technology department prohibited individual units from utilizing software or cloud-based tools that were not fully tested, vetted, and approved at corporate level. This constrained GSURR from adopting, or even experimenting with, any of the tools for online collaboration and community management that were emerging in other industries. As a result, the GSURR knowledge management team was forced to rely on tools that were inadequate and not fit for purpose when it came to supporting its communities of practice. One particular constraint was the inability to provide external access to the various communities' databases, curated solutions, online discussions, and recorded events. This severely restricted their ability to realize the vision of becoming global communities, bringing together like-minded experts and practitioners not only from the World Bank but from across the world.

A lesson derived from the experience of the *Thirty Minutes on Thursdays* initiative is that successful programs need more than a grievance for sustenance. The *Thirty Minutes on Thursdays* sessions were designed specifically to address concerns about the inconvenient timing and headquarters-centric nature of many of the World Bank's knowledge and learning offerings. However, a meaningful program of such exchanges should have been built on a more concrete demand for knowledge from the targeted audience and should have been integrated into larger professional development plans for field office staff.

On the positive side, GSURR's experience demonstrates the benefits that can be derived from attention, and a strategic approach, to knowledge management. By fully integrating knowledge management principles, approaches, and staff into the Global Practice's strategy, organizational structure, and leadership team, GSURR was able to derive benefits both upstream, during formulation of programs and strategy, and downstream, during implementation. Indeed, this integrated approach was critical to allowing the GSURR knowledge ecosystem to catalyze the impressive organizational transformation that is described throughout this book.

Note

1 Inputs for the *Thirty Minutes on Thursdays* section of this chapter were provided by Barjor Mehta, lead urban specialist.

Chapter 5

Communities of Practice for Action

Ivan Butina

Communities of Practice at the World Bank

The History of Communities of Practice

The formal introduction of communities of practice—called thematic groups at the time—happened in the late 1990s under "The Knowledge Bank" vision of the late World Bank president James Wolfensohn and the leadership of the former program director for knowledge management Steve Denning (see Chapter 2). After Wolfensohn and Denning left the organization, in 2005 and 2000 respectively, communities of practice, like knowledge management, had their highs and lows in terms of senior management's attention. However, once introduced and intentionally cultivated they never left the organization. At any given time, there were some 300 operational communities of practice across the organization. They had different names, such as thematic groups or beams. Some of them were fully internal to the World Bank, while others were mostly external. Some had management support and resources, while others were fully driven by staff commitment (see Box 5.1 for a typology of communities of practice at the World Bank). Some fully embraced the introduction of videoconferencing and/or virtual platforms or were even born on them, while others maintained "old-school" ways of interacting via email, or—when possible—in person. But they never ceased to exist, and some of them thrived over the years.

Communities of Practice in the New Organizational Structure of the World Bank

When the leadership team of the newly formed Global Practice for Social, Urban, Rural, and Resilience (GSURR) decided in 2014 to fully embrace and invest in communities of practice, they were working on fertile ground. The leadership team saw the communities of practice as a core tool to achieve its strategic objectives, including offering better services and new business lines to clients that brought together diverse technical disciplines to solve wicked development challenges. The expectation was that the communities would also serve as a vehicle to create a new culture and vision for the large and diverse GSURR group with its more than 700 staff in 70 offices around the world and with a wide range of technical disciplines that had not worked together before.

DOI: 10.4324/9781003199083-6

Box 5.1   —Definition and Typologies of Communities of Practice

Communities of practice, as defined by the World Bank, are gatherings of individuals motivated by the desire to share professional experience, work across organizational boundaries, relate to one another, and build a body of actionable knowledge through coordination and collaboration.

The most common types of communities of practice over the history of the World Bank include:

- *Informal*: initiated and maintained only by community members.
- *Formal*: initiated and/or sponsored by management with specific mandates
- *Cross-cutting*: members are from different thematic areas/practices of the WBG.
- *Open*: anyone can join.
- *Restricted*: by invitation or vetting only.
- *Internal*: members are WBG staff only.
- *External*: created and maintained by the WBG for its clients.
- *Hybrid*: created and maintained by the WBG for its staff as well as external members.

The GSURR communities of practice were defined—using the typology presented in Box 5.1—as *informal, cross-cutting, and open* groups designed to connect staff across technical disciplines within GSURR, across other Global Practices, and externally. The mandate, thus, was to work either in an *internal, external, or in a hybrid format*, depending on the level of maturity of the underlying community. The communities of practice were conceptualized as a core component of the GSURR knowledge ecosystem (Chapter 3) to connect dispersed staff and knowledge, enable collaboration, and support operational business, through practitioner or project support, business development, quality enhancement, or product innovation.

From the beginning, GSURR leadership's intention was to connect groups even *across* organizational boxes. To communicate this objective, the new communities of practice were called "knowledge silo breakers" or KSBs, for short. The name inspired the nascent communities and gave them permission to connect with other teams inside or outside organizational boundaries without sensing restrictions.

The intention within GSURR was to build upon success and good practices from existing communities of practice while, at the same time, encouraging innovation and collaboration. One important difference, and this was a clear strategic choice of the GSURR leadership team, was to ensure that every KSB was closely linked to World Bank business and to client needs rather than focusing only on knowledge sharing.

Soon after GSURR management launched its ecosystem of KSBs, the World Bank senior management decided to set up a new category of communities of practice called global solutions groups (GSGs). The GSGs were defined, using the typology of Box 5.1, as *formal, internal*, and generally focused on a *single sector or topic*. They were formal communities because their scope of work, mandate, and leadership were selected by management. They focused, with a few exceptions, on technical topics within each Global Practice rather than having a cross-sectoral mandate.

While both KSBs and GSGs maintained the traditional functions of World Bank communities of practice, they had a new strengthened emphasis on being closely linked to business and operational needs. However, while the GSGs were mandated top down by the management of each Global Practice, GSURR's KSBs were proposed by staff in a bottom-up process through an open call for proposals. The leadership of the KSBs was self-selected by its members, while the leadership of the GSGs was selected by management among the top technical experts of the institution. The areas of work of KSBs were selected by its members, while those of GSGs were decided by management teams. GSGs were seen as large groups with institutional backing, while KSBs were flexible, agile, and lean groups with different community sizes.

After a year of experimentation with the bottom-up (KSB) and top-down (GSG) communities, the GSURR leadership found that each of them had strengths and weaknesses. The KSBs were more vibrant, innovative, and agile. However, many of the KSB leaders did not have enough operational experience to strongly connect their communities' activities with World Bank business. The GSGs were more structured and traditional in approach. The GSG leaders had a lot more operational experience, and they shaped the work program to better support client services.

The GSURR leadership decided to merge the two approaches. Each KSB was placed under the umbrella of a GSG depending on the thematic and business areas they covered. The GSG leaders were tasked to provide some guidance to KSB leaders without crushing their innovation and energy. The GSG benefited from the energy of the KSBs, and the KSBs' influence on new business lines and client services grew stronger.

Corporate Support to the GSURR Communities of Practice

At the time the KSBs were conceptualized, in another corner of the World Bank, a team in the Learning, Leadership, and Innovation Vice Presidency developed a comprehensive program to support the development and strengthening of communities of practice across the organization. Under its learning division, this Vice Presidency brought together teams, previously scattered across the World Bank, that were supporting the organization in building communities of practice and online collaboration. Thus, the corporate community of practice support program was created, combining in-house expertise on establishing communities of practice with that of helping World Bank teams collaborate online via its internal and external networking platforms. GSURR's GSGs and KSBs became a primary client for this program tapping into its community management training, community leadership workshops, peer learning facilitation, advisory services, and templates and tools.[1] Hence, KSBs were not only launched on fertile ground and within the context of a somewhat renewed attention to community of practice–like structures, but GSURR was also able to tap into existing learning resources and expertise as well.

Foundational Elements of the GSURR Knowledge Communities

The evolution of GSURR knowledge communities—KSBs and GSGs—had four main foundational elements: leadership engagement, a strong central knowledge management team, connections to technical leaders in GSURR, and a clear pathway to growth.

Leadership engagement—The vision for the KSBs was to become—over time and in a gradual manner—the go-to knowledge communities for all relevant practitioners worldwide, increasing operational impact, driving new projects, and ultimately influencing the global agenda. This vision and the role of the KSBs within the business context of the Global Practice were regularly communicated by GSURR management throughout their development.

KSBs were discussed at management meetings and the leadership team members discussed them with staff at unit meetings. The message about the importance of the KSBs was clear, providing an incentive for staff to propose KSBs or get engaged with them: KSBs meant business.

Additionally, KSBs provided opportunities to staff of all grades to exercise leadership either as KSB leads or as active members, and staff were recognized accordingly in annual performance evaluations.

A central knowledge management team—GSURR had another key element that supported the successful launch and development of KSBs—the largest knowledge management and learning team among the Global Practices, counting five full-time staff and several consultants. The leader of this team was part of the GSURR management team, thus ensuring a direct connection between knowledge management and learning work—with KSBs at its center—and the business priorities of the Global Practice (see also Chapter 3).

This team ensured that the KSBs were indeed at the center of the GSURR knowledge ecosystem by connecting other knowledge and learning activities to them, and vice versa, while also providing key support to the roll-out and development of KSBs either through their expertise or by connecting them to existing resources within the organization, such as the corporate community of practice support program mentioned previously.

Thanks to the support provided by the GSURR knowledge management and learning team, KSB leads were ever more able to dedicate time to leading their community and its technical agenda rather than having to worry about the organizational and administrative aspects of communities of practice. KSB leads could focus on strategizing, identifying opportunities, establishing collaborations and partnerships, and ensuring the business relevance of the work undertaken with their KSBs, while specialists from the knowledge management and learning team assisted with organization of events, establishment of performance metrics, and development of online platforms.

Linkages to Global Practice technical leadership—The third foundational element that characterized KSBs was their link to the Global Practice's technical leadership. By connecting the KSBs to the GSGs, each KSB was represented and supported by a global technical lead in charge of the GSG. These staff were also part of the GSURR technical leadership team, along with the managers.

The strong connection between KSBs and GSGs ensured that ideas, practices, and innovations emerging from KSBs were easily surfaced to Global Leads and, in turn, to GSURR management. Conversely, the global technical leaders were able to exercise their technical leadership by providing feedback and direction to the KSBs in their portfolios.

A clear pathway to KSB growth—Finally, the gradual evolution approach that GSURR followed with KSBs was key, first focusing on the bottom-up emergence of the technical and

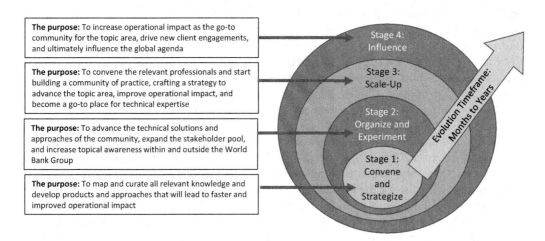

Figure 5.1 Knowledge Silo Breakers Impact Evolution

business areas they would cover and letting them manage themselves, to then gradually developing a whole program intended to support them towards fulfilling the purpose and vision for which they were created. Such an approach was important for two reasons. First, KSBs were at different stages of development, some having been just launched, while others already existed, before the 2014 World Bank reorganization, as thematic groups, beams, or other forms of communities of practice. Second, to become global "go-to" communities, KSBs had to go through earlier stages of development exemplified by the "KSB Impact Evolution" (see Figure 5.1)

Three Steps in the Communities Journey

The gradual evolution of the KSB ecosystem of knowledge communities also allowed for learning and adaptation along the way. This development happened in three different phases:

1. An intentional bottom-up "garden approach."
2. Introduction of a centralized community management support.
3. Introduction of a gradual impact framework to guide KSBs towards fulfilling their purpose.

A Garden Approach—Not Simply Letting One Thousand Flowers Bloom

"Letting one thousand flowers bloom" is an aphorism usually used to describe a non-interventionist approach by an organization to encourage the emergence of many ideas from many sources and waiting to see which ones stick and which ones fail. The GSURR leadership wanted to encourage the emergence of ideas, giving all staff the opportunity to participate in the process; however, the "flowers" resulting from the emergence of these ideas—the KSBs—were going to be tended to through a "garden approach."

In this approach, the GSURR leadership would provide the basic support for KSBs to grow. After a year of letting the "flowers bloom," the "garden approach" called for a detailed evaluation of progress and results prior to *pruning*. KSBs that did not make sufficient progress, usually because their leaders or members did not have the time or energy to build the community, were put in "hibernation."

The first KSBs emerged through an open call for proposals clearly stating that any staff member could propose establishment of and lead a KSB. Even staff from other Global Practices could propose a KSB as long as it had a GSURR member as one of its leaders. GSURR management indeed encouraged cross-practice proposals and even partnerships with external organizations.

Some communities of practice that existed before the establishment of the GSURR, such as the Land Thematic Group, the Urban Floods Community, and the Violence Prevention Global Beam, were also asked to submit applications to become KSBs. This was in their interest not only because of the formal recognition granted with KSB status but also because of the additional budget they would then be able to receive. They would also receive hands-on support and training from the central knowledge management and learning team.

A committee composed of members of the GSURR management team plus representatives from World Bank country offices reviewed all the proposals and either approved them, rejected them, or suggested adjustments such as mergers with other proposals, refocusing of the objectives, or a modification of activities. To emphasize the importance assigned to initiative by GSURR leadership, the Global Practice's senior director chaired the committee.

While rejections were few because of the high quality of most submissions, several KSB proponents were asked to merge with others to avoid overlap, ensure better alignment with GSURR business priorities, promote cross-practice or cross-disciplinary collaboration (e.g., between economists and engineers working on disaster resiliency), or prevent dispersion of resources, including staff time dedicated to participating in KSBs.

Interestingly, during this first and only open call for proposals, some of the KSBs that ended up being approved were not technical in nature but were affiliate communities such as the Grasshopper Youth Network KSB and the Women in Urban Development KSB. Also, a mentoring initiative for community-driven development and a technical team of 12 social development specialists working on global resettlement intelligence were given the status of KSBs.

In line with its bottom-up approach, seeking wide staff involvement, and the spirit of learning, innovation, and risk-taking that it was encouraging, the call for proposals stressed that it was okay for a KSB to fail. Indeed, documented failure to achieve planned outcomes, alongside with lessons learned from it, was mentioned as a positive outcome.

During the first year, new KSBs focused on establishing their presence by recruiting members, creating their convening spaces and communication channels, and launching their first activities. Most KSB leaders understood from the beginning the time commitment that building and managing a community required. They used a portion of the funds allocated to hire consultants to help them with community management. The GSURR knowledge and learning team took note of this.

A Change in the Second Year—Centralized Community Management

After their first year of activities, all KSBs were asked to submit a progress report for review by the GSURR leadership team. The evaluation served several objectives. First, to promote a disciplined approach to measure progress on knowledge management. This is a particularly difficult task. Nevertheless, it forced community leaders to describe in quantitative and qualitative terms their achievements. Second, the evaluation helped the GSURR leadership team understand the innovations and the bottlenecks as the knowledge ecosystem developed organically. Third, the evaluation served as the basis for "pruning the garden." A few communities that did not operate as a KSB were moved to different categories. For example, support communities such as a group of women in urban development or a group designed to match mentors and mentees continued to receive support in a different way. Other KSBs did not make much progress during the year and were put in hibernation.

The first-year evaluation highlighted an important inefficiency. Many KSBs were hiring separate consultants to support them with community mobilization, communications, and overall knowledge management support. Some of these consultants had community management experience, but many did not.

To ensure consistency in the level and quality of community management support across KSBs, GSURR decided to centralize this function. First, a knowledge management consultant specialized in communities of practice was hired to coordinate this new central function. His first assignment was to recruit a five-person team to support all GSURR communities (GSGs and KSBs). Meanwhile, GSURR management and the Practice's knowledge management and learning team convinced the KSB leads of the merits of this change. The KSBs would receive higher-quality knowledge management professional support and would not need to individually search for and hire such expertise.

All five community managers hired had completed the training organized by the corporate communities of practice program and were accredited as community managers, thus ensuring a common and consistent approach and skill set. GSURR's establishment of a centralized team of community managers represented a significant departure from past practice in the World Bank. It recognized that it is important to have knowledge management professionals with specialized skills to support communities. By the time of the second annual evaluation, KSB leaders could not imagine their communities without their centrally assigned community managers.

Another benefit KSBs received from the centralized community management team was the cross-pollination of effective ways to engage members, how to use available platforms, and new approaches to curate and share knowledge. In addition to sharing tips and tricks of the craft among themselves, the five community managers also coordinated respective events to avoid overlaps or to join forces when it made sense. Finally, the team facilitated the adoption of common basic knowledge management and community management standards across the KSBs, while also improving their branding across the World Bank.

The centralized community management team met weekly to discuss plans, challenges, and learnings and to ensure overall coordination with the GSURR knowledge ecosystem. The added value of the centralized community management team also became clear during the biggest knowledge and learning event for the Global Practice, the weeklong GSURR Forums (see Chapter 8). KSBs were assigned the role of providing the technical learning sessions to their GSURR colleagues, choosing topics and formats on how to deliver most effectively. This allowed for a unique community-building and learning experience among the more than 700 GSURR staff and further demonstrated the value of specialized knowledge management staff.

The centralized community management team, however, had one big challenge: how many communities can one knowledge management specialist support? In GSURR, the number ranged from 5 to 12 communities. The community manager who had 12 KSBs ended up providing standardized services such as the creation and maintenance of a knowledge hub in the intranet, the organization of knowledge-sharing events, or the collection of key information to compile a newsletter. These all were activities on the lower end of the value a trained community manager can add. The community managers who could focus on fewer KSBs had the bandwidth to strategize with the KSB leads and their core teams, build relationships with key members, or intentionally initiate and maintain community-building activities. An important lesson was to keep the number of communities per knowledge community manager low for greater effectiveness and impact.

Thanks to their work, over their second year of operation, KSBs improved overall staff engagement, increased collaboration across communities, continued to break thematic silos, improved efficiency in use of resources, and allowed KSB leads to focus their time on technical leadership and the alignment of KSB activities with business goals. The KSBs, indeed, were maturing, and it was time to further strengthen the support provided and to create a new model to assess their impact.

A Clear Path to Fulfill the Purpose and Vision of KSBs

In their third year of existence, the number of KSBs grew to 36 communities aligned across 9 GSGs. KSBs were not only covering traditional areas of work in the Global Practice but also were becoming even more of a channel to emerging business areas, several of which were cross-sectoral. The total membership of these KSBs grew to more than 2,000 staff across the organization.

In the third year, the KSB support program was expanded to include additional services such as product or service development support, team strategy sessions, and peer learning and knowledge exchange sessions among KSB leads, thus expanding the cross-pollination opportunities.

The GSURR knowledge management and learning team mapped out the dozens of products and services KSBs had introduced since inception. This rich repository of practices was a testament to the innovation and experimentation KSBs were encouraged to undertake. These products and services included different formats for knowledge sharing such as talks with experts, post–business trip knowledge sharing, or e-discussions. They also included project support initiatives such as project clinics, peer reviews, or sourcing of members for project teams. The inventory of products included learning initiatives and knowledge and operational products such as briefs, toolkits, and templates. And much more.

A particularly interesting innovation introduced by some of the KSBs was crowdsourced project and report reviews. The World Bank regularly uses peer reviews as a quality assurance mechanism for new projects and for publications. Traditionally, peer reviewers are senior technical experts, handpicked by the project manager for the project or report being reviewed or by their supervisor. Junior staff have limited opportunities to be involved, even if they have interesting ideas or experience. By crowdsourcing peer review comments from their members—in a very public and transparent manner—KSBs not only were able to bring in a broader set of perspectives, but they also "democratized" the review process, offering an opportunity for everyone, irrespective of seniority, to contribute.

Team strategy sessions led by community managers were offered to the core team of each KSB. These sessions were particularly beneficial to the new KSBs that were starting from scratch and could now benefit not only from the expertise of the knowledge management and learning team but also from the lessons learned from the KSBs that preceded them.

These sessions were also useful to older KSBs, as they were maturing to become technical centers of expertise for World Bank's business operations and its clients.

A challenge taken on by the GSURR leadership team was how to assess the impact of KSBs at different stages of development. The knowledge management and learning team set out to create a KSB Impact Framework that recognized the very diverse range of KSBs and their different stages of development. To do this, they once again partnered up with the corporate community of practice program, which, in turn, engaged an external vendor to help with the conceptualization of the framework.

The KSB Impact Framework that emerged sought to balance the need for a solid assessment approach, based on metrics that could demonstrate the progress of a KSB or lack thereof, with the need for flexibility due to differences among KSBs as well as the need to have a reasonable framework that could track and analyze metrics within a reasonable budget level. The KSB Impact Framework adopted was based on the following principles:

- Track KSB impact over time using a common methodology.
- Take into consideration the different stages of KSB development.
- Leave room for KSB leadership and the sponsoring GSG to choose the metrics that are most meaningful to their community given its stage of development and strategic goals.
- Instead of comparing KSBs with one another, focus on the progress of each KSB over time.

As part of the rollout, KSBs were each asked to choose at least three metrics to track performance and impact over the year. The KSB Impact Framework illustrated the four stages of development for KSBs. The highest level corresponded to the long-term vision set out for the KSBs when launched. The Impact Framework proposed 23 metrics KSBs could choose from. These metrics were distributed across the four stages of the KSB Impact Evolution.

The KSB Impact Framework helped KSB leads and their core teams plan their third-year activities according to a path that was now clearer, enabling them to choose goals that would help them to advance to the next level of impact. The centralized community management team played a key role in helping with the adoption of the KSB Impact Framework, by helping the KSB leads chose the right metrics, track them throughout the year, and report back at the end of the fiscal year.

Leadership Lessons

GSURR's knowledge communities (KSBs and GSGs) were largely successful in fulfilling their purpose of connecting staff within the Global Practice and other parts of the organization, breaking silos through knowledge sharing and increased collaboration, and strengthening the technical support provided to business operations while also demonstrating the potential of new business lines.

The evolution of GSURR's knowledge communities carries five lessons for other organizations:

First, senior management support was essential to the success of KSBs—While the communities of practice were a knowledge management approach that was already established at the World Bank, GSURR management decided to use such communities as the core element of the Global Practice's knowledge ecosystem and as an integral element of how the Practice would carry out its business.

The GSURR leadership team developed a unique label for the communities of practice—*knowledge silo breakers*—to signal the desire to break down traditional organizational barriers to knowledge flows and collaboration. But GSURR management did not stop at ideation. It did not create the concept and leave it to the knowledge management and learning team to implement while they moved to the next task. Instead, the senior leadership of the Global Practice consistently and clearly communicated about the role and importance of KSBs. This approach provided an authorizing environment for the KSBs to pursue their ambitions and innovations. It also gave an informal incentive to ambitious staff who saw KSBs as an opportunity to pursue business ideas, develop and strengthen leadership skills, and gain visibility and recognition from their peers and management.

Finally, GSURR management put financial resources behind their vision, including for seed cash and knowledge and community management support. The clear support from GSURR leadership made the work of the knowledge management and learning team much easier, as the technical practitioners leading and actively participating in KSBs were invested in their success, hence appreciated their expertise.

Second, a clear vision of their purpose and role made the evolution of KSBs much easier—Even during the first year, when KSBs were encouraged to experiment, the reason for their creation was clear, namely to become an integral part of how business would be done within the practice, providing technical leadership to ensure that the best available knowledge was embedded within GSURR products and services. The clarity of this vision was an essential foundation for the connection between KSBs and business operations. This connection ensured alignment of incentives and reinforced the importance for team members to participate in KSBs. The vision also gave direction to KSB leads as they were setting up and defining the work programs of their communities. When there is a clear vision from management, it is easier to create the structures and the tools to support the creation and evolution of communities of practice. If the destination is clear, envisioning a path forward is simpler.

Third, having KSBs at the center of the GSURR knowledge ecosystem helped make the mantra that "knowledge management is everyone's job" a reality—Through KSBs technical practitioners were directly in charge of generating, curating, and sharing knowledge. They were "living" knowledge management in these activities and were supported by knowledge management specialists who demonstrated their added value and technical expertise by providing guidance, supporting access to platforms and tools, and providing both strategic and logistical support.

The annual GSURR Forum (Chapter 8) exemplified the essential knowledge and learning role played by KSBs, not only because they were providing the technical learning content for these events but also because they were directly involved in the design and delivery of learning and knowledge-sharing sessions, thus creating a sense of ownership. Through the KSBs, technical practitioners were empowered to focus on the knowledge that mattered to them and to access it and share it through the formats that worked for them. The users had access to the knowledge they needed because they also were contributing to its generation.

Fourth, the centralized team of trained community managers played a critical role for success—They helped with improved coordination, ongoing cross-pollination and learning, resource optimization, and better coherence, while respecting the uniqueness of each community.

Fifth, succession plans are critical for communities of practice—The formal nature of the GSGs meant that their succession plans were structured through an open competitive selection of the community leaders about every three years. In contrast, the bottom-up nature of the KSBs meant that their succession approach was not clear from the beginning. While some KSBs held bi-annual leadership elections that involved the whole community of practitioners, most KSBs didn't have a clear succession model, thus running the risk of becoming dormant if the founding KSB leads were to step down or have less time to dedicate to this function.

The question of the continuity of communities of practice after senior management changes was an important one. GSURR management provided the top-level leadership that enabled several KSBs to emerge, develop, and provide business value in a short amount of time. While the GSURR model was picked up and adopted by at least one other Global Practice (Governance), it didn't become a standard across the whole organization.

In 2019, the GSURR Global Practice was split into two, with corresponding leadership changes, and in 2020, another institutional reorganization changed the World Bank structure and leadership positions. Despite these changes, many of the communities have continued because they provide a unique value to their members. Even if the incentives and support at the corporate level changed, the social capital and the tools and platforms of the former GSURR communities of practice have continued in several areas and have been adopted by other units and departments.

As has been shown by their rather long history at the World Bank Group, once created, communities of practice continue to live, evolve, die, and come into existence. Even without formal recognition or support, the ones that are most successful in building a strong community of practitioners and delivering value will continue to exist. In the end the basic promise of a more connected organization survives all the organizational changes and shifts in priorities.

Note

1 The guidance, tools, and templates provided by the CoP Program were collected in the World Bank Group's publication: "Building Community: A Primer. 2018 Update," World Bank, 2018, https://documents1.worldbank.org/curated/en/188671504682900121/pdf/119411-REVISED-PUBLIC-Community-Primer-2018-Final-2–21–2018.pdf

Chapter 5.1

Disrupting Creatively
How the Urbanscapes Community Sought to Change the Status Quo

Jon Kher Kaw

The Role of Communities of Practice (CoPs) as Disruptors

Large organizations often have established systems in place to streamline processes and shape business and project design. However, their focus on efficiency, productivity, sales volumes, and existing entrenched business lines can often stifle innovation. Consequently, even proven innovative solutions from other stakeholders or organizations often face significant barriers to adoption within large organizations, requiring substantial effort and institutional support.

At the World Bank, addressing client challenges and finding technical solutions, particularly through financing instruments like loans or grants for infrastructure and reforms, depend heavily on how well the proposed engagement aligns with development objectives, stringent operational requirements, risk management, and corporate mandates. This raises the question: how can innovation thrive in such a context, and where can it find entry points?

First, there is a growing recognition that there exists a significant untapped opportunity for creative new urban solutions within the Social, Urban, Rural, and Resilience Global Practice (GSURR), which focuses on supporting the development needs of cities and urban areas. Traditionally, the World Bank's support for cities has centered around well-defined and established sectors, such as investing in large-scale infrastructure (e.g., urban roads, flood protection), expanding urban services (e.g., water and sanitation, solid waste management, mobility), and reforming financial and governance systems—as part of top-down national programs or projects.

However, some of the most groundbreaking urban transformations defy traditional molds. These transformations transcend sectors, extending beyond the boundaries of GSURR, and are often most effective when implemented at the city or smaller neighborhood scale. Cities like Barcelona, Medellín, Seoul, and Singapore serve as prime examples, showcasing the power of smart city-level policies and high-quality infrastructure, even when focusing on seemingly "small" and "agile" interventions. These initiatives prioritize the development of people-centered urban environments, concentrate on regenerating neighborhoods, foster creative placemaking, unlock the potential of public spaces and cultural heritage, and seamlessly integrate urban planning with transit-oriented development. As a result of these bottom-up interventions at the street and neighborhood levels, these cities have successfully cultivated vibrant, creative, inclusive, and productive communities.

Second, the driving force behind truly innovative operations within the World Bank often came from individual team leaders who act as change agents, passionate about challenging

DOI: 10.4324/9781003199083-7

the status quo in project or program design. These team leaders possess the ability to not only navigate institutional hurdles and push the boundaries of established systems but also identify customized and novel solutions that go beyond traditional business lines and build collaborative teams that draw expertise from different sectors within and outside the Practice and the organization. What if we could remove the frictions for innovation and empower them for these changes?

This chapter traces the journey of a community of practitioners that decided to find new relevance for these "discarded, small, and/or hidden," yet "agile and transformative" urban solutions—working more closely with mayors and city leaders rather than just national governments—to create new business opportunities and ask critical questions such as—do cities need more costly infrastructure? Or can they better leverage the often-underutilized public assets that they already have to achieve similar or better outcomes? These innovators also held a strong belief that the cities of today need rapid but impactful transformation from the ground up and that smart policies, coupled with local leadership and agility, had to be part of the solution. These innovators decided to foster a new community as a force of disruption. What critical steps did they take to build a successful community of practice? What worked and what didn't?

Step One: Create a Unique Community Identity, Communicate an Aspiration

When a handful of like-minded team leaders and specialists got together and decided to form a CoP focused on transforming urban spaces in cities, they knew from the outset that they faced an uphill battle to implement their ideas on a larger scale, challenging established top-down practices and adopting fresh approaches to address long-standing issues from a bottom-up perspective. They also recognized the excitement and potential for change that lay before them, and it wasn't long before they decided that their disruption needed to be creative, engaging, and even "playful" despite the critical importance of providing serious evidence to support their ideas and fast proofs of concept.

One of their initial challenges was effectively conveying the purpose and character of the community. The members envisioned a vast array of possibilities for creative urban solutions spanning various domains, including urban planning and design of streetscapes and cityscapes, placemaking, land-value capture, municipal asset and land management, and urban technology solutions. In search of a unifying identity for the group, the Urbanscapes Community of Practice was conceived—an anagram for "urban spaces" and an unconventional name for a unique community.

Unlike many other communities within the GSURR knowledge ecosystem, the Urbanscapes Community of Practice chose to craft a mission statement to highlight its unique purpose and aspirations—rather than the technical focus of the CoP. For the participants, the "why?" was as important as the "what?" Figure 5.1–1 shows the approach they used to explain how they wanted to tackle urban challenges.

Step Two: Cultivate the Community's Culture

Right from the start, the Urbanscapes Community embraced a culture of openness and experimentation and a determination to challenge the status quo. While deepening knowledge and expertise among members was an integral part of its approach, it also focused on

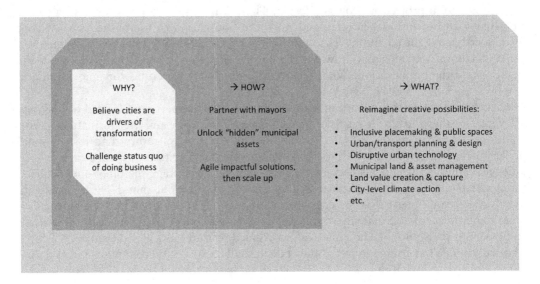

Figure 5.1–1 The Urbanscapes Community Strategy

Source: World Bank Urbanscapes CoP, framework based on Sinek (2009)

Figure 5.1–2 Bringing the Urbanscapes Community's Knowledge and Methods to the Real Challenges of Dhaka, Bangladesh

Source: Ishita Alam Abonee

encouraging a culture of creativity. Setting themselves apart from other communities and the institution as a whole, the Urbanscapes CoP established a distinctive visual and imaginative communication style. Its community announcements, communications, and documents were thoughtfully crafted to convey the expertise and artistry it aimed to bring to its community. Its messages were clever, visually appealing, and contextual. (See example in Figure 5.1–2.)

(Excerpt from Urbanscapes presentation at the World Bank. Quote from: Dan Reed, founder of "*Just Up the Pike*")

THE POPSICLE TEST

"You can measure the walkability of a neighborhood by how easily a child can go out, buy a popsicle, and make it home before it melts."

- Dan Reed, founder of *"Just Up the Pike"*

Figure 5.1–3 Experimentation With Problem-Solving Tools
Source: World Bank Urbanscapes CoP

Additionally, the community ventured into unconventional problem-solving and design thinking methods rarely used at the World Bank during that time. For instance, it sought to foster interactivity and design thinking by employing colored Lego building blocks to simulate and visualize land use and transport planning across teams with diverse technical backgrounds. Furthermore, it developed and harnessed virtual reality tools for participatory urban planning and design (see Figure 5.1–3).

By embracing these innovative approaches, the Urbanscapes Community not only expanded its creative toolbox but also cultivated an environment where fresh ideas could thrive and where collaboration among members from various fields was encouraged.

Step Three: Engage With Change Agents, Meet the Needs of Community Members

In contrast to other types of team-based institutional structures, CoPs operate on a self-organizing basis. Members choose to join and actively participate based on the benefits they derive from their involvement. As a result, different tiers of membership naturally emerge within each CoP, whether explicitly or implicitly. Recognizing this, the Urbanscapes Community explicitly identified these tiers to facilitate more targeted engagement.

The first group consisted of core team members (typically about five to ten people) who actively participate and shape the community's agenda. They served as change agents, driving the community forward. The second group comprised extended members who closely follow the community's activities and contribute opportunistically. Finally, observers made up the third group, identifying themselves with the community but participating to varying degrees.

The Urbanscapes Community of Practice also played several roles in fostering a vibrant and inclusive environment that facilitated collaboration, knowledge sharing, and the advancement of innovative urban solutions across different roles:

- Technical specialists and practitioners within the community of practice, such as economists, urban development specialists, transport specialists, and social development specialists, saw the community as a platform to explore shared interests in the latest advancements and global best practices across various disciplines—ranging from urban planning and design, urban transport, green infrastructure, placemaking, urban technologies, and local economic development.
- For team leaders and country-based management responsible for client engagement, the community of practice presented a new range of possible project and program designs centered on leveraging municipally owned assets and land through local government action.
- Wider community members saw the community of practice as an opportunity to test new ideas and seek support for practical implementation. This ranged from utilizing technology and data to shape evidence-based policies to employing tactical urbanism and placemaking processes as implementation strategies. Others used the community as a platform to showcase their recent achievements and gain recognition for their work.

Step Four: Connect With the Global Community

The Urbanscapes CoP recognized the importance of establishing strong professional networks, both within and beyond the World Bank, as the cornerstone of a thriving community. In addition to fostering internal collaboration, the community actively sought to strengthen its connections with external practitioners.

To cultivate expertise and credibility within the World Bank on relevant topics, concerted effort was made to incorporate cutting-edge knowledge and global best practices. In 2016, the community embarked on an initiative to facilitate meaningful engagements between project team leaders and prominent practitioners, think tanks, and thought leaders worldwide. These interactions took place through symposiums and knowledge platforms, with some relationships blossoming into collaborative partnerships that contributed to World Bank operations and research programs.

By 2020, the Urbanscapes Community had established robust connections with global thought leaders and had engaged in collaborations with entities such as the Singapore and Korean governments, the European Space Agency's Earth Observation for Sustainable Development, and the United Nations Human Settlements Program (UN-Habitat). The community published a book, launched at the World Urban Forum 10 in Abu Dhabi, which showcased a collection of crowdsourced stories and documented global case studies on public-space initiatives. These efforts aimed to extract valuable insights from on-the-ground experiences, focusing on the institutional dynamics and actions taken throughout the life cycle of public-space assets, encompassing their creation, design, funding, and management.

Step Five: Accelerate Concepts to Pilots

From its inception, the Urbanscapes CoP made a deliberate decision to gather and curate exemplary practices while fostering a diverse range of knowledge exchange mechanisms. These platforms served as fertile ground for cultivating synergies and forging connections across a wide spectrum of topics that captivated the community's interest.

Moreover, these platforms played a crucial role in fueling new ideas and nurturing their growth, guiding them from conceptualization to tangible pilot projects. The ultimate objective was to showcase these pilots and garner the necessary credibility to integrate concepts into large-scale projects funded by the World Bank.

For instance, the community's exploration of the innovative use of high-resolution satellite imaging and remote-sensing technology to analyze land use in expansive cities commenced with a seminal community seminar talk. Subsequently, a dedicated team advanced this idea by establishing a partnership with the European Space Agency. The Urbanscapes Community actively contributed to its refinement through an iterative process involving peer reviews and focused technical discussions. As a result, the tool's applications empowered policymakers to effectively identify and prioritize investments for a project in Dhaka, Bangladesh, saving substantial time and resources for both World Bank staff and government teams compared to laborious on-site surveys.

In another compelling example, the utilization of virtual reality to enhance participatory urban design within an operation in Karachi, Pakistan, emerged from a prototype that underwent rigorous beta testing during several technical deep dives organized by the Tokyo Development Learning Center (refer to Chapter 6 for more details). This iterative approach ensured the robust development and validation of the virtual reality solution within the context of real-world implementation.

By leveraging these mechanisms and experiences, the Urbanscapes Community actively facilitated and expedited the progression from conceptualization to pilot testing, bolstering innovation and propelling transformative impact.

Step Six: Find Opportunities for Scaling Concepts

Karachi, a bustling metropolis in Pakistan with a population exceeding 15 million, holds significant economic and commercial importance within the country. Despite this, the city faces numerous challenges: the absence of a public transport system, a substantial portion of the population residing in informal settlements, and limited access to piped water supply for a quarter of its residents. The complexities of Karachi's urban issues are formidable.

For over a decade, the World Bank had not actively engaged with the city as substantial policy reforms or large-scale investment programs were considered high-risk endeavors. The social and political landscapes further complicated matters. Additionally, there existed a general mistrust and resistance among the city's population towards any involvement with international organizations, while participatory planning was nearly absent from the city government's discourse. However, in 2017, the World Bank's country director for Pakistan expressed interest in exploring a new avenue for engagement with Karachi. The innovative ideas put forth by the Urbanscapes CoP piqued the country director's curiosity, opening a window of opportunity.

Collaborating with Karachi city officials, a team from the Urbanscapes Community embarked on a city diagnostic process to identify feasible steps for a phased transformation strategy. This approach led to the development of a strategy focused on a bottom-up, catalytic platform aimed at revitalizing specific areas of the city and public services through an intensely participatory neighborhood-based initiative.

Initially, the program interventions would commence as small-scale transformations. However, the overarching vision was to leverage these impactful incremental improvements in the urban environment, which would garner visibility and build trust among stakeholders.

This, in turn, would pave the way for broader reform-driven programs encompassing urban development, transportation, and water management sectors.

The Karachi Neighborhood Improvement Project, approved in 2017 (totaling US$98 million), sought to revitalize three neighborhoods in Karachi and enhance the government's service delivery capacity. The project aimed to benefit approximately 1.5 million residents living in these neighborhoods. Success in this initial phase would generate support for expanding the approach to other neighborhoods and programs throughout the city. The project's achievements led to an additional US$800 million of investments in water, transportation, urban management, and the business environment.

The ideas championed by the Urbanscapes CoP were no longer perceived as small-scale pilots but rather as evidence that demanded serious attention. The Karachi project served as proof of concept, prompting a shift towards rapidly replicating its innovative concepts in large-scale projects while maintaining a relentless commitment to fostering innovation (refer to Figure 5.1–4 from Bangladesh). Furthermore, there was an effort to broaden the community's expertise to address emerging and evolving demands from cities and municipalities. For example, community members provided support for frontier land value capture initiatives in Saudi Arabia's municipalities and contributed to smart city and green infrastructure programs in Amman, among various other endeavors.

Step Seven: Evolve the Community

Since its establishment in 2016, the Urbanscapes CoP has experienced remarkable growth, expanding from a small group of active members to over 300 professionals representing diverse disciplines. Over the course of five years, the community has achieved significant milestones, including the establishment of various platforms for knowledge exchange, the successful piloting of new operational business lines, the expansion of its global professional network, and contributions to corporate and global agendas. However, navigating the growth trajectory of the community has not been straightforward as its activities often do not align neatly with the formal strategies and structures of a large organization.

With that said, the World Bank recognized and acknowledged the vibrancy and creativity of the CoP. The Urbanscapes Community of Practice received several awards for collaboration and impact within the Global Practice. Furthermore, the CoP was also recognized as a finalist for the IFC's KNOWbel Prize in 2018 (refer to Chapter 13), highlighting the community's achievements in establishing a new operational business line.

Following the initial success, the COVID-19 pandemic necessitated a shift in approach and tactics. Travel and work restrictions posed challenges to the community's operations, prompting a reevaluation of traditional methods for exchanging explicit and tacit knowledge. New approaches were required to maintain and grow the informal and organic networks that form the foundation of communities of practice.

For instance, in 2021, the Urbanscapes Community collaborated with the Transit-Oriented Development Community of Practice (refer to Chapter 5.5) and the Tokyo Development Learning Center (refer to Chapter 6) to experiment with the use of technology and customized conferencing platforms for a virtual deep-dive technical workshop. These innovative efforts inspired further advancements within teams—through the use of interactive virtual whiteboards, coupled with design-thinking approaches involving large groups of participants, that enabled the World Bank Group to gather extensive datasets and distill ideas in several other engagements.

Simultaneously, the needs of mayors and city leaders underwent a shift in scope and urgency due to the pandemic. The economic crisis severely impacted urban economies worldwide. In response, the Urbanscapes Community adapted its integrated multi-disciplinary perspective to the new reality. The tools and approaches developed are now invaluable in assisting municipalities to leverage their land resources, infrastructure, and assets to address financial sustainability, urban health, and climate action simultaneously.

Chapter 5.2

Breaking Silos for New Client Services

The Affordable Housing Community

Angélica Nuñez, Yan Zhang, and Rodica Tomescu-Olariu

Communities of practice can be effective in breaking institutional silos across diverse technical disciplines, even when these groups have very different cultures, approaches, and tools, when working in closely related areas. This chapter looks at the Affordable Housing Community of Practice and its journey in bringing together three diverse groups engaging in the housing sector—two working with the public sector (urban sector and financial/mortgage sector) and one working with the private sector (private developers and financial institutions). This chapter describes the practical steps the community of practice took to build bridges of trust and develop new multidimensional tools and a comprehensive suite of services that was more attuned to the needs of client countries.

The Story of the Affordable Housing Community of Practice in Three Acts

Act 1: Three Families Fighting in a Village

The World Bank Group has been active in the housing sector since its establishment more than 70 years ago. Work in this sector is usually delivered by one of three practices or "families." Each of them has a distinct value proposition, identity, and technical area of expertise. The Urban Development family has been the Group's largest practice in the housing business for several decades. Their business lines include slum upgrading and regularization, urban sites and services schemes, and urban regulations. The Financial Sector family specializes in building and expanding housing finance markets. They help clients strengthen the legal and regulatory framework for housing finance and mobilize longer-term funding for housing, which is often missing in emerging markets. The Housing family at the International Finance Corporation (IFC)—part of the private sector arm of the World Bank Group—specializes in "downstream" interventions such as providing loans and equity to housing developers and lenders in emerging markets.

Previously, when a client country requested World Bank support for affordable housing, the three families often rushed to offer their own separate solutions. Internally, disagreements were sometimes seen as attacks on the other family's approach and methodology. The competition and disagreements among the three families was seen by clients as a "fight." In the best of cases, this led to inefficiencies. In the worst cases, clients received different or contradictory policy advice.

DOI: 10.4324/9781003199083-8

The family "fights" took different forms. In the best of cases, the three families avoided each other or divided the markets upfront to avoid stepping on each other. In the worst cases, there were conflicts to obtain project leadership.

At times, clients with strong capacity would clearly define the problem they wanted to solve and would force either the selection of a leading family or the organization of a team with multiple technical areas of expertise to solve the housing challenge they were facing. This situation was not common.

Act 2: The Birth of a Community of Practice Focused on Affordable Housing (2016)

Triggered by an open call for proposals from GSURR management to set up communities of practice (called knowledge silo breakers, or KSBs), a small group of housing professionals got inspired by the leadership's invitation to set up informal structures to connect across departments and break knowledge silos.

This initial group understood well the two main challenges created by those silos. First, the housing strategies of the three families had only a partial view of the sector. Sometimes one family would lament that the sites and services projects were captured by the well-to-do, losing sight of the fact that even middle-class families were facing affordable housing challenges. In other cases, financial instruments were developed to support new buyers, but there was no supply of affordable housing to purchase.

Second, the technical expertise in the housing sector was scattered across the World Bank Group. The affordable housing challenges in the developing world are immense, and the situation was not improving. During those initial conversations, the group asked how to restore the World Bank Group's competitive edge in the affordable housing space and offer the best solutions in an agile way to clients around the world.

The proposal sent in response to the call for new communities of practice was written around a vision to rebuild the institutional capacity in the housing sector by creating a safe space and a common platform for holistic solutions, breaking knowledge silos. The hope was that the housing offers to clients would be much stronger if all three housing "families" were to cooperate and thrive together.

Act 3: Five Years Later (2021)

By 2021, the Affordable Housing KSB had become a community of practice with about 200 members across the entire World Bank Group and external members from the International Monetary Fund (IMF) and leading NGOs working in housing, such as Habitat for Humanity, Urban Housing Practitioners Hub, Center for Housing Finance in Africa, and more.

The community members have a wide range of technical backgrounds, including housing policymakers, city administrators, housing and community development staff of local governments, mortgage bankers, developers and builders, housing finance companies, community-based shelter advocacy groups, and academics.

Community members from the three urban "families" now seek each other's expertise and support formally and informally. Crowdsourcing of ideas and sharing information and suggestions to ad hoc inquiries are now commonplace in the community. Members are also invited to provide formal reviews of projects under preparation by teams in different departments. A new generation of projects has been jointly prepared by the families, offering clients with more holistic solutions. Innovation has also flourished in this new collaborative environment, for example, in the recent projects in Tamil Nadu (India), Punjab (Pakistan), and Senegal, among others.

The community has also organized joint learning and co-design events with clients, such as a technical deep dive on affordable housing held at the Tokyo Development Learning Center (see Chapter 6). The design of this event was developed through a collaborative process with a team that included specialists from across the three housing families. This event helped to crystalize a vision for the World Bank Group's housing sector: The World Bank would work across the entire housing value chain to enable and deepen the market to deliver safe, affordable, and sustainable housing for all.

In parallel, senior and frontline managers within the World Bank Group have also stepped up their efforts in cross-organizational collaboration in the housing sector: a team consisting of key staff of the three housing families jointly identified challenges and opportunities in the sector over a yearlong progress. Key thought leaders and clients were also invited—public and private sector alike—to share their insights. This process crystalized a vision for the World Bank Group's housing sector: work across the housing value chain to enable and deepen the market to deliver safe, affordable, and sustainable housing for all. Several countries were identified as a priority for cross-organizational collaboration in affordable housing. Progress made in priority countries is regularly reported and discussed at the regional management meetings.

Five Ways of Working of the Affordable Housing Community of Practice at the Core of Its Success

The journey from 2016 to 2021 was successful in some core areas thanks to five ways of working that evolved as the community developed its identity and tools. These five factors of success are:

The community leveraged the innate desire of team members to collaborate across internal boundaries—The most complex challenge faced by the community was the pressures against cross-sector collaboration created by the internal incentive and resource allocation system of the World Bank. The institution has set up mechanisms to foster collaboration, such as co-leadership of projects, formal peer review requirements by specialists from other regions and sectors, among others. However, these mechanisms were not enough to build strong bridges of collaboration.

The Affordable Housing KSB leadership was convinced that technical staff are naturally interested in collaboration. The multidimensional development challenges that they observe in developing countries, and where clients want support, require multisectoral solutions.

The KSB leadership also knew that collaboration thrives when there is shared understanding, knowledge, and appreciation of the value added by others across the table. The Affordable Housing KSB sought to capitalize on this aspiration by creating a platform for informal discussion, knowledge exchanges, and transfer of operational know-how across professional disciplines.

Collaboration and trust begin with a few "bread and butter" items—The KSB focused at the beginning on a few simple products: a crowdsourcing help desk, a seminar series, an engaging and carefully crafted newsletter, and a matchmaking platform:

- The crowdsourcing platform became the "go-to" place to ask questions for anything related to housing. Examples include ad hoc requests for recommendations on good housing practices, on global subject-matter experts, or on sources for data and statistics needed to prepare an urgent briefing note requested by a client.

  Some of the questions asked and knowledge mobilized were complex. For example, a request for comments on how to define "slums" or low-income communities was asked. Such a definition has important implications on the 11th Sustainable Development Goal, and its indicator 11.1.1 "Proportion of urban population living in slums, informal settlements, or inadequate housing." The many views and practical ideas from across the community were summarized and submitted to the UN agency in charge of the definition of slums and its computation. The crowdsourced inputs were influential in expanding and making more inclusive the definition of slums.

- A carefully curated newsletter—"House Buzz"—was instrumental in building a sense of community in the Affordable Housing KSB. The quarterly newsletter brings together important housing industry news around the world, noteworthy studies and reports from practitioners and academics, and highlights from social media on affordable housing to keep its members abreast of the latest developments in the affordable housing agenda.

- A seminar series was organized early on by the community. The speakers were purposefully selected to discuss topics that were of interest to the three housing families. The seminar series was instrumental in building a shared understanding across diverse technical disciplines.

- A "matchmaking" platform was designed to help project leaders express their demand for new team members with specific areas of expertise. The platform allowed community members interested in supporting teams across regions and professional practices to equally express their interest. The matching between demand and supply was an effective tool to mix teams and build new professional contacts.

Targeted "safe space" reviews for new projects lead to better design of solutions—To strengthen the linkage between knowledge sharing and new business opportunities, the Affordable Housing KSB organized a new modality of peer technical support across institutional boundaries. In these reviews, the Affordable Housing KSB strives to link knowledge with real-world challenges. Targeted "safe space" reviews for new projects are one such modality, offering peer technical support across institutional boundaries. Affordable housing solutions included in World Bank projects are often components of larger projects. At times, these components do not receive enough attention in technical reviews given the complexity and broader development challenges of the larger projects. At the request of a housing specialist working on a project, the KSB began to organize a safe space review. For these sessions, the KSB would mobilize technical specialists with deep operational knowledge on the issues identified by the requester. These specialists would volunteer their time because the knowledge exchanges during the safe space reviews were also quite valuable to them. These brainstorming sessions offered a forum to explore new operational frontiers by leveraging global tacit knowledge from experts working in different regions on similar issues. As the reviews were designed to influence the design of new operations under preparation, the connection between knowledge and solutions was strong. Teams working in countries as diverse as India, Argentina, and Djibouti took advantage of this tool.

Operational toolkits support rapid response and action—The KSB also developed select "toolkits" to provide focused technical input to sophisticated clients. Examples include

---

Box 5.2.1   An Example of Knowledge in Action—The Case of Pakistan Housing Sector Engagement

The World Bank Group engagement in the housing sector in Pakistan was focused on housing finance through a US$145 million project designed to increase access to housing finance for households and support capital market development in Pakistan. In early 2019, the Government of Pakistan launched the Naya Pakistan Housing Program (NPHP) to provide five million houses across the country. During the design phase, the Government turned to the World Bank for advice and support to its flagship housing program.

The Affordable Housing KSB provided significant value addition to shape the housing sector support in Pakistan: a high-level housing conference was organized to showcase and reflect with the Government on global experiences in housing policy and programs. The three housing families closely worked together and quickly mobilized the most appropriate expertise via the Affordable Housing KSB network.

The conference was the first step to identify a suite of solutions to support the housing sector in Pakistan. These solutions ranged from deepened engagement with an additional US$85 million for housing finance to expand the nascent mortgage market through a scaled-up risk financing facility. IFC—the private sector arm of the World Bank Group—made an equity investment of US$3.2 million in Pakistan Mortgage Refinance Company Limited. Other IFC studies analyzed underwriting informal income for mortgages, the microfinance industry in the country (which included a section on housing). A US$200 million Punjab Affordable Housing Project aimed at increasing the quantity and quality of affordable housing supply at the provincial level, by focusing on addressing supply-side bottlenecks—infrastructure provision. The program will enhance government systems to create an enabling environment that attracts private financing for mixed-income housing developments. It will also help the government better target subsidies of the NPHP for low-income households. Finally, the Punjab Urban Land Systems Enhancement Project will digitize urban land records and establish a unified, provincial land administration system. This system will help verify land ownership efficiently and facilitate housing development.

These three projects processed in parallel, and with a closely coordinated design, demonstrated that the World Bank Group can offer a suite of services to tackle simultaneously the housing supply, demand, and land development challenges. The Affordable Housing KSB was key to facilitating these coordinated engagements.

rapid assessment tools and support to the design of complex studies. A request that emerged early on during the initial phase of the KSB work was a basic diagnostic tool for rapid housing sector assessment. This tool helped World Bank teams or client agencies to conduct a quick but insightful diagnostic of the sector, leading to incorporating technically sound advice in policy formulation and/or project design. When the needs of the clients were more sophisticated and the general diagnostics was insufficient, the KSB provided support to design the scope of work for in-depth analyses on specific housing topics, such as assessment and design of subsidy schemes, rental housing policies, and affordable housing PPPs, among others.

Upskilling KSB members was a strong driver of community engagement—The KSB sought to deepen the skills of community members from the beginning, using new formats. Three examples of these upskilling efforts are:

- A customized Wharton School of Business international housing finance course to gain economies of scale by bringing the instructors to the World Bank instead of sending three to four staff per year to the course. The KSB worked closely with Wharton faculty in designing and customizing the course to fill specific knowledge and skill gaps identified by KSB members. This approach was not only cost-effective but also leveraged existing experiences within the three housing families to make the training more relevant for World Bank business.
- An affordable housing technical deep dive in Tokyo, which provided an opportunity for peer-to-peer learning and co-creation of solutions with clients. A group of clients, bank practitioners, and international experts had an opportunity to review case studies and live examples of how affordable housing is being addressed in different contexts. Delegations from Argentina, Azerbaijan, Bhutan, Brazil, Bulgaria, Colombia, Djibouti, Ethiopia, India, Iraq, Kenya, Malaysia, and South Africa participated. Examples from all these countries were analyzed in addition to those from other reference cases such as Chile, Japan, the UK, France, and the US. The KSB leveraged this event by maintaining the network of participants beyond the four days spent on the event and acting as institutional memory.
- A housing finance conference that had been organized regularly for more than a decade—and was closely guarded—by one of the three housing families evolved into a multidisciplinary event. The expanded scope did not dilute the technical depth of the conference. Rather, it deepened the multidimensional nature of the topics discussed and speakers invited.

Nourishing a Community to Shape the Next Generation of Housing Sector Engagement

The KSB's journey to collaboration has been also propelled by the search for the "next generation" of housing sector engagement. The KSB leaders recognized that it "takes the entire village" to move the needle in innovation and that both senior management involvement and grassroots efforts of the KSB had roles to play.

It began with an Africa-focused One World Bank Group Housing Strategy, the result of a senior management request that an integrated approach to be jointly prepared by IFC and the World Bank. Soon the integrated approach was expanded to cover all the regions, either formally or informally. The process involved reviewing past engagements and what worked and what didn't, embracing the value chain framework to analyze how the different pieces of the housing sector fit together, and exploring the different business lines that the World Bank and the IFC offer (e.g., public investment, liquidity facilities, guarantees, equity, debt), how they could be better utilized, and, more importantly, how each group best adds value in the sector.

The Affordable Housing KSB initiated a series of events to "sensitize" the One World Bank Group Housing Strategy and to cultivate collaboration across the urban, competitiveness and private sector teams, and to inspire more strategic thinking and practical actions.

The Importance of the GSURR Global Knowledge Ecosystem for the Success of the Affordable Housing KSB

The tools and central support provided by the global knowledge ecosystem were important for the Affordable Housing KSB during its establishment and growth phases. Four areas of support are particularly noticeable:

First, the GSURR leadership through its global knowledge ecosystem encouraged and rewarded KSBs for cross-sector collaboration. The Affordable Housing KSB was one the earliest recipients of the GSURR Collaboration for Impact Awards because of its efforts to break organizational silos across the World Bank Group. These incentives gave an impetus to the Affordable Housing KSB to deepen collaboration across the three housing families in the World Bank Group.

Second, the centrally designed KSB Impact Framework was rolled out during the second year of the KSBs operations to help community leaders and members think through the output-to-impact value chain. While it was mainly used by the GSURR leadership to evaluate the performance and growth of KSBs, it was also helpful to improve the codification—and replication—of best practices among KSBs. The framework and associated reporting were also used to identify at-risk KSBs early in the process so they could be strengthened in timely ways.

The KSB Impact Framework helped the Affordable Housing KSB in identifying their preferred priority activities and the multiyear journey they wanted to follow. The KSB selected three indicators of success for the first couple of years:

- Number of member inquiries received and answered on time—to measure the effectiveness of the crowdsourcing platform.
- Number of products (e.g., projects, policy and research reports, evaluation reports) supported by the KSB—to measure the linkage of the community to the business.
- Number of projects designed using new approaches developed by the KSB—to measure the degree of innovation and impact of the community activities.

Third, the central GSURR knowledge management team organized the support of a community manager (see Chapter 5) who had specific training on community mobilization and knowledge management tools. The community manager helped the KSB with the development of the knowledge management tools and platforms. She was part of a central team of community managers that helped with the coordination and cross-fertilization among KSBs. The community manager helped facilitate access to training opportunities in KSB value pitch making, design and delivery of Ignite/TED-style presentations, and pedagogical design of workshops and global events.

Finally, the Affordable Housing KSB also benefited from the TDLC knowledge hub and platform (see Chapter 6), using it to deliver a multicountry peer-to-peer learning program that benefited a dozen client country delegations.

Leadership Lessons

The experience of the Affordable Housing KSB has three main lessons for leaders of communities of practice:

- *Persistence and patience pay*: A community cannot be built overnight. Trust-building is indispensable for communities, and it takes time. While it is tempting to try to measure success by number of activities or products completed, it is not easy to measure the change process of building a community, especially in the early days. A community changes perspectives, one person at a time. It takes practice and time until new knowledge behaviors take hold. One event or a joint initiative will not be enough. Running a community takes commitment, grit, and staying power. It needs to be sustained by a critical mass of individuals who believe in collaboration, stay the course, and continue to build trust through providing genuine and sustained service to the community.
- *Sustained and "conditional" management support to the bottom-up process is critical*: The Affordable Housing KSB grew out of a bottom-up process, led by a few passionate technical staff willing to spend time and energy. The support from the GSURR leadership team to these bottom-up processes proved to be critical. That support was not unconditional. It was conditional upon the demonstration of value addition to the business. The approach of "letting a thousand flowers bloom" was modified to have continued support only to those communities growing and thriving. Other communities withered. This may seem a bit harsh at first sight, but such discipline introduced a sense of responsibility for community leaders and members. This approach rewarded performance and gave space to grow in a resource-constrained environment.
- *Communities need centrally managed support and training*: This support included coaching sessions for the "elevator pitch" the community developed to convince potential supporters and prospective members of the value addition of the KSB. This support also included the "knowledge fairs," global events designed to generate awareness and interest. At these fairs, participants voted for the most popular knowledge communities, with commensurate increased funding allocations to the winners. These methods may sound unconventional for large organizations like the World Bank, but they provided a clear "authorizing" environment and brought in excitement, energy, and different perspectives to community-building and knowledge curation.
- *Do not expect a paradigm shift in behaviors overnight*: Despite the senior management support for multisectoral operations, the incentive structure of the World Bank, like many other organizations, guides middle managers and their teams. Spending time working for another department is not always welcome by managers who have specific deliverable and lending targets. "Grassroots" efforts like the Affordable Housing KSB helped colleagues from different technical disciplines and departments to understand each other's point of view, language, and tools. The community nurtured open-mindedness and created a genuine belief in collaboration.

Future Areas

The dream of the Affordable Housing KSB leaders and members is for this community to become the world's "go-to" place for affordable housing knowledge, not just for the World Bank Group. The ambition is to grow into a community that:

- Connects housing practitioners in developing countries worldwide.
- Curates and shares relevant knowledge and experiences.
- Matches quickly the most relevant technical expertise or experience for a specific housing sector challenge: for example, how to design housing subsidy programs? How to set up a real estate regulatory agency? What is the most effective way of incentivizing private developers to supply affordable housing? How to structure an affordable housing PPP project? and many more.

Developing New Business Lines and Innovation

The Disaster Risk Management Community of Communities

Ede Ijjasz-Vasquez[1]

The Disaster Risk Management and Resilience Global Solutions Group was one of the largest of GSURR's formal communities of practice (see Chapter 5 for a classification of GSURR communities). This community was unique in the GSURR global knowledge ecosystem for three reasons. First, it was a community of communities. This formal community embraced and nurtured more than a dozen informal communities (knowledge silo breakers (KSB)). Second, the community had a dual objective to develop and deepen several new business lines for clients and, at the same time, to upskill team members in these new areas. Third, it had an experienced knowledge management staff as community manager right from the start, leading to several innovations in knowledge asset production and dissemination. This chapter presents the journey and lessons of this community of communities.

A Special Community of Communities

The GSURR ecosystem of communities of practice had two categories: formal and informal (see Chapter 5 for details). The formal communities, called global solutions groups (GSG), were selected by the GSURR leadership team to cover broad themes with significant areas of work for the Global Practice. The informal communities, called knowledge silo breakers (KSBs), resulted from a bottom-up process of nominations by interested staff from all corners of the Practice. After a year of learning with this structure, the GSURR leadership combined the system and placed each informal community under the umbrella of a formal community to help with technical and strategic guidance.

The Disaster Risk Management and Resilience Global Solutions Group was one of the largest of the formal communities. Disaster risk management was a growing area of engagement for the World Bank and included financial support and technical advice for reconstructing infrastructure and livelihoods after natural disasters. In recent years, the recognition of the growing frequency and intensity of disasters due to climate shocks led to an expanded focus of this line of work to help countries and communities get ready and become more resilient to climate shocks. The disaster risk management teams had about 200 staff working in developing countries all across the world, with large portfolios in East Asia, South Asia, and Latin America and a growing portfolio in Africa. In the years leading up to the 2014 World Bank reorganization, these teams had grown rapidly in response to increasing client demand. The new team members were younger and had very diverse technical profiles, offering interesting opportunities for innovation.

The vision of the Disaster Risk Management Global Solutions Group leadership was to unleash and foster the creativity and innovation of its generally younger teams to create

DOI: 10.4324/9781003199083-9

new business lines through informal communities of practice. The global solutions group leadership launched a structured process to encourage and guide the establishment of these informal communities.

The group leadership believed that an effective community of practice cannot have a scope of work that is too broad but rather needs to have a narrower focus to be engaging and attractive to technical team members. Very busy staff may join knowledge exchange events and discussions once or twice to test their interest, but they will only return if they can connect with other professionals working on client solutions close enough to their own client challenges. This proximity does not happen easily when the topic of conversation is too broad.

The Knowledge Silo Breakers in Disaster Risk Management and Resilience

The global solutions group leadership initially authorized eight communities, with the list eventually growing to more than a dozen (see Box 5.3–1).

Box 5.3–1—Knowledge Silo Breakers in Disaster Risk Management and Resilience

Analytics for resilience
Emergency preparedness and response
Gender and disaster risk management
Hydromet, climate services, and resilience
Nature-based solutions
Resilience of energy systems
Resilient housing
Resilient infrastructure
Resilient recovery
Resilient transport
Resilient water supply and sanitation
Safer schools
Small island resilience
Urban floods

The new community hurdle—In keeping with the "gardening approach" to community of practice building described in Chapter 5, the Disaster Risk Management and Resilience Global Solutions Group leadership decided that there was a greater risk in not experimenting than in having informal communities be born and then fail. That said, the leadership defined a few basic criteria in the consideration of the knowledge silo breakers that would be established under its umbrella:

- Several initial solutions to similar client challenges in disaster risk management and resilience were being developed or tested. A new community could not start with only one or two solutions under development.

- These initial solutions were in countries located in different regions. A new community had to prove its multiregional reach.
- The informal community proponents had a clear vision for the group's growth path and the relevance of their topic to clients. Ideally, the community proponents had a path to develop a new business line or product to serve a well-defined client need.
- A core team had to show strong interest in establishing the informal community. A new community could not be the idea of a single individual.
- The topic could not be academic. There were great ideas for research on the topic of climate resilience. If the proponents were not able to show the potential and clear relevance to client challenges, it was a no-go.
- The term *resilience* can be very broad and can encompass a wide range of development issues. For example, a household that is less poor is more resilient to disasters because it can bounce back. However, poverty reduction programs were seen as too far away from the core theme of disaster risk management. The relationship of proposed topics for new communities could not be too far from the core area of the global solutions group.
- Existing communities of practice in topics related to disaster risk management that existed before the World Bank reorganization into Global Practices (see Chapter 2) had to apply to be upgraded to become a knowledge silo breaker. This established discipline in the process and helped everybody understand the new way of operating as a community.
- The community proponents had to prepare a proposal for review by the central GSURR leadership. While the proposal was not complicated, it proved to be a good hurdle as a first product the community had to deliver. It was a test of whether they could work together.

The regional managers responsible for client relations were consulted informally on the ideas for new communities.

Once these conditions were clearly presented by the proponents of a new community, the global solutions group leadership was generally positive and inclined to support new ideas, even if they sounded far-fetched at first. The group leadership recognized that they did not know everything in the disaster risk management area nor did they have a crystal ball to guess the trajectory of new community development. This spirit of openness and experimentation served the group well in its development and innovation journey.

Communities' establishment: In retrospect, the hurdle approach worked. The enthusiasm of several groups of committed individuals led to the establishment of an initial group of about eight new knowledge silo breakers. This number is larger than for other global solutions groups that started as a single coherent group and slowly developed working groups around themes that evolved into KSBs.

The proponents were attracted by the opportunity for leadership—even if informal and without authority. They were also interested in the opportunity to deepen their technical specialization, promote their ideas and innovations, and get recognition beyond their immediate work units and clients.

The World Bank tends to hire professionals who are interested in influencing and leading change—in policies, institutions, and solutions across the world—and the informal communities gave an opportunity to younger team members to gradually expand their influence.

The most effective leaders of informal communities had three key skills: a strong interest in finding innovative solutions to challenging problems, a good sense of business opportunities, and networking skills. Leading a KSB allowed them to further develop their ability to influence across boundaries and without supervisory authority.

The structure provided by the GSURR global knowledge ecosystem allowed these opportunities for leadership and innovation, and most of the informal communities developed, some of them quite rapidly.

The role of the global solutions group—The global solutions group did not try to establish a separate identity from the aggregation of the individual informal communities. The group leadership believed that their role was of facilitator, guide, and monitor of results. They created a community of knowledge silo breaker leaders to help the learning and cross-fertilization among them and to explore synergies and areas to work across communities.

The only major activity the global solutions group organized at its level was a core training course on risk analysis tools. The leadership believed that a core skill for all staff working on disaster risk management should be on risk analysis as a technical differentiator from other technical disciplines in the World Bank. Whether staff in the practice were trained as engineers, water specialists, or urban planners, it was deemed important that they had a common understanding of the rapidly developing field of risk analysis. The identification of "critical knowledge" for each community is important to ensure all members, especially new members who joined later in the community journey, have the same basic understanding of concepts and tools.

An interesting signal that the Disaster Risk Management Global Solutions Group leadership gave to the informal communities was that size was not an indicator of success. Many communities in the GSURR Global Practice did membership drives to promote their theme across the organization to find new ideas through members working in diverse areas and geographies. For the Disaster Risk Management and Resilience GSG, it was more important to focus on the core members and the operational impact on new business lines. The group size was more of a corollary than a primary objective.

Challenges—Some informal communities did not survive the passage of time. In some cases, the topic was too small or niche, the community could not develop a new business line, or the interest of members waned. In other cases, the community leader did not have enough networking or influencing without authority skills to generate excitement among potential members and build coalitions across silos. Finally, in some cases, the leadership succession was not planned well in advance. If a community has a single leader and that person changes jobs, then the continuity of the community will be at risk. In these circumstances, communities sometimes go through a "dormant" period until a new leader or core group emerges and reinvigorates the group.

The Disaster Risk Management Global Solutions Group leadership was disciplined in engaging with each informal community and following up with groups that were losing energy or productivity. The leadership wanted to keep active knowledge sharing spaces for each community. If somebody were to come to one of the internal web sites or repositories of knowledge assets and find all of them old and no longer relevant, this situation would lower the credibility of the overall community of communities. Therefore, the leadership actively monitored the number of visitors and downloads of materials to determine whether a knowledge silo breaker was truly dormant and its knowledge assets no longer useful to the institution.

A second challenge was related to the existence of a formal unit in the World Bank structure with the mandate to develop innovative tools and solutions in disaster risk reduction. Many organizations set up innovation labs or similar centers of excellence to bring together highly specialized expertise to develop frontier solutions. The development of communities of practice in areas that overlap with those of these innovation labs can create tensions. In the case of disaster risk management, the tensions were unexpected because the individuals knew each other and had worked together in the past. The "perceived threat" was handled through a supportive environment by management, open dialogue, and—above all—time and patience for the groups to find their complementarities. In the end, the communities of practice benefited from building connections with staff in the innovation lab with highly specialized skills. The lab benefited from the communities because they accelerated the diffusion of their tools, enhanced the cycle from development to scaled-up use, and helped with the improvement of tools through the rapid communication of lessons learned in applications.

Examples of Successful Knowledge Silo Breakers in Disaster Risk Management

This section reviews interesting features of some of the informal communities:

Nature-based solutions—These disaster risk management solutions based in nature are a rapidly emerging concept in the climate resilience space. In this approach, gray infrastructure solutions (e.g., dikes, flood canals, drainage systems, sea barriers) are combined with green solutions (e.g., mangroves, restored floodplains, landscape management) to reduce the impacts of climate shocks in a more balanced and cost-effective manner.

Nature-based solutions were a fringe topic at the World Bank in 2016 with only a few staff experimenting in some projects. These staff were in the Water Global Practice, the Environment Global Practice, and the Disaster Risk Management team in the GSURR Global Practice.

Fast forward to 2022 and the topic of nature-based solutions has been widely embraced in a number of fields. Thanks to the initial efforts of the knowledge silo breaker, the World Bank has been ahead of the curve on the use of this modality, and it has been mainstreamed throughout the World Bank portfolio as a recognized business line used by numerous practices. This community was at the right time with the right topic and took several steps to catalyze this change.

First, they undertook a "portfolio review," a compilation of components in dispersed projects in different sectors that used nature-based solutions. This was a key step to know what is happening and to prepare a who's who on the topic. Second, they commissioned—in partnership with top class organizations and research centers with recognized expertise in the topic—a few initial papers of very high quality. These papers gave the community recognition and standing in the World Bank. As the community members were all relatively young professionals, they needed the rigor of these papers to demonstrate the value of the nature-based solutions approach.

Third, the community defined their new business line not as an independent one with separate projects and loans. Rather, they decided to go the "mainstreaming" way. In this approach they worked as a "service team," helping others incorporate nature-based solutions into their projects (e.g., roads, dams, water supply, urban flood mitigation). Instead of convincing ministries of environment to work on nature-based resilience initiatives, they worked with other ministries to bring nature to them.

Analytical tools for disasters—After a natural disaster, like an earthquake or cyclone, occurs, it used to take several months to calculate the damage to infrastructure, housing, and agriculture in the disaster area, especially when those areas were remote. Governments did not have the information to budget for the reconstruction and recovery process or to request for additional support from donor countries and financial institutions.

A team of data scientists and engineers in the Latin America region began using machine learning, satellite data, and other remote-sensing information to develop a new tool to calculate damages faster. The team tested the tool following a couple of disasters in the region and then teams in Africa tested it with good results.

When the call for proposals for new communities came out, this small team and some staff who had used the tool across regions came together to propose a knowledge silo breaker. Fast forward to 2022 and the tool has been improved continuously. Damage analysis and cost calculation now takes as few as eight days. The World Bank now uses it regularly as the tool to prepare requests for emergency funding under its various financing windows.

The knowledge silo breaker structure allowed a group of these data scientists to demonstrate that their tools could play a central role in disaster risk management and changed the landscape of disaster needs assessments.

Safer schools—School buildings are not always built to the specifications needed to withstand earthquakes or cyclones. A group of disaster risk management professionals broke the silos with the Education Global Practice to set up a global program. This community first focused its attention externally to compile country data worldwide, promote countries to understand the challenge, and mobilize donor funding to finance the activities needed to support the design of national programs for construction and/or retrofitting of schools to ensure resilience to natural disasters.

Fast forward to 2022 and this knowledge silo breaker has developed completely new business lines, supporting 18 countries across the developing world. It has also compiled and curated a practical set of tools and national studies to define national road maps to retrofit schools and ensure new schools are built with resilient standards.

Using the Tools of the GSURR Global Knowledge Ecosystem

The Disaster Risk Management and Resilience Global Solutions Group and its informal communities made good use of the various tools of the GSURR global knowledge ecosystem. For example:

- Given the highly distributed location of team members of the global solutions group, the leadership decided to focus on online training using the Open Learning Campus platform of the World Bank (see Chapter 11). The platform became the standard way of sharing knowledge through training for all the informal communities. The library of e-courses was one of the most robust knowledge assets of these communities.

Box 5.3–2—Knowledge Management Expert and Communities of Practice: Lessons From a Practitioner

- An effective knowledge management specialist does not work in the abstract. Some knowledge of the subject matter and of the technical community team members' work helps immensely in connecting, forging alliances, and identifying trends that can be useful to generate new knowledge assets.
- An effective knowledge management expert engages with teams early on to help them prepare a knowledge management approach that serves the community and the clients. When the team calls the knowledge management specialist at the last minute, the products are suboptimal and rushed.
- Knowledge management and communications need to work hand in hand (see Chapter 7). The best packages follow the "Disney" approach (not only the movie but the books, toys, etc.) This means that a publication is never enough for good knowledge sharing—a package of repurposed knowledge assets (e.g., infographics, videos, blogs, factsheets) targeted at different audiences is fundamental. This approach requires detailed thinking of the audience—Is it the general public? Technical practitioners? Government decision-makers? Potential clients?
- Newsletters are important knowledge assets, but standardization and process simplification are key. They can be a unique channel to collate and curate dispersed knowledge assets. If designed well, they can connect to the repository of the community's knowledge.
- An effective knowledge management specialist should be, at times, a cheerleader of teams to encourage them to share their work, to help them complement their skills (writing or presenting or positioning), and to support them to connect with other teams working with clients that face similar challenges.
- Sometimes available information technology systems are not fit-for-purpose for knowledge management functions, but a good knowledge management specialist knows how to work around this. Change of information technology systems needs to be with caution. The learning curve of communities that change systems can be high and discourage knowledge sharing and use.
- A dashboard—even a simple one—is critical to understand how different communities are working. Even basic indicators of readership or participation in knowledge-sharing events can be useful to understand what leading communities are doing and to identify which communities need extra support. Public sharing of indicators can be the basis for a healthy competition across communities.
- Conferences are great opportunities for knowledge asset generation, but they need advanced preparation: Who takes notes? Who prepares the blogs? Who can be interviewed on video to share lessons? What other knowledge assets can be prepared and by whom? Sharing the knowledge assets soon after the event helps reinforce the message and drives more readership to the knowledge catalog.
- Do not confuse knowledge management specialists with event planners! Big events require both skill sets, and the quality of the event can be compromised if the knowledge management specialist is pulled into functions such as venue and travel planning. At the same time, it is important that knowledge management specialists participate in logistical arrangements such as room configuration, determination of audiovisual requirements, etc. so as to ensure that these are conducive to a good learning experience on the part of participants.

- The technical deep dives organized by the Tokyo Development Learning Center (see Chapter 6) were an invaluable tool to co-create solutions with clients. The global leadership and expertise of Japan in disaster risk management made these technical deep dives some of the most useful and impactful.
- The GSURR Forums (see Chapter 8) served all the disaster risk management platforms well to build awareness across the GSURR Global Practice and its many technical disciplines. The Forums helped the disaster risk management teams connect with social development professionals (out of which new initiatives of disaster and post-conflict reconstruction programs emerged). These activities also served as an opportunity for the GSURR leadership to engage with the informal community leaders and recognize their work, which gave them an enormous boost of confidence and energy to continue on their innovation path.

The Invaluable Role of a Knowledge Management Expert

The Disaster Risk Management and Resilience Global Solutions Group was supported by a highly experienced knowledge management professional from the GSURR knowledge and learning team. She joined GSURR with years of practical experience on knowledge management collaborating with technical teams on disaster risk management projects. Box 5.3–2 summarizes some of the lessons of experience on ways an experienced knowledge management specialist can work with communities of practice.

The Future

Strong communities of practice that develop deep social capital and relations among members can survive organizational changes and restructuring. In 2020, the World Bank went through a reorganization that changed the integrated Global Practices into separate regional teams and a global unit. The practices developed to break silos have been invaluable in continuing the work.

The informal communities that were strong in knowledge-sharing behaviors and innovation continue to grow. Communities that were dormant have disappeared. The informal communities have found new sources of funding and support. In short, the creativity and energy that was at the core of the community's establishment and growth keep them going regardless of the underlying organizational structure.

Note

1 Niels Holm-Nielsen, head of the GSURR Disaster Risk Management Global Solutions Group, and Erika Vargas, senior knowledge management specialist in the Global Facility for Disaster Risk and Recovery, provided extensive inputs for this chapter.

Chapter 5.4

Shortening "Time to Market" for Research

The Territorial Development Community

Ede Ijjasz-Vasquez[1]

The World Bank has a central research department and sectoral units specialized in developing new methodologies and tools to analyze development challenges and offer insights to help develop or improve new solutions. Just like for any other large organization, a key challenge is to connect with and translate its own research the services offered to clients on the other. The research team needs to be useful for the organization's products and services. Usefulness is a result of relevance, effectiveness, and speed. Timing is of essence for building the competitive advantage of the organization. The faster the cycle from research to client services—and back with feedback and new research questions— the more agile and effective the organization. This chapter illustrates how a community of practice was successfully mobilized in the World Bank to leverage research: first, by making the research questions asked more relevant to clients' problems; second, by improving the effectiveness of tools developed by the research teams; and third, by shortening the time from research to new or improved business lines and products—the "time to market."

Introduction

The World Bank's research department investigates a wide range of issues, from basic research on development challenges to the management of development data (e.g., international statistics, statistical capacity building, and results monitoring), global indicators (e.g., comparable cross-country measures on a range of policy issues), and impact evaluations (e.g., to understand whether, how, and why development programs achieve their intended objectives).

Other World Bank units conduct more applied research on specific sectors, such as trade, education, or transport. These units are tasked to bring into the institution external research done by academia or think tanks and translate it to the needs of World Bank clients. These units also develop new methodologies or tools for analysis of development challenges. The end result is intended to support teams providing better financing or advisory services to their clients, either by applying research findings and tools to problems faced by clients or by developing new services and product lines for use across regions or worldwide. The "time to market" is an important indicator not only for the research department itself but also for the teams undertaking applied research.

DOI: 10.4324/9781003199083-10

Box 5.4–1:   An Example of a Typical Path From Research to Field Applications

A good example to illustrate the "time to market" challenge at the World Bank is the experience with *solutions for spatial inequality*. The unequal concentration of production and economic activity in countries has important impacts on people's livelihoods and living standards. Spatial concentration is common. Half of the world's entire economic production is done in only 1.5 percent of its land. For example, the capital of Egypt, Cairo, generates more than half of the country's GDP, using about half a percent of its area. As economic activity is concentrated, people living in other regions are less well off. In all major emerging economies—from Brazil to China to India—the poverty rate in economically lagging states is more than twice as high as the rate in economically dynamic states. More than two-thirds of the developing world's *poor* live in villages and not in large cities even though only half of the *population overall* lives in cities. These patterns clearly indicate that economic development does not bring economic prosperity everywhere at the same time. Markets prefer some areas over others. The solution, however, does not reside in dispersing production. Instead, economically prosperous nations do two things. First, they support the concentration of production. Second, they set up policies and programs to provide key public goods that have the potential to lift everybody's living standards, no matter where they are, including education, health, nutrition, sanitation, and social protection.

How should developing nations deal with spatial inequality? In 2008, the World Bank initiated a large research effort to investigate this question. The results were published in its annual flagship report—the *World Development Report 2009: Reshaping Economic Geography*.[2] This research report reframed the debate on urbanization, territorial development, and regional integration. This study put forward recommendations to resolve the challenge of spatial inequality through a combination of institutional cooperation, shared infrastructure, and special incentives.

These concepts were incorporated in the 2009 World Bank's Urban and Local Government Strategy[3] to guide the World Bank approach to support cities and regions. The central research team working on urban issues began to develop tools that would translate the concepts from the global research and the urban strategy into practical tools. These tools were tested initially in Vietnam and Sri Lanka in 2011 and in Uganda, Indonesia, and Colombia in 2012.

Lessons learned from the initial application of the new tool were summarized in 2013 in the form of an internal "urbanization review" report, and subsequently synthesized in a formal publication, *Planning, Connecting, and Financing Cities Now*.[4] In the subsequent years, the analytical tools developed as part of the urbanization review began to be applied in numerous countries around the world, from India to China and Turkey, and in regional analyses like South Asia (2015)[5] and Africa (2017).[6]

These studies would then form the basis for designing financing services offered by the World Bank. These investments typically start one to two years after completion of the country or regional reports. The "time to market" for the spatial inequality research had taken from 2008—when the *World Development Report* team initiated the first studies—to the first project approval in 2014: six years!

When the freshly appointed leadership team of the new Social, Urban, Rural, and Resilience global practice came together to build its strategy, they identified the reduction of the "time to market" as a critical factor for success. The department needed new tools and fresh ideas for business lines, as the competitive pressures from other providers of financial and advisory services were quite high.

The leadership team tasked one of the newly formed global solutions groups (GSGs)—the *Spatial and Territorial Development* team—to tackle the "time to market" challenge (see Chapter 5 for a description of the GSGs). This community of practice was selected because its members had lots of experience with research and had been closely associated with the *World Development Report 2008* (see Box 5.4–1) and the tools derived from it. The GSURR leadership tasked this community with the development of new tools based on fresh data and research. But the real challenge was to reduce the time to market. The target set was ambitious: two years, instead of six. This chapter tells their story.

The Spatial and Territorial Development Global Solutions Group had taken on a tough challenge. Its area of work—understanding and addressing spatial inequalities—was a topic that involved many more internal players and technical disciplines than was typically the case with other topics. The client experience at the time was a mirror of this situation. Depending on the technical department of the World Bank with whom a client country government talked, solutions proposed to address spatial inequality might have varied starkly. For example, the Competitiveness Department might recommend focusing on special economic zones, the Transport Department would propose infrastructure solutions, and the Social Development Department would recommend small-scale community-based investments in infrastructure or social services, just to name a few. Every department recommended what they knew best.

The journey of the Spatial and Territorial Development Global Solutions Group can be described in four steps.

Step 1: Identify and onboard the dispersed expertise from across the organization—In setting themselves up as a new community of practice from scratch, the first step taken by the Urban Analytics and Territorial Development Global Solutions Group involved identifying and connecting experts—whatever their organizational affiliation—who had the technical training and personal preference for more analytical and research-type work. The early success of the urbanization reviews (see Box 5.4–1) and the investments that followed had led many operational teams to hire specialists able to undertake this type of work in different countries.

As many of these experts were new to the World Bank, having been recruited from outside the organization, they had no easy way to even know of each other, let alone to connect with these peers, learn from each other, and coordinate their efforts globally. Joining the newly created global solutions group would make all this possible.

The first conversations were of mutual discovery. The original tools developed by the central research team had evolved and adapted to specific country needs. The new hires' fresh knowledge and technical expertise helped to swiftly create new solutions in different countries. Putting these together—through coordination and learning—began quite rapidly to shape a "garden of ideas" where mutual strengthening and reinforcement took place naturally.

The new global solutions group attracted technical specialists from a range of disciplines related to spatial inequality, from urban development to competitiveness, environment, and social development, among many others. The global solutions group provided an informal platform to connect across regions and disciplines, with less tension linked to the otherwise strong sense of competition between different business units. Everyone's shared interest in the topic—spatial inequality—and the opportunity to connect with professionals across the World Bank working on similar challenges were attractive enough to overcome institutional barriers to collaboration.

Step 2: Create a new—composite—toolkit and promote it with a standard pitch—The second step was to create a shared vision for how the global solutions group would operate. The members of this new community, supported by periodic engagements with the GSURR leadership, decided that instead of creating a "solve-it-all" tool or focusing on the latest frontier research developed outside the World Bank, they would follow a different path.

The new approach was to break the development of new tools into bite-size products that could be designed and rolled out fast to respond to clients' requests. Instead of having a single tool, the goal was to have a toolkit with a broader menu of more focused instruments.

The new path could be described as follows: diversifying the research menu, developing tools fast, testing them in the field, learning from initial results, and then iterating and improving without delay. This approach resulted in a complete turnaround of the research-to-services cycle.

The diversity of the global solutions group's members was a core strength. Their expertise ranged from a specialist in political economy and demographics to an expert on environmental economics and spatial policies, from a trade expert to a spatial econometrician, to name a few. The initial conversations within the core team were not easy. Terminology, traditions, and culture got in the way. However, after developing a shared understanding and a uniform language of what they could offer to clients, they were keen to present and pitch their ideas to internal and external clients.

The global solutions group crafted a pitch for the following hypothetical situation: if you meet a government counterpart, for example, a minister of a client country at the airport and you have ten minutes before flight departure, how would you describe what analyses can be done to help the country diagnose the spatial inequality challenge, compile data through innovative means, and present practical solutions for investments and policies to solve the minister's problem. They had to do it in simple language suitable for fast but substantive communication? The pitch had to be exciting and, more importantly, offer a feasible pathway to specific solutions.

In parallel, the community worked with the GSURR leadership to convince internal clients of the new toolkit's benefits. The World Bank's leadership structure includes a group of directors—the country directors—that manage client relations and serve as the decision-making point on what investment and advisory programs will be delivered to clients. The country directors make these decisions in agreement with their main counterpart in the government, the minister of finance. Given the country directors' pivotal role in client engagement, the Urban Analytics and Territorial Development Group decided to enlist the GSURR leadership to accelerate the World Bank's internal "buy-in." Within six months, several country directors had agreed to support the application of the new toolkit in a few pilots. The challenge for the global solutions group was to deliver on these new opportunities. It had to earn the reputation of speed and results in ways that had not been achieved before in the organization.

Step 3: Test and learn fast—In getting ahead of what would be a steep challenge, the global solutions group designed a series of knowledge-sharing mechanisms to ensure teams working on the pilots—and the community members at large—were connected, learned from each other, gave advice across countries, and improved the analytical tools quickly. The community set up periodic knowledge-sharing sessions of 30 minutes in the early mornings in Washington, DC, corresponding with late evenings in East Asia, as well as sessions throughout the day to "catch" all other time zones in between. The specialists would present interim results from the country they were working on and would share their challenges. The exchange of ideas was fast, and the offline conversations continued between sessions.

The different tools of the toolkit were applied in very diverse ways across countries. This allowed for parallel experiments with different spatial inequality and development characteristics. Instead of sequential experimentation, the community was learning concurrently. This approach accelerated the improvement process.

Also, a few highly specialized training opportunities were offered to the younger team members of the community to learn about the latest techniques on spatial analysis or urban economics. Building the capacity of the next generation of specialists was considered core to strengthening the team for the future and to increasing the ability to replicate the toolkit application in other countries down the line.

The central GSURR knowledge management team helped set up an a website to serve as an internal repository to help all team members (see Chapter 4), no matter their location, find the latest information on all the pilots and the latest external research on the topic.

These tools were indispensable in a large global decentralized institution to accelerate the "conveyor belt" from research to client services.

Country clients and World Bank country directors began to see results much faster than usual. For example, the entire client engagement program with the Democratic Republic of Congo would be based on a program to reduce spatial inequality. The community's members earned a reputation of delivery internally and with clients that allowed them to move to the investment phase. The programs and policies that followed as part of investment projects were designed based on the toolkit results in each country.

Step 4: Spread the word and break more silos—Based on these initial successes, the Spatial and Territorial Development Group decided that it could not grow the new business line if it stayed working only within its community. It then sought out new ways to build bridges with technical specialists in other disciplines.

The first attempt was to write *knowledge briefs* to disseminate the initial lessons. This was the easiest and most natural way of communicating given the members' backgrounds as researchers and policy analysts. However, the group soon realized that uptake of those products outside its community was minimal. It needed to move into more attractive, bite-sized, and easy to consume modalities, such as using videos and storytelling. After overcoming the initial discomfort with these communication channels and with the support of the GSURR's communications and knowledge management teams, the stories told by community members conveyed the excitement of the new tools to new audiences. The stories described the initial results in ways that a difficult-to-understand dry paper could not achieve. The skills the community members had developed building the "sales pitch" to the minister came in handy.

In identifying new audiences, the community members decided to focus on connecting and influencing specialists from disciplines they had never worked with, from municipal engineers to anthropologists. Increasing the technical diversity of their teams and tools could only improve client services. The GSURR Forum, described in Chapter 8, was an excellent opportunity to break the existing silos preventing productive cross-sectoral engagements. For the Forum, the group designed a series of inclusive events and proactively carried out conversations outside the community. The members did not see the Forum as a vehicle to build deeper connections among themselves, as they had already done that. They wanted to reach out and have conversations and linkages with staff far off from their regular spheres of influence.

Some connections worked. Others didn't. For example, breaking the silo with the teams working on fragile and conflict-affected environments paid off. Lagging regions far from the centers of power and development not only have high levels of poverty but are also—in many countries—the location of insurgency and armed conflict with non-state actors. Bringing together these two technical disciplines allowed for a new analysis of lagging regions and conflict-affected regions.

Some of the group's members observed that it was more challenging to break silos with long-established communities. These groups have well-defined techniques and solutions to the problems they work on. Even for the same concepts, the technical language they use is different. The professional-cultural barriers across teams can be challenging to solve. Newer groups developing innovative business lines are more flexible and interested in experimentation. Leadership interventions to help break old modes of thinking are needed in these situations.

The "Time to Market" Journey: Drivers of Success

Most of GSURR's communities of practice were grounded in existing operational business lines. The GSURR knowledge ecosystem encouraged them to extract lessons from implementation, using knowledge learned from field engagements to design new business lines and rapidly share knowledge from investments across countries. The Spatial and Territorial Development Group had a different challenge. It was born from a group of researchers and analytically minded team members. The explicit goal was to accelerate the conveyor belt from research to new business lines. Creating and growing a community of practice to achieve this goal proved that speed and effectiveness on the road from research to client services can be radically improved.

The Spatial and Territorial Development Group did not create subcommunities early on (known as knowledge silo breakers—see Chapter 5 for a full description of the GSURR communities of practice). It was already a relatively small group (less than 100 members at the beginning), and it decided to stay as a single group through the initial phases. This period allowed the participants to find a common language, connect across regions and technical subdisciplines, and build a cohesive vision of where they wanted to go and how they wanted to operate. After achieving these milestones, they established the first subgroups in areas such as competitive cities, spatial planning and investments, and urban spatial economics. This was an important lesson: do not rush to subdivide the community until you have a cohesive group.

The GSURR leadership was heavily involved in this group's evolution. The World Bank and its clients highly value economic research and new insights. The Urban Analytics and

Territorial Development Group was identified as a potential source of such research for the entire Global Practice. The leadership was clear, right from the start, on the need to connect upstream research and final investment offerings to clients. This mandate and the leadership support to realize it were crucial to the success achieved. The periodic evaluation of the work program and the regular feedback by the group's leadership provided the guidance that this community of practice needed to keep its course and strategic direction.

Leadership Lessons

Many organizations struggle to define an innovation strategy and pathways to create and scale new services to clients. Leadership needs to invest in the (sometimes hidden) pockets of creativity and research in the teams. But research and new ideas alone will not grow into new business lines. Well-designed communities of practice that connect research and operations can be the critical missing element to deliver new services and products.

The temptation to reorganize teams—either by bringing together research and field operations or creating newly integrated units—can be strong. As noted in several chapters in this book, a key lesson learned from the GSURR experience is that it is better to spend energy cutting through organizational boxes rather than moving, mixing, and creating new boxes within the formal organizational structure. Agile communities of practice with clear visions and strong support from leadership can achieve the same objectives with less institutional and human disruption.

Researchers and innovators many times feel alone and misunderstood by large organizations. The leadership support to create communities of practice that connect them can offer them the sense of feeling valued. These communities can trigger new ideas and creative energy. The focus of leadership on accelerating the translation of research into new services and products can be invigorating for these innovators.

Top-down mandates to innovators and researchers rarely work. The creativity and diversity of a community, combined with the right amount of guidance and push from leadership, can shape the right chemistry for disruptive innovation.

Future Areas

As with other communities of practice, the mandate and final goal were to become a global center of excellence in its work areas. The expansion of the global solutions group activities to include think tanks and research centers in developing countries was always part of the future work program of this community. Building the capacity of clients to undertake the global solutions group work using the tools developed was always part of their scaling-up strategy, namely to create new tools, pilot them in a few countries, improve the approaches, use them in a larger group of countries, leverage their results for investments and policies, enhance the capacity of think tanks in client countries to use these tools, and move on to the next set of frontier questions.

Notes

1 Somik Lall, former leader of the Spatial and Territorial Development Global Solutions Group, provided extensive input to this chapter.
2 The full list of World Development Reports can be found at: www.worldbank.org/en/publication/wdr/wdr-archive

3 World Bank. 2009. *World Bank Urban and Local Government Strategy: Systems of Cities*. Washington, DC: World Bank.
4 World Bank. 2013. *Planning, Connecting, and Financing Cities—Now: Priorities for City Leaders*. Washington, DC: World Bank. DOI: 10.1596/978–0–8213–9839–5.
5 Ellis, Peter, and Mark Roberts. 2016. *Leveraging Urbanization in South Asia: Managing Spatial Transformation for Prosperity and Livability. South Asia Development Matters*. Washington, DC: World Bank. DOI: 10.1596/978-1-4648-0662-9.
6 Lall, Somik Vinay, J. Vernon Henderson, and Anthony J. Venables. 2017. *Africa's Cities: Opening Doors to the World*. Washington, DC: World Bank.

Convening for Innovation

The Transit-Oriented Development Community of Practice

Ede Ijjasz-Vasquez[1]

Knowledge communities have distinct cultures, reflecting the diversity of their members. This chapter reviews the Transit-Oriented Development Community of Practice, a successful group that focused from the beginning on the production of an outstanding report designed to offer state-of-the art insight into the complex field of questions covered by the community. The community had to overcome important challenges, most notably the geographic distribution of its members around the globe and the wide diversity in technical expertise among its ranks. Building terminology "bridges," creating a common vision early on, and defining specific measures of success for its work program were key elements for the results it achieved in a short time.

A Community Shaped by Its Members' Needs

The Transit-Oriented Development Knowledge Silo Breaker (KSB) had unique and interesting features among the group of GSURR communities of practice. These features emerged from the specific needs of its members. The community's operating rules and its products emerged from a practical problem-solving attitude shown by the core members.

What helped the community solve challenges common to many other practices were four distinct characteristics. First, being associated with and recognized by two different Global Practice departments in the World Bank-urban and transport—rather than one (dual technical recognition). Second, early focus on content curation to prepare one core product. Third, a purposeful mapping of its member "types" to leverage their diverse interest and time availability for the good of the community. Fourth, development of engagement practices to keep a highly decentralized membership connected. The following sections explain each of these features in detail.

Dual technical recognition—The members of the Transit-Oriented Development Knowledge Silo Breaker mainly came from two technical disciplines within the respective departments: urban planners and urban transport specialists. Of course, the multidisciplinary nature of the topic attracted a wide range of other experts, too—from social inclusion to municipal finance, road safety, and urban environment—but these were a minority. From the beginning, the members wanted to have strong linkages and support from the management teams of GSURR (as the Global Practice for urban development) and the Transport Global Practice. This was important for the community members to ensure their managers saw this knowledge platform as an activity worthy of their time. Having the dual recognition also allowed the community to tap

DOI: 10.4324/9781003199083-11

Box 5.5–1   What Is Transit-Oriented Development?

Transit-oriented development, commonly known as TOD, is a planning and urban design approach that focuses on facilitating the use of public transit, walking, and cycling and that supports livable communities. Transit-oriented development looks to achieve higher urban densities that allow for most community activities to be within reach by walking only 5–10 minutes from mass rapid transit stations (bus or subways/ metros). The TOD approach also works to develop high-quality urban space and a diverse mix of land uses. Transit-oriented development is a multidisciplinary approach that brings together elements of urban transport planning, land use planning, urban design and regeneration, and real estate development. At the same time, the approach uses tools such as land value capture and municipal financing to mobilize the resources needed to build and maintain the urban infrastructure needed. Well-prepared transit-oriented interventions balance diverse urban priorities in a people-centered approach that is inclusive of all citizens.[2]

The urban transport community and city mayors have understood that the benefits of bus and metro stations cannot be fully achieved without transit-oriented development. Cities like Singapore, London, and Tokyo have demonstrated the increased ridership, economic activity, and quality of life that can be achieved with TOD approaches.

---

into financial resources from diverse sources, thanks to the credibility earned in both Global Practices.

Early focus on one core product—Many communities in their early stages explore a variety of products or activities until they find their own rhythm for the productive development of knowledge assets. The Transit-Oriented Development KSB members very early on settled on addressing an urgent need: the rapid curation of a broad range of informal and uncatalogued knowledge, both tacit and written. The members decided that preparation of an integrated toolkit that would go deeper than the general concepts of transit-oriented development would be the ideal product. This clarity of purpose and the immediate need for such a product galvanized the community.

Once the first phase of the toolkit was completed after about a year of work, additional topics were added but always kept in close relation to the main toolkit. This architecture of community products was a practical way to maintain the group's focus and energy.

Mapping of members into categories for proactive engagement at different levels—The community members naturally gravitated towards three levels of engagement. First, a core team that devoted the most time and energy, led specific products, and proactively engaged in knowledge exchange with all members. The core team made up about ten percent of the community members. Second, "interested" members were those that liked the transit-oriented development concept and were working with clients on its applications. These members did not lead the development of new knowledge assets but would contribute with inputs when curating exercises were underway. They would also answer questions from colleagues for lessons of experience. The "interested" members made up about 40 percent of the whole group. The third category of members were those that had a general interest in the topic, would participate in knowledge-sharing events, and would actively read summary materials produced by the community such as its quarterly newsletter. They would rarely engage actively in knowledge exchange, and they would not lead products. This category was about 50 percent of the community.

The Transit-Oriented Development KSB's leadership catered activities differently to each group and designed engagement programs to keep all three groups connected. In later sections of this chapter, several examples of this approach are described.

Specific engagement approaches for a highly distributed team—the Transit-Oriented Development KSB was one of the communities with the most decentralized membership. Many other communities struggled when engaging members located outside of the World Bank headquarters in Washington, DC. The Transit-Oriented Development KSB, in contrast, had active members in a couple dozen offices, and the community leader worked in the Singapore office.

The community organized itself to cater to the multiple locations of its members. First, it identified regional coordinators who would be focal points for anything related to the larger community. Regional coordinators were part of the KSB's core team. This responsibility gave them visibility. Their energy kept the community members in the same region (Latin America or Africa, for example) engaged.

Second, it designed a very high-quality newsletter with less general news and more focused on specific knowledge assets. The active readership of the newsletter was close to 75 percent of the target group—extremely high for a periodic publication of a knowledge community.

Third, the community worked in "sprints." It would organize periodic regional or global gatherings. The design of these events was not only focused on knowledge exchange activities, but also they were purposeful in advancing the production of knowledge assets—either ideation, conceptualization, or peer review of each other's work. Once it had built the building blocks of the next phase of work, it could continue engaging remotely from the members' respective offices around the world.

One Core Product—Serving a Core Need and Mobilizing the Community

The first task of the Transit-Oriented Development KSB was to bridge the "language barrier" and understand the city needs from the different perspectives of two groups of professionals: the World Bank's urban planners and its urban transport specialists. These two groups understood in general terms what their counterparts were doing. But the key word here was "generally"—when it came to specifics, each side had its own technical terms and nomenclature.

The first step was to develop awareness and a common nomenclature. That step did not take long. World Bank city clients were not asking for the general concept of transit-oriented development. They wanted more. They were asking "how" to do it.

As a first step, the community did a knowledge-mapping exercise. About 30 cities in different regions of the world were receiving financial or advisory support from the World Bank. The community unpacked the types of support being provided into 15 transit-oriented development themes. Based on this 30 x 15 matrix, the community began compiling all its knowledge "assets" (e.g., reports, lessons learned, lists of local and international experts trusted by the community, terms of reference for specialized consultancies)

The knowledge-mapping exercise was useful but not easy to digest. The community decided, as a second step, to prepare a toolkit. From the long list of fifteen themes, the community prioritized the top six and began the work of compiling the best lessons, interesting cases, and practical advice to client cities. The report "Transit-Oriented Development Implementation Resources and Tools"[3] was the first flagship product of the community. The most interesting findings and lessons from reports compiled in the knowledge-mapping exercise were distilled for this toolkit. The lessons learned and recommendations proposed in the toolkit were collectively agreed upon by the community members.

In the area of partnerships, the Transit-Oriented Development Community of Practice decided not to overextend its external outreach at the beginning. It selected one single partner—a well-known think tank and research center with global presence and a strong reputation on urban transport—to work together on the toolkit. The World Resources Institute was the partner of choice for this work because of the complementarities in skills and expertise with the World Bank.

The dispersed location of the community members meant that it was difficult for them to get together to have face-to-face brainstorming and knowledge-exchange sessions. They took advantage of the technical deep dive program of the Tokyo Development Learning Center (see details in Chapter 6). Transit-oriented development deep dives were organized annually in Tokyo, with each delving deeper into the topic.

The first technical deep dive covered the experience of Japanese cities with the "basics" of transit-oriented development. The second gathering focused on "compact cities." The third event focused on "public spaces." This fourth technical deep dive was prepared together with the Urbanscapes Community of Practice (see Chapter 5.1)

This approach of preparing knowledge events and co-creation exchanges with city clients served two purposes. First, it allowed the community to continue compiling, exploring, and deepening the toolkit. Second, as city clients' knowledge and implementation practice with transit-oriented development was evolving rapidly, this approach allowed the World Bank to move as fast as its clients in its knowledge and practice. The community's membership of GSURR and transport global practice staff and the growing and evolving group of client cities built strong relationships through the technical deep dives. The co-creation process to find innovative solutions became easier with each round.

Once the community completed the first edition of the transit-oriented development toolkit, the ideas for additional topics continued to bubble up—from road safety to railway stations, social inclusion, and many more. Preparing the second edition of the toolkit kept the community engaged and productive. An approach that proved quite useful to prepare new knowledge assets jointly agreed by the community was to assign the production to teams of two members. This pairing was designed to bring diversity of perspectives to the knowledge asset being prepared. It also strengthened the resilience of the production process as the asset would be delivered even if one member of the team left. Finally, this approach provided peer pressure for timely delivery.

Leadership Lessons

There are four areas where the Transit-Oriented Development KSB's leadership saw the greatest benefits from GSURR managerial support:

- The KSB Impact Framework (Chapter 5) developed by the GSURR knowledge management team played a particularly useful role in forcing communities to clarify their journey ahead and the specific milestones they wanted to achieve. The flexibility of the Impact Framework was useful because it recognized that communities were at distinct stages of growth and development. Furthermore, the Impact Framework allowed for different visions of knowledge community development.
- The GSURR leadership's attention to the communities of practice gave the credibility needed to mobilize additional financial resources from different World Bank and external sources. The typical community of practice was seen elsewhere in the institution as an informal group without management oversight. The structured GSURR global knowledge ecosystem and the use of the KSB Impact Framework gave communities the leadership backing and a more formal standing (without being absorbed in the formal structure of the organization).
- The GSURR knowledge fairs and annual Forums (Chapter 8) where all communities of practice (KSBs and GSGs) presented their progress and deliverables were useful. The push to report against each individual community's Impact Framework brought discipline to the process. These knowledge-sharing events were an opportunity for each community to reflect on its achievements and ways to catch up in areas that were not working as well. The events created peer pressure and a bit of friendly competition among communities. This atmosphere encouraged them to grow and deliver results. The Transit-Oriented Development KSB appreciated the direct feedback from the GSURR leadership, as it demonstrated the continued interest of the community members' managers for their knowledge work. Finally, the knowledge fairs were an opportunity to rapidly share (and copy!) innovations in the organization and tools across communities.
- The community manager (Chapter 5) assigned by the GSURR knowledge management team was especially important for the success of the Transit-Oriented Development Community of Practice. The community manager was instrumental in the membership drive and in efforts to find World Bank specialists from across the institution that might be interested in the community's work. As part of this membership drive, the community manager kept a skills map of members updated. The community leadership leveraged this information to mobilize skills and experiences of new members for the group. Finally, the community manager's focus on new activities designed to keep the connections and excitement among team members was invaluable.

Box 5.5–2 presents a summary of lessons for community leaders based on the experiences of the Transit-Oriented Development Community.

Box 5.5–2 —Lessons for Community Leaders

The experience of the Transit-Oriented Development Community of Practice holds some practical lessons for community leaders, including:

- Community leaders need to identify "core" team members early on who bring enough passion and interest in developing knowledge assets and contributing to the sharing of tacit knowledge. The success of a community depends on motivating these core members to deliver. Different individuals have diverse factors that motivate them—either helping the next generation of technical staff, visibility in the organization, or genuine interest in connecting across silos. The community leader needs to identify those motivating factors and find opportunities to leverage them individually.
- It is important to equip the community with high-value knowledge assets that raise the standing of the collective in the organization. The asset's value depends on how relevant it is for its members—not only the core group but the entire community in its relations with clients.
- The community's core group needs to constantly explore how to add value to internal and external clients. A disciplined approach to understand the potential impact of each activity and to prioritize the knowledge products and activities is critical for the community's success.
- Knowledge communities give a unique opportunity to members to deepen their technical skills. Through innovative applications of new tools and cross-fertilization with other sectors and organizations, the community members will stay at the forefront of their technical disciplines in ways that regular training and upskilling programs cannot achieve or, at least, not at scale.
- Community leaders need to understand that mobilizing and guiding a knowledge community will always take more energy and time than originally envisioned.
- Succession planning is indispensable for a community to thrive. Community leaders cannot sustain over the medium term the level of energy and innovation to keep the community moving forward. New leadership is required to refresh the community's innovation and future directions.
- Finally, solving problems together as a community is the most rewarding part of the work. A community that only focuses on knowledge-sharing activities would not reach its full potential.

The Future

The Transit-Oriented Development Community of Practice plans to continue expanding the toolkit with greater diversity of formats and topics. Two additional areas of possible engagement are the following:

- Deepening the knowledge-asset mapping and including other categories. The initial mapping focused on the reports, lessons learned, and community members' tacit knowledge. The mapping did not cover knowledge assets from other financing organizations (like regional development banks or bilateral funding agencies) or the studies, research, and reports done by client countries and cities themselves. These additional categories may provide a wealth of practical experience with different perspectives from those internal to the World Bank.

- Bringing new members up to speed on what the community has done in the past is difficult. Also, the time difference is a challenge for participation of all community members distributed over 14 time zones. The written documents, even if short and punchy, are not enough to share knowledge effectively. The setup of a video library of events, lessons learned, panel discussions on the community knowledge assets, among others, could be an effective way to allow more members to catch up at their own pace with the community conversations.

Notes

1 Gerald Ollivier, leader of the Transit-Oriented Development Community of Practice, provided extensive inputs for this chapter.
2 Ollivier, Gerald, Ghate Ashish, Bankim Kalra, and Mehta Prerna. 2021. *Transit-Oriented Development Implementation Resources and Tools* (2nd edition). Washington, DC: Global Platform for Sustainable Cities.
3 https://openknowledge.worldbank.org/handle/10986/34870

Partnering to Influence

The Urban Infrastructure and Services Community

Ede Ijjasz-Vasquez[1]

Many Paths to Becoming a Globally Recognized Community

The charge that the GSURR leadership gave to their communities of practice was to become—over three to five years—global virtual centers of excellence in their topics. The leadership asked them to become "the" place to go to get the latest innovations and lessons of experience in their work areas. They were encouraged to connect with other practitioners and networks and replicate at scale the internal transformation process they were achieving at the World Bank. This challenge had two objectives: learn and influence. Both goals were linked to improved client services. Despite its size, global reach, and focus on knowledge, the World Bank is, at times, quite insular, with technical staff in a given field or business area relying mainly on their peers within the organization for knowledge and solutions to client challenges. There are some individuals with strong external networks, but this is the exception rather than the rule. The knowledge silo breakers were asked to not only promote collaboration across organizational boundaries within the World Bank but also to break the "institutional silo" and connect globally.

The first objective of these global connections was to learn and to learn fast. The GSURR leadership wanted to tap more systematically into external networks to ensure its clients received and learned from the most up-to-date knowledge and real-world experiences as part of its services.

The second objective was to influence development practitioners within the respective technical fields. The GSURR leadership saw the usual approach of influence via formal publications (e.g., policy papers, project evaluations, opinion pieces) and the narrow dissemination of new ideas and solutions only to direct clients and in technical conferences as too limited and slow. The vision was to bring the World Bank knowledge to a larger group of development professionals faster and, hopefully, invite them to co-create new knowledge.

Not every GSURR community was ready for this challenge. The GSURR leadership did not push them to take this step from the beginning. Rather, the message was for them to take their time building the internal community but not to forget that there is an ocean of knowledge outside the organization that needs to be explored, brought inside, and used to co-create solutions with clients and partners.

Some communities were ready to tackle this challenge early on. They took different approaches. The Community-Driven Development Global Solutions Group (GSG) grew its external membership organically, one specialist at a time, through an external website, open knowledge-sharing events, and a newsletter. The Transit-Oriented Development Knowledge Silo Breaker (see Chapter 5.5) established a partnership with a think tank and created a dual

DOI: 10.4324/9781003199083-12

internal-external work program centered on a specific platform product. The Urban Infrastructure and Services GSG decided to work with existing and well-recognized external networks to rapidly multiply the exchange of knowledge and connections and develop new or deeper relations with client cities worldwide. This chapter describes the journey of this latter community.

The Urban Infrastructure and Services Global Solutions Group

This GSG was one of the largest in the GSURR Global Practice, covering several of its main business lines. When selecting the scope of work of the GSGs, the management team wanted to experiment and explore whether large or small groups would be most effective. Some GSGs were set up with narrow, more specialized topics like land and geospatial or municipal finance, which only had about 100 active members. These small GSGs only had one or two communities of practice (KSBs) associated with them. At the other side of the spectrum, some GSGs focused on much broader topics such as disaster risk management and resilience or urban infrastructure and services with several hundred members across different Global Practices and numerous KSBs connected to them. As discussed in Chapter 5, size was not a determinant of success. There were highly successful communities and less effective groups in both the large and small categories.

The Urban Infrastructure and Services GSG included several active KSBs. This presented a challenge to the GSG leadership: should it focus on individual flagship initiatives above its KSB's activities, or should it simply facilitate coordination and technical support to the individual KSBs? The team's answer was to follow a third way. It decided to connect to and collaborate with external networks and, in doing so, to leverage the power of the individual KSBs to offer client cities a more integrated package of services. A network of networks would leverage the knowledge generated by the individual KSBs to a much larger audience and influence than anything that the individual KSBs could do. In short, the Urban Infrastructure and Services GSG became a broker of knowledge with external audiences and clients through networks.

A Community Connecting to External Networks

The global urban development space has many organizations and networks. Rapidly growing urbanization is recognized worldwide as one of the most essential megatrends in development. The role of cities in climate change—both as generators of greenhouse gases and the location of the most significant economic damages from climate disasters (from floods to forest fires), on the one hand, and as leading edge innovators in addressing climate change, on the other—is central. The tensions between central and municipal governments are common. Associations and peer networks of cities are essential outlets for knowledge sharing across cities and countries. Several of these networks have become powerful platforms for political mobilization for global action on climate change and on the Sustainable Development Goals.

While most urban networks and associations have knowledge generation and sharing as one of their core functions, their approaches and organizational cultures vary widely. Some are focused mainly on influencing policy and on political mobilization for global action (C40 on climate change or the United States Conference of Mayors on federal policy change). Others focus on professional development (the International City/County Management Association). A third group focuses on supporting cities with innovations and action on frontier issues (Global Resilient Cities Network on resilience and climate change). Others are membership associations of cities with broad agendas that respond to their city members (such as ICLEI or United Cities and Local Governments [UCLG]).

The Urban Infrastructure and Services GSG faced a critical dilemma: how to select which of these networks to engage with. Should they focus on the largest networks for the broadest reach? Or work with networks having highly specialized technical focus to solve wicked urban problems? In a crowded space of networks, prioritization of engagements was critical.

How to Prioritize Engagements? Factors of Success for Productive Relations Between Internal and External Communities

Based on the World Bank experience, knowledge partnerships among networks or communities need three elements for success. First, the two groups need to have a shared vision of services to clients. For example, a research network and a community of practitioners may have visions of success that are too different to reconcile. Also, their clients may be too different for these networks to have a productive working relationship.

A second element for success is the diversity of approaches among the networks. This may seem contradictory to the first criteria, but it is not. If the two communities have a shared vision of who their clients are and their needs, then complementary approaches and skills can be beneficial. In the earlier example, if the network of researchers and the community of practitioners see local low-income communities as the clients they serve, then their diverse approaches—research and field programs—can enrich each other. If the networks understand and respect each other's skills and expertise, the partnership can be productive. There will be fewer jealousies between the network members, and the mix of perspectives will help them find more innovative solutions.

The third element for success is the willingness of the networks' leadership to put aside the usual competition for resources, clients, or visibility. All participants should see the alliance between networks as an opportunity to provide better services, enlarge the client base, mobilize more financial resources, and earn the respect of beneficiaries and network members for the association and partnership's value-added.

A First Story of Success: The Urban 20[2]

The Urban 20 (U20) was launched in 2017 as a city diplomacy initiative under the leadership of the mayors of Buenos Aires (Argentina) and Paris (France). The U20 brings together mayors from major cities in G20 countries in a forum to develop a message to collectively inform G20 negotiations.

The U20 runs parallel to the G20 process and strives to propose solutions to enhance climate action and sustainable economic development, in recognition of the fact that cities consume 75 percent of the world's energy and generate 75 percent of greenhouse emissions. The network also covers the cross-cutting theme of access to finance. Finally, it aims to enrich the G20 agenda by contributing the unique perspectives and good practices from cities and by carrying out annual discussions on critical urban subjects requiring joint efforts of national and local governments.

The C40 Cities (C40)[3] and United Cities and Local Governments (UCLG)[4] convene the U20 under the leadership of a chair city that rotates annually, based in the G20 host country. Its membership includes 25 principal cities and a group of observer cities invited to bring their experiences to the discussion.

The U20 group invites partners to support the process with knowledge contributions and evidence-based research in the topics decided by member cities in each cycle. For example, the 2018 cycle included topics that ranged from affordable housing to the future of work in cities, gender inequality, and sub-national financing.

The U20, under the leadership of the city of Buenos Aires, invited the World Bank as a knowledge partner. Before the creation of the GSURR communities of practice, this invitation would have been handled by the urban team working in Latin America. The Urban Infrastructure and Services GSG saw this invitation as an opportunity to build a longer-term partnership that could pass on from region to region with the U20 rotating chair.

The engagement with the U20 secretariat team and the city officials of Buenos Aires showed that the opportunities for effective engagement with this external network were quite positive. The U20 group wanted to bring the best global knowledge to inspire participating cities to act on climate change and sustainability. It also wanted to influence the G20 deliberations and national government policies. The World Bank's financial and knowledge support to urban centers and the policy work with national governments were similar in objectives. At the same time, the tools from each network (the U20 and the GSG) were quite different and complementary: the high-level political discourse and advocacy engagement of the U20 benefited from the technical knowledge brought by the GSG team members. Vice versa, the visibility with city leaders from G20 countries was a unique opportunity to open new avenues to expand the World Bank's client services.

The opportunity to work with the U20 was a strong motivator to the Urban Infrastructure and Services GSG members. The GSG leadership leveraged this motivation to build links across urban teams working on different regions and diverse subtopics (e.g., finance or water). Defining a knowledge product of global scope with a specific deadline and client in mind focused the attention of community members. Having access to city leaders from many large potential client cities was a strong motivator. The knowledge products had to be quite innovative as requested by the U20. This required the engagement of both experienced and younger team members to combine traditional and disruptive solutions to urban challenges. This engagement with an external network proved to be energizing for the new GSG.

When Tokyo took over the leadership of the U20, the GSG was well-positioned to continue the global engagement. The client relation leadership transferred from the Latin America to the East Asia teams, but the entire community already knew how to engage with the external network, and the relations deepened. Moreover, GSURR was able to leverage its partnerships with Japanese cities through the Tokyo Development Learning Center (see Chapter 6) to further the engagement with the U20 during this period.

GSURR's formal organizational structure had different managers for Latin America and East Asia and still a different manager overseeing the TDLC partnership. Even if the responsible managers were interested in collaborating and transferring the relations, it would have been far more challenging to do so without a strong community of practitioners. The aligned interests of community members across formal silos allowed for a new way of providing services seamlessly.

A Second Story of Success: The Global Resilient Cities Network[5]

In 2013, the Rockefeller Foundation established a partnership known as the 100 Resilient Cities Network. The objective of this network was to support cities around the world in building resilience to the economic, social, and physical risks of the 21st century. After a competitive selection process, a group of 100 cities was selected to join the network. Support from the Rockefeller Foundation included financial support to hire a chief resilience officer (CRO), expert support to prepare a city resilience strategy, and access to partners from the private, public, and NGO sectors who could help the city develop and implement projects identified in their resilience strategies. The community of CROs became an effective platform for peer-to-peer learning as they embarked on the resilience journey.

The CRO network soon realized that many of the challenges faced by economically advanced cities and urban centers in developing countries were quite similar, from air pollution to crime and flood risks. This realization built new bridges of exchanges different from the traditional North-South transfer of knowledge and expertise. The cities worked on shared challenges and diverse solutions, recognizing their different contexts and cultures.

The potential partnership between the Urban Infrastructure and Services GSG and the 100 Resilient Cities Network had several things going for it. First, both networks were focused on solving specific city resilience challenges. Second, the approaches were complementary: the 100 Resilient Cities Network had a CRO in each participating city (usually in the mayor's office or in a specialized resilience department) and resources for upstream work to prepare a resilience strategy; the World Bank had a wealth of global knowledge and experience from a much larger set of countries (particularly in the design of specific projects emerging from upstream resilience strategies) and financial resources to support the implementation of projects, if approved by the national government. Third, both organizations, especially the teams working in specific cities, quickly understood the complementarities and the leverage that working together would bring.

GSURR teams worked with the 100 Resilient Cities Network in various ways. At the project level, CROs were included in discussions regarding World Bank support for resilience-related infrastructure and policy advice. In several instances, this resulted in improved coordination as the implementing agency for the World Bank resilience projects was not always connected with the CRO. Beyond project-level coordination, GSURR partnered with 100 Resilient Cities Network and/or with individual CROs in a number of knowledge-sharing programs including those of its City Resilience Program and of the Tokyo Development Learning Center.

In 2019, the 100 Resilient Cities Network concluded its work, and a new organization—the Global Resilient City Network (R-cities[6]) was established to support the former 100 Resilient Cities Network members and their CROs in future-proofing their communities and critical infrastructure. The emphasis on knowledge, lesson sharing, and common platforms for action is at the core of the new network. The relation with the World Bank team evolved to one where structured participation in each other's knowledge events fosters a rapid exchange of experiences and innovations.

Three Leadership Lessons

Growing knowledge networks through partnerships requires specific leadership attention in three areas:

1. *Rigorous analysis and prioritization of possible partnerships using the three factors for success discussed earlier*: In a desire to grow their communities, leaders often want to push for fast establishment of partnerships without undertaking adequate due diligence. The push to reach a larger number of members and partners cannot be the sole criteria if

the ultimate objective is to offer better services to clients. This approach may look good in terms of numbers. It can also sound attractive for public relations purposes. Signing of partnership agreements or memorandums of understanding can be good photo ops. However, this approach does not always lead to specific products, new client relations, or innovation. The role of these partnerships is not always optimal. The leaders' role in bringing discipline and selectivity is essential.

2. *Clear objectives and milestones*: The growth and deepening of partnerships need a road map with clear milestones and expected results. These results need to go beyond the general partnership agreements with well-meaning intentions. Partnerships go through distinct phases, and the communities themselves evolve. A rigorous periodic review of partnership results in terms of knowledge assets, innovation, and client engagement is necessary. Effective knowledge partnerships need to go beyond knowledge exchange events and explore ways to deepen the knowledge relation, moving to co-creation, joint or coordinated client engagement, and deeper trust.

3. *Skills of community leaders for successful partnerships with external communities*: Community leaders need an additional set of skills to be effective in analyzing, defining, and nurturing knowledge partnerships with external groups. In GSURR's experience, these community leaders need to be trust builders, have a long-term vision combined with short-term urgency for results, and be good at mobilizing a combination of community members who are doers and networkers for an effective relationship. These leaders need to be comfortable understanding the motivations and culture of other networks and analyzing strengths and complementarities. They should identify early on practical results and ensure a connection with client services leveraging both the internal and external community.

Future Areas

The partnerships described in this chapter did not have sufficient time at the time of writing this book to explore or face three issues, as follows:

First, the knowledge partnerships discussed were between an internal community and one external community. The expectation is that this working model would be replicated through organic growth of the collaboration with new communities. The original idea was to grow the partnership until it became a "federation" of communities. Another idea was to eventually create a separate entity that would play the role of connecting tissue and coordinator of the various communities engaged. There was insufficient time to explore whether a formal structure is needed after reaching a large enough scale, how to share functions and resources, and how to evolve and co-create the identity of this agglomeration. As the GSGs and KSBs were tasked to become global centers of excellence in their focus areas, these questions would emerge in due course.

Second, the internal and external communities had similar perspectives and visions for solving urban development challenges. Innovation requires diversity: diversity of perspectives, backgrounds, experiences, and approaches. Figuring out how to work with entirely different communities can bring important dividends. For example, a partnership with a community of urban low-income neighborhood NGOs or a community of data science researchers might generate vastly different and potentially disruptive solutions. Community leaders who can bridge cultures and lexicons, and build trust, are indispensable in making such associations work.

Third, it may be inevitable that tensions between the participating communities will emerge. The competition for clients, funding (in the not-for-profit world) or revenues (in the profit world), or visibility will arise. Open and transparent discussion among community leaders may resolve these differences or at least identify rules of the game for a productive relationship that combines cooperation and competition.

Notes

1 Horacio Terraza, leader of the GSURR Urban Infrastructure and Services Global Solutions Group provided extensive input for this chapter.
2 www.urban20.org/
3 www.c40.org/
4 www.uclg.org/
5 www.rockefellerfoundation.org/100-resilient-cities/
6 www.resilientcitiesnetwork.org

Building a Global Community

The Understanding Risk Community and Forums

Francis Ghesquiere

The Understanding Risk (UR) Community of Practice brings together professionals and practitioners from the field of disaster risk management to share knowledge on the latest innovations in risk assessment and to build partnerships and collaboration. The flagship activity of the community is the biennial Understanding Risk Forum, the first of which took place in June 2010, at a time when risk modeling and digital mapping technologies were opening an entirely new era in disaster risk management. The Understanding Risk Community was founded to bring together different experts and practitioners who typically do not interact in their regular course of business in order to spur discussions and strike up nontraditional partnerships. This chapter introduces the Understanding Risk Community, its genesis, activities, lessons learned, and the evolution to adapt to COVID-19 constraints.

Genesis and Rationale

The Understanding Risk Community emerged from a successful conference (Understanding Risk 2010) held at the World Bank in the aftermath of the 2010 Haiti earthquake. At the time, the field of disaster risk management (DRM) was the domain of a limited number of specialized "experts," mostly engineers using "black box" and proprietary models and platforms. As Understanding Risk 2010 demonstrated, the advent of computing power, open-source software, satellite imagery, and many other innovative technologies provided exciting opportunities for disruption to the traditional model of business. It became clear that providing the space to explore new concepts and share ideas would benefit disaster risk management professionals across the spectrum of practitioners and experts.

Since its establishment, the Understanding Risk Community has grown with each biennial forum, taking stock of new concepts and new technologies used to assess and communicate risk. Multiple independent UR events have also been organized, mostly at a regional level, expanding the geographical reach of the community (See Figure 5.7–1). Today the community, which operates both virtually and through the biennial events, comprises close to 20,000 experts and practitioners from nearly 180 countries and represents about 2,200 organizations. Community members include representatives of government agencies, multilateral organizations, nongovernmental organizations, the private sector,[1] research institutions, academia, community-based organizations, and civil society.

DOI: 10.4324/9781003199083-13

Figure 5.7–1 Understanding Risk Spinoffs

Box 5.7–1   —Understanding Risk 2010 and the Haiti Earthquake

The first Understanding Risk Forum took place in the aftermath of a devastating 7.1 magnitude earthquake that struck Haiti in January 2010 claiming in excess of 300,000 lives, an event that raised public consciousness about the potential impact of natural hazards. The World Bank was at the forefront of the recovery and reconstruction efforts. A team was dispatched to Haiti barely a week after the disaster to support the government in assessing the damage and planning the reconstruction. It was immediately clear that detailed mapping of the affected area was a requirement to guide the reconstruction. To map the affected area, the World Bank team quickly organized a collaborative effort[2] to capture and open satellite imagery and crowdsource the damage assessment to expert volunteers. More than 800 people volunteered to help with the rapid damage assessment in what became the first large-scale, post-disaster crowdsourced analysis of the impact of an event. The analysis, conducted in record time, provided detailed information about the extent of the damage and the crowdsourced maps of the area proved to be crucial to the reconstruction program and are still in use today.

In addition, the World Bank supported the deployment of OpenStreetMap (OSM) volunteers to support community-mapping activities. This was one of the first major applications of the OSM platform to disaster response. Using OSM—also known as the Wikipedia of maps, an open and editable map of the world—450 volunteers used the open satellite and other remote-sensing imagery to digitize roads, buildings, and other features, thus creating the most up-to-date map of Port-au-Prince (Haiti) in a few weeks. Risk modeling, geospatial information and open-source platforms, satellite imagery, and crowdsourcing were all on the agenda of the first UR Forum in 2010.

How Is the Understanding Risk Community Organized?

The biennial Understanding Risk Forums, which are the flagship events of the Understanding Risk Community, are crowdsourced events consisting of two elements: the Understanding Risk Community days and the Forum itself. During the community days, organizations

Box 5.7–2 —Ten Years of Understanding Risk

2010 Understanding Risk Forum, Washington, DC, USA

The inaugural *Understanding Risk: Innovation in Disaster Risk Assessment* conference sought to address several key questions, notably, what is risk? Can we measure it? If we understand it, can we manage it better? The event explored best practices in a variety of topics ranging from open-source risk modeling to community-based risk assessments. New approaches in risk assessment included the use of geospatial platforms, the crowdsourcing of information, and the benefits of partnerships across sectors. Understanding Risk 2010 was also the first global Random Hacks of Kindness hackathon—a collaboration with Google, Yahoo!, Microsoft, NASA, and the World Bank, where volunteers with expertise in computer programming or hacking came together with disaster risk management practitioners to develop tech solutions to identified challenges over a 24-hour period, fueled by passion and pizza.

2012 Understanding Risk Forum, Cape Town, South Africa

Understanding Risk 2012: Mapping Global Risks convened 500 risk assessment experts and practitioners from more than 86 countries, this time on the continent of Africa. Organized in partnership with the Government of South Africa and the Africa, Caribbean, and Pacific—European Union (ACP-EU) Program, the conference introduced new approaches to risk assessment including techniques for decision-making under uncertainty. Crowdsourcing, a topic that was completely new just two years earlier, had become part of the mainstream and examples of how this could be applied to risk assessment for financial applications was shared. There was also a growing consensus about the need for more open data. Many initiatives demonstrated that this could be done for the benefit of all. Finally, the two years since the first Understanding Risk Forum confirmed the need for the world to continue thinking about the unthinkable. The Great Japanese Earthquake and Tsunami of March 2011 and floods in Thailand came as stark reminders that the world faces a future of increasing uncertainty about extreme events. The Forum helped strengthen regional and global partnerships and built technical capacity in the Africa region through a series of training events.

2014 Understanding Risk Forum, London, UK

The *Understanding Risk 2014: Producing Actionable Information* conference included multiple technical sessions and workshops led by various organizations and covered topics such as risk modeling in the financial sector, risk communication, community-based risk assessments, and assessing risk in a changing climate with a call to move the needle on producing risk information that can be acted upon by decision-makers. New technologies showcased that year included the use of drones and other earth observation tools. The event saw a spike in the number of attendees, reaching 840 participants from 60 countries and 285 organizations. The 2014 conference saw Google and Airbus committing to provide the first global high-resolution digital elevation model of Earth's entire land surface, benefitting a multitude of applications including disaster risk identification. Risk Management Solutions (RMS) announced free access to RMS-One, a risk modeling platform for catastrophic risk, to governments in developing and developed countries. One prominent focus of the 2014 conference was small island developing states (SIDS) with a special set of events organized around financial protection. Many senior leaders from numerous nations participated in these events, including Tonga, Maldives, Grenada, and Madagascar.

2016 Understanding Risk Forum, Venice, Italy

The fourth edition of the Understanding Risk Forum, *Understanding Risk 2016: Building Evidence for Action,* was a resounding success, bringing together practitioners from more than 100 countries to meet, learn, and share best practices. This was the most ambitious and global forum yet. More than 2,000 meetings and networking opportunities saw policymakers, risk modelers, urban planners, economists, psychologists, communicators, and others meet in the inspiring setting of the 12th-century Venetian Arsenale. Set in the city's medieval shipyard, the 2016 Forum paid particular attention to flood risks. The main innovations presented that year were in big data and social media analytics. Several speakers showed how social media can be used to improve early warning systems, to map vulnerable infrastructure, to assess damage immediately after an event, and to monitor reconstruction programs.

2018 Understanding Risk Forum, Mexico City, Mexico

Understanding Risk 2018: Disrupt, Communicate, Influence marked the emergence of artificial intelligence and cloud computing as new tools for hazard assessment, risk modeling, and collaborative work. The event was held in the Palacio de Minería, the 18th-century building that belongs to the National Autonomous University of Mexico, and saw a record number of community sessions with 1,050 participants representing 101 countries and 550 organizations

2020 Understanding Risk Forum, Global, Online

As a result of the COVID-19 pandemic, the ten-year anniversary of the Understanding Risk Forum took place online, enabling attendees to participate in their local business hours regardless of their location. Built around the theme *Understanding Risk 2020: Looking Back, Looking Forward,* the Forum took stock of ten years of Understanding Risk events and explored avenues for the future. Building on sessions from the 2018 conference, the forum included important sessions related to pandemic risk assessment, risk and crisis communication, and social inequality as a key driver of risk. Six thousand people registered for the event, which is an outstanding number and shows the growth of the community. The agenda was designed to ensure maximum participation—with sessions and content available in three time zones, and with a focus on interactive sessions to keep the audience engaged. Ultimately the event reached 2,558 participants from 179 countries; representing 1,310 organizations.

and individuals that are part of the Understanding Risk Community organize their own events and sessions. These includes annual meetings, dedicated training events, site visits, and even specialized conferences. The community days usually take place during the first two days of the week, after which everyone is invited to join the main Understanding Risk Forum, which usually spans 2.5 additional days.

The main forum aims to maximize interactions between participants through plenaries and smaller technical sessions but also art exhibitions, networking spaces, an expo on the latest cutting-edge technologies and trends, and other activities. Partners and community members are consulted in developing the agenda for the main forum, with technical sessions being selected from entries submitted in a call for proposals. These two days allow experts and practitioners from different walks of life to interact, discuss, and exchange views. The Forum is designed to open opportunities for reflection, knowledge sharing, and collaboration in addition to providing inspiration to members to keep up the important work of building resilience for all.

The Understanding Risk Community is managed on a voluntary basis by dedicated individuals. Community members are the real owners of the forum and the secret to its success. By providing a platform for members to hold their own events, the forums bring together many individuals from various fields of expertise and different parts of the world. This diversity is one reason for its strength.

What Were the Results?

In 2017, Understanding Risk undertook an independent evaluation to ascertain if and how the community was contributing positively to the disaster and climate risk management field. The internal evaluation found that the *Understanding Risk Community* has improved understanding of risk, strengthened disaster risk assessment capacity, [created] new partnerships, [advanced] knowledge sharing, strengthened communities of practice, and [supported] application of technical expertise at the country level. A few of these results are explained in more detail:

A *field transformed*—Understanding Risk was born at a time when disaster risk management was the purview of a limited number of experts largely disconnected from each other. Experts of risk assessment and risk communication were even more difficult to find. Limited employment opportunities were partially a reason for the lack of interest in the field. The world has changed since then. The concept of "resilience" is now at the core of every development program. The Understanding Risk Community and its events can be credited, in large measure, for this transformation.

A *vibrant community*—Understanding Risk is now a vibrant community of close to 20,000 members. Apart from the biennial events, 19 "local" Understanding Risk events have taken place around the world (See Figure 5.7–1). Beyond guidance provided by the core Understanding Risk team, these events emerged from the initiative of individuals and organizations that had attended Understanding Risk Forums. The scale and quality of these events have helped expand the reach of the community and advanced its objective to promote new ideas and encourage collaboration in the field of risk assessment and risk communication, leading to increased and better informed resilience projects at the World Bank and other external organizations.

A *multitude of atypical partnerships*—The Understanding Risk Community has helped generate multiple atypical collaborations, for example, providing the catalyst for a highly successful partnership between NGOs and insurance companies or between development agencies and Silicon Valley companies. The diverse nature of membership as well as possibilities for networking and collaboration are the highest ranked outcomes of the Understanding Risk Forums, according to the participants.[3] The program has not only helped create standard partnerships between experts in similar fields but has also managed to reduce silos by connecting individuals and organizations that would otherwise not find synergies—the forums have encouraged technology companies, academia, experts from the financial sector, nonprofit organizations and even artists to work together.

An innovative platform—The first Understanding Risk Forum was born with a clear vision that the cross-fertilization of ideas between experts and practitioners from different walks of life would help generate innovation. Each biennial forum brought new concepts and technology to the forefront, leveraging already known concepts and generating new ideas, including new concepts that the World Bank has successfully demonstrated in projects, as well as exposing the World Bank and others to new concepts and ideas. Box 5.7–2 provides a summary of the new ideas that emerged at each forum and have been mainstreamed at the next.

A *fertile talent pool*—According to some participants quoted in the Understanding Risk evaluation report, the community and events have "made DRM cool." Indeed, the Understanding Risk Community has catalyzed an entire new generation of people interested in risk assessment and risk communication, resulting in an increase in participation from youth and young professionals. This community has provided the World Bank, other development agencies, and specialized companies with a fertile talent pool at a time when demand for such expertise has been rapidly growing.

Five Lessons Learned During Ten Years of the Understanding Risk Community

Inspiration is at the core of the Understanding Risk formula—Understanding Risk Forums aim to inspire and promote the cross-fertilization of ideas. The balance between serious discussions and inspiring or experiential sessions has been at the core of Understanding Risk since its inception. Art, humor, and interactive learning have proven to be powerful ways to engage participants, transmit knowledge, and build the community. As with other GSURR knowledge events such as technical deep dives (see Chapter 6), and drawing on the World Bank's *Art of Knowledge Exchange* methodology (see Chapter 9) this element is what sets Understanding Risk apart from typical conferences. Sessions and speeches in the Forums are highly curated to be short, engaging, visual, and inspiring—moving away from traditional forms of information sharing that consist of long panels and "death by PPT."

Active participation is key—Keeping the participants engaged throughout the event requires changing formats, making various voices heard, and utilizing a range of media. Some of the instruments and activities used in Understanding Risk Forums over the years are described in Box 5.7–3. Inspiring, visual, and emotional keynotes are used to set the stage and close the event. The opening "Ignites" lure participants to join technical sessions, which themselves follow a wide variety of formats. An expo and a networking space, which is always infused with creativity itself to stimulate out-of-the-box thinking, help promote collaboration and partnerships and the spread of new ideas

Empowering the community in session planning makes for richer content—As with the GSURR Forums and other events organized by the Global Practice, different disaster risk management communities of practice are given the freedom to organize their own sessions. This is because, as professionals in their own fields, they are likely to be the best ones to plan and manage the session structure and content. Taking this a step further, the Understanding

Risk Community nudges session organizers to be interactive, save ample time for Q and A, engage the audience, be creative, and make sure that the panels are diverse.

Mixing people from different backgrounds but same interests produces new ideas— Communities that work in fields related to risk might not have a direct link to disasters. These experts and professionals are still relevant to the Understanding Risk Community. Risk in the financial world, nuclear risk, cyber risk, even risk analysis for launching a space shuttle are all relevant from the point of view of disaster risk management. All these groups look at risk from different perspectives, and it is useful for them to learn from each other. For example, cyber risk does not include just risks related to technology: reducing cyber risk must cover the whole ecosystem of regulation, specialized companies, and technology that a country needs to build resilience. By bringing in professionals from these diverse fields, we have seen the cross-pollination of knowledge and a better understanding of disaster and climate risk.

Avoids mission creep—The organizing team has been under pressure over the years to widen the topic of the Understanding Risk Forum beyond risk assessment and risk communication but has remained steadfast in the focus on keeping on topic. By avoiding mission creep, the community has managed to build a very specific brand and identity. Over the years, many more conferences and communities have emerged that deal with resilience and disaster risk management; some with many more resources. But Understanding Risk has remained one of the prime events in the field thanks to its strong focus and identity.

Box 5.7–3 —Keeping the Audience Engaged

Varying formats, interesting speakers, and different outreach channels have proven effective at keeping UR participants engaged throughout the biennial Forums. Some tools and techniques for knowledge sharing in UR include:

- *Ignites:* Understanding Risk was the first team at the World Bank to pilot the "Ignite" format—5-minute presentations with 20 slides advancing automatically every 15 seconds. This format is now mainstreamed. It ensures time-keeping and more exciting presentations that focus on key messages and visuals to capture the imagination of the audience and not lose its interest. Ignites have been used at the beginning of the Forum to help participants decide which session to attend—session leads "pitch" their ideas, and audience members show up to the best sessions.
- *Keynote addresses:* These are talks that establish the underlying tone, summarize the spirit, and communicate the core message of the Forum. At Understanding Risk Forums, keynotes are usually used at the opening and closing ceremony and are always meant to serve as inspiration for the next few days of the Forum or to keep the community's energy up until the next event.
- *Plenary sessions:* These sessions usually involve hard-hitting speakers addressing a broad audience. In most cases, three to four speakers are given five minutes to introduce their ideas. These presentations are followed by a panel discussion led by a well-prepared moderator.
- *Hard talks:* These sessions usually involve a well-known figure interviewed by a "no-nonsense" journalist. Hard talks are casual but direct conversations, allowing for a flowing dialogue between the speaker and the journalist.

- *Rapid talk*: Another format is this pre-prepared dialogue between two individuals of opposing views allowing for rapid exchanges on a generally controversial topic (e.g., geo-engineering).
- *Fireside chat*: This format is a more relaxed conversation between a moderator and a topic expert.
- *Interactive sessions*: These sessions designed to get the audience (sometimes more than 500 people) to actively participate, generally with the help of improvisation techniques.
- *Serious games*: Participants are put into a scenario where they are required to make decisions about risk that have consequences, ultimately revealing various challenges of decision-making under uncertainty and complexity in systems. These games can last for as short as five minutes or as long as two days.
- *Cartoon-a-thons*: A "cartoon-a-thon" is a participatory session that harnesses the power of intelligent visual humor to enable learning and dialogue on challenging topics. Like a hackathon, but with professional cartoonists instead of computer coders, the cartoon-a-thon process invites people and organizations interested in a serious issue to co-create visual depictions that are serious and fun, inspiring and useful.
- *Doodling or murals*: Art is usually drawn during sessions or the entire conference to help participants take stock and look at the topic from an additional perspective.
- *"5 × 15"*: In collaboration with event team 5 × 15, UR has held evening sessions that feature 5 speakers that are given 15 minutes each to share an inspiring, and often personal, story around the topic of risk.
- *Hackathons*: This is a sprint-like event in which computer programmers and domain experts collaborate intensively to propose a software solution to a particular problem. The goal of a hackathon is usually to create functioning solutions by the end of the event. The hackathon organized at Understanding Risk 2010 in collaboration with NASA, Google, Microsoft, and Yahoo! was one of the world's first global hackathons.
- *Interdisciplinary pressure cooker*: Teams of youth and young professionals from diverse backgrounds are provided real-world, local challenges around a topic that necessitates an interdisciplinary approach, working through the night for 24 hours.
- *Innovation expo*: The expo is a dedicated space where agencies and specialized companies can present their programs and products.
- *Connecting the venue to risk*: The venue and its look and feel are designed to evoke risk and the community, often through art and stage design.
- *Infusing music and art*: Music and art are used to connect to the topic and to highlight a new way for attendees to think about the field, such as music created out of risk data. For example, the Climate Music Project did an orchestral performance at Understanding Risk 2018 to capture the sound of climate change.
- *Comedy*: Comedians walking around during the breaks would often engage with the participants to add fun and reflect on some of the sessions.

While the Understanding Risk Community has not invented these concepts, it has served as a catalyst in making them better known in the World Bank and in the disaster risk management community.

Reinventing Understanding Risk in the Context of COVID-19

The 10th anniversary of Understanding Risk was meant to take place in Singapore in May 2020. Unfortunately, due to the occurrence of COVID-19, in March 2020, barely two months before the planned date, the decision had to be taken to postpone the event. Two months later, it was decided that Understanding Risk 2020 would be a fully virtual event.

No one within the Understanding Risk core team had ever organized a virtual event of this magnitude. Everyone was wondering whether it was even possible to create an event as interactive and inspiring as the previous forums had been. In the end, Understanding Risk 2020 proved to be a success as the team built on delivering the core elements of the Understanding Risk formula, namely crowdsourcing sessions from the community and encouraging interaction within and beyond sessions.

After a challenging test run of an online event where the potential technical difficulties were exposed, the team opted for a simple format, inviting community members to run their own sessions, which were broadcast through a common platform. This structure made it possible to broadcast 105 online community sessions that were organized by 150 different organizations. The agenda was designed so that anyone, anywhere in the world could watch at least some of Understanding Risk 2020 during their local business hours. Many sessions were prerecorded but included interactive elements such as a chat box and polling, which allowed people to communicate and contribute to the sessions while it was broadcast.

Another new feature added was the recycling of curated material from the sessions, broadcasting them during the following months to help keep the community active. Like other organizations and communities that were prompted to shift to virtual delivery modalities due to COVID-19, Understanding Risk Forums of the future are likely to adopt a hybrid model wherein an in-person event will take place while, at the same time, people unable to travel to the physical location of the event will be able to follow broadcast sessions interactively from their own locations.

Notes

1 Mostly, technology companies, insurance and reinsurance, engineering and consulting firms, and specialized risk modeling firms.
2 Key actors in this effort included ImageCat and the Humanitarian Open Street Map Community.
3 Independent UR Evaluation Report 2017

Exporting the Knowledge Ecosystem

The Global Platform for Sustainable Cities

Ede Ijjasz-Vasquez[1]

The Global Environmental Facility (GEF), the world's largest funder of environmentally oriented programs, created a new modality for its grants in 2016. Instead of supporting only individual projects focused on an environmental issue, it opened the possibility to tackle the underlying causes of environmental degradation in an integrated manner. Cities were one of the focus areas for the new program. The GEF also wanted to support a knowledge-sharing and learning network among participating cities. The GSURR Global Practice's knowledge ecosystem was an attractive solution. The World Bank partnered with the GEF to create the Global Platform for Sustainable Cities. This network connected more than 30 cities receiving funding for environmental action, implementing partners, and knowledge partners to innovate, learn, and exchange knowledge from environmental action. This chapter tells the journey to leverage an internal knowledge ecosystem of tools and behaviors as a new service line to clients. The World Bank was used to provide financial and advisory support to cities. How to provide knowledge management services was a new challenge.

The Global Environmental Facility and a New Approach to Solve Environmental Challenges

The Global Environmental Facility (GEF) was established during the 1992 Rio Earth Summit as a multilateral trust fund to provide grants to developing countries in support of the implementation of major international environmental conventions. Today, GEF works on biodiversity, climate change, chemicals, desertification, and related global environmental challenges. Since its establishment, the GEF has provided more than US$21 billion in grants for more than 5,000 projects and programs. These grant resources have mobilized close to US$120 billion in additional financing. More than 40 donor countries contribute funds to the GEF for its environmental work.

As part of its 2020 strategy, GEF introduced a new modality of support to countries, called the integrated approach modality. In this new way of working, GEF expanded its standard operational modality focused on individual projects tackling a single environmental issue (e.g. biodiversity or chemicals). The new approach was more holistic, allowing countries to receive resources to tackle several environmental challenges at a time. The goal was to work on the underlying drivers of environmental degradation.

For example, the GEF would support country programs on agricultural transformation and intensification to reduce impacts on biodiversity, reduce chemical use, and reduce greenhouse gas emissions from agriculture at the same time.

One of the work areas for the integrated approach modality was urban development. Cities in developing countries are growing fast. Nearly 90 percent of the increase in urban

DOI: 10.4324/9781003199083-14

population is taking place in Asian or African cities. Furthermore, cities are responsible for about 70 percent of all greenhouse gas emissions; they use and emit chemicals of a wide range, including through inadequate solid waste management; and they cause significant strain on natural resources, such as biodiversity or water. By tackling environmental issues in cities, GEF expected to work on several environmental topics in an integrated manner.

The Institutional Challenge

The GEF had worked with many cities before 2020 on environmental issues. However, the institution felt that the typical project, with few exceptions, had a narrow perspective (for example, wastewater treatment to improve the quality of international waters or restoration of urban wetlands). GEF's ambition was to work with cities in more integrated platforms tackling the root causes of multiple environmental problems. The intergated pilot approach was a significant step change in direction and approach for the GEF.

A second challenge was GEF's desire to move from a series of individual programs with a few cities in developing countries to an integrated platform where participating cities would learn from each other during the design and implementation of environmental solutions. The ambition was for this platform to provide lessons of experience that could be replicated through city networks and financial institutions to hundreds of cities worldwide.

The Approach

The GEF cities program had four innovative features:[2]

- An emphasis on evidence-based urban planning as a key tool for improved quality of urban life and enhanced environmental performance of cities.
- A comprehensive suite of support services to cities connecting the latest thinking and research on environmental sustainability with cities in developing countries.
- A "network" approach that would connect the GEF program with global city-based associations and networks to enlarge its influence through the tools developed and experienced learned.
- Contribution to global discourse on urban environmental sustainability.

The GEF cities program was designed around two major lines of action. First, direct grant financing to individual cities to support an integrated urban planning approach and priority investments with global environmental benefits. Second, a global platform for knowledge sharing connecting the cities receiving funds from GEF but also open to other interested cities. The objectives of this platform were to bring the state-of-the-art thinking and methods of integrated urban planning with an environmental perspective. At the same time, the lessons learned would be disseminated through networks of mayors and city experts.

The first phase of the direct grant financing window of the GEF cities program supported about 30 cities across 11 pilot countries: Brazil, China, Cote d'Ivoire, India, Malaysia, Mexico, Paraguay, Peru, Senegal, South Africa, and Vietnam. Several agencies—Multilateral Development Bank and UN organizations—supported the implementation of these projects and mobilized additional financing.

A New Platform Is Born

At the time it decided to shift its approach to supporting urban development, including the establishment of a mechanism to share knowledge among cities, the GEF did not have much experience with knowledge-sharing platforms. It decided to engage a partner with deep experience in both urban development and knowledge management. The World Bank's GSURR Global Practice emerged as the preferred candidate for the Platform. The *Global Platform for Sustainable Cities* (GPSC) was born with a financial contribution of more than US$5 million from the GEF. This was one of the first times the World Bank provided knowledge management services to another organization.

The GSURR leadership team saw in this new platform an opportunity to expand the reach from its internal communities of practice to a global platform. The GEF appreciated the World Bank's commitment to its vision and the practical experience of the GSURR global knowledge ecosystem that matched its objectives.

The new platform had three unique characteristics that enhanced its knowledge flows and impact: connections with three types of city networks, a top-down and bottom-up selection of topics for research and action, and a connection with the GSURR communities of practice.

Three networks—Neither the GEF nor GSURR wanted to build a knowledge-sharing platform exclusively for the participating cities receiving grants. Rather, the objective was to reach as many cities as possible through the platform. To achieve this objective, the World Bank and GEF focused on building connections with three city groups:

- *Cities receiving financing from multilateral development organizations*: The platform developed connections with financial institutions working with cities in developing countries and the GEF, such as the Interamerican Development Bank or the Asian Development Bank. The platform membership included one national development bank—the Development Bank of South Africa (DBSA). The platform also built informal connections with other financial institutions working with cities, such as the European Bank for Reconstruction and Development. Working with these institutions opened avenues for the knowledge generated by the Sustainable Cities platform to be directly relevant to programs financed by these institutions, shortening the time from lessons learned to replication. Furthermore, the platform built trust among financial institutions that sometimes compete to find common ground for a joint global policy declaration on urban development for the first time.
- *Cities working with United Nations organizations*:[3] these organizations had a unique role in global advocacy and mobilization of global stakeholders for global discourse processes on the urban environmental agenda. They also brought highly specialized expertise on specific topics that allowed technical silos to be broken.
- *City networks and membership associations*: Associations and networks such as ICLEI and C40, which connect thousands of cities around the world and have the unique position and representation given their broad membership, are another area for platform. Their role as amplifiers of messages and lessons was seen as invaluable.

Top-down and bottom-up selection of topics—The lessons of the GSURR global knowledge ecosystem were used to chart the course of technical topic selection for the Global Platform for Sustainable Cities. An important function of the platform was to identify "frontier" issues on urban environment, prepare position and research papers, and discuss them with participating cities and affiliate organizations. The combination of top-down selection and bottom-up call for ideas allowed the platform to fulfill its knowledge-generation function.

Three topics were selected from the top: 1) integrated urban planning and management, a critical factor in making cities greener; 2) municipal finance to ensure adequate resources are mobilized for urban environmental action; 3) sustainability indicators and tools to support cities in monitoring progress towards their objectives.

The discussions with participating cities and affiliate organizations led to a series of bottom-up lines of work, including affordable green housing, transit-oriented development, solid waste management, and urban biodiversity, among others. The question of green urban post-COVID recovery took renewed importance beginning in 2021.

Connection to GSURR communities of practice and knowledge tools—Many of the working topics matched the areas of focus of GSURR communities of practice (KSBs and GSGs), such as solid waste management, housing, and municipal finance. This correspondence offered a unique opportunity for the communities to expand their reach to external audiences: client cities, other multilateral banks, UN organizations, and networks of cities.

Some organizations were eager to exchange knowledge and views with the World Bank's urban communities of practice and the Global Platform for Sustainable Cities. For example, the European Bank for Reconstruction and Development was an active partner, even if it did not receive GEF grants for its client cities. Its objective was to exchange knowledge and lessons on urban environment, as it was developing a new program for Green Cities in Eastern Europe. The Sustainable Cities platform benefited from its research work and initial lessons of implementation. This approach was replicated, to some extent, with other financiers and their urban environment portfolios.

The Global Platform for Sustainable Cities provided financial resources for the GSURR communities of practice to develop new tools and methodologies that were replicated across cities in the platform and among World Bank client cities. This symbiotic relation served the communities well and increased their impact beyond the immediate World Bank clients. Furthermore, the platform served as a platform to promote the large number of policy and research reports on urban environment published by the World Bank.

The Sustainable Cities Platform learned from several of the experiments and tools developed as part of the GSURR global knowledge ecosystem (Chapter 4). For example, the GPSC worked with the Tokyo Development Learning Center to prepare a technical deep dive (unfortunately postponed due to the COVID pandemic). Its newsletter, knowledge-sharing events, and development of informal working groups benefited from the lessons of GSURR knowledge management tools.

From Informal Brainstorming to a New Business Line—A Case Study

The Global Platform for Sustainable Cities established an annual knowledge-sharing and learning event that borrowed elements from the GSURR annual forum and added some interesting features. These annual forums included:

- High-level policy discussions with the participation of ministers of urban development and mayors from around the world.
- Expert workshops on topics selected by the GPSC partners.

- Training through a GPSC City Academy on topics of greatest interest to most participating cities.
- Launch of flagship technical reports on frontier urban environment issues.

The connections between the city investment programs, their implementation lessons learned, the frontier research answering emerging questions in those city programs, and the global policy dialogue helped to reinforce the various lines of the Platform work.

In one of the brainstorming sessions during the Platform's global meeting in Sao Paulo (Brazil), the deputy mayor of Paris (France) began a conversation on the importance of green spaces and biodiversity for the quality of life of urban citizens. The conversation highlighted the many benefits of biodiversity and green spaces for resilience to climate change impacts such as heatwaves and flooding. Participants discussed the climate mitigation benefits—from increased vegetative cover to reduced housing cooling needs. The idea of a new working group and line of work on cities for biodiversity was born.

The Global Platform for Sustainable Cities searched for and mobilized a group of global technical leaders from academia and innovative cities working on biodiversity. Based on inputs from cities and organizations in the working group, an initial background report on cities and biodiversity was prepared. The Platform mobilized organizations working on the topic, from the World Economic Forum to the International Union for Conservation of Nature.

The Sustainable Cities Platform work on cities and biodiversity was an excellent match to the work of the Nature-Based Solutions KSB in GSURR. The coordination of the research and learning agenda and the opportunities for financing of biodiversity action in cities through the Nature-Based Solutions team in the World Bank were an ideal match.

This case study shows how structured knowledge management tools can accelerate and scale-up the process from ideation and co-creation to investments across countries eventually reaching a global scale.

Leadership Lessons

The World Bank engagement in setting up and coordinating the Global Platform for Sustainable Cities was not seen as core to the GSURR business. That way of thinking would have led to missed opportunities with important returns. Here are three leadership lessons from this experience:

- Once the basic elements of a knowledge management system are in place, it is important to keep an eye for "lateral" opportunities to leverage them, even if—at first—they are not necessarily core to the business. The use of GSURR communities of practice, knowledge management tools, and lessons learned on conference design, the "garden" approach for new ideas, among others, were extremely useful in building a platform that reverted in new business opportunities and raised the standing of the World Bank among urban practitioners globally.
- Knowledge management can be a productive business line, provided the technical topics are closely related to the main business of the organization. Leaders need to understand the unexpected linkages and business opportunities that new platform can bring. The return on investment of knowledge management as a business line needs to consider the collateral benefits of such an engagement.

- As with all platform, a detailed analysis of strengths and overlaps of participating organizations is critical. A source of tension in the Sustainable Cities Platform was the overlap of strengths—real or perceived—among organizations. Open and frank discussions with partners to reach a shared understanding of the value added of each member can save time and unproductive engagements down the line.

The Future

The Platform proved its value early on during implementation. The participating cities recognized the value of belonging to a network where all members had financing available to implement related solutions. The Platform was—to some degree—a global laboratory of new solutions for urban environment challenges.

There are three potential areas for future development, including:

- *Stronger connection between the Platform and the knowledge management systems (including communities of practice) of participating organizations*: The connections that were built between the platform and the GSURR knowledge ecosystem can be replicated with other partners.
- *New modalities of support by the Platform to the city*: A pilot engagement with the city of Malaka (Malaysia), where the Platform financed deeper engagement of partners with the city authorities led to excellent results. However, the financing required for this type of deep engagement of platforms with individual members needs a cost-benefit analysis.
- *Development of robust methodologies*: New methods to monitor and measure the results of urban environment interventions supported by the GEF-financed programs are a key goal. Many of the frontier areas in urban environment—from biodiversity to remote-sensing and disruptive technologies—can benefit from a platform that fosters experimentation and robust lesson learning.

Notes

1 Xueman Wang, program coordinator for the Global Platform for Sustainable Cities, provided extensive inputs for this chapter.
2 Tackling the Drivers of Global Environmental Degradation Through the Integrated Approach Pilot Programs—Progress Report. Global Environmental Facility (2017)
3 The United Nations Industrial Development Organization that works on solid waste management; the United Nations Environmental Programme; and the United Nations Human Settlements Program.

Chapter 6

A Platform for Knowledge Sharing and Co-Creation of Solutions

The Tokyo Development Learning Center (TDLC)

Philip Karp, Daniel A. Levine and Dean Cira

The Context

The Challenge of Organizing Knowledge Exchange on a Sustainable Basis

During GSURR's journey in using knowledge and learning concepts to inspire organizational change and drive innovation, the enormous benefits of peer-to-peer knowledge exchange had become amply clear. A methodology and set of materials had been introduced to all GSURR staff that allowed them to support clients from different countries in learning with and from each other while identifying and creating new solutions to common challenges. (see Chapter 9).

However, such knowledge exchanges face a number of difficulties. First, knowledge sharing is typically not part of the core or primary mandate or mission of the institutions or organizations that most often have direct experience with development solutions. For example, a ministry of the environment may have excellent solutions to share, but its primary mandate is to protect its country's environment and not to document or share successful solutions with other countries or organizations. Even if it has documented its solutions, the demand from other countries to learn from its successful experiences can, in many cases, far outstrip its limited capacity to share its lessons.

Second, knowledge exchanges are often conceived to be unidirectional. The learning group goes through a learning and inquiry process. The knowledge-sharing "provider" tells its story, shares the challenges and solutions, and may react to questions from the visiting party to compare and contrast the situations. This type of exchange can be helpful but is also limited in that it does not build on the existing wealth of experience and knowledge already available and does not offer an opportunity to use—and thus contextualize—the newly acquired knowledge right away.

Third, individual knowledge-exchange events can be expensive. One-to-one knowledge exchanges where one agency visits another are intensive exercises that require lots of preparation to be truly effective. Moreover, the organizers of this type of knowledge exchange often face budget challenges that limit the number of organizations that can benefit.

From Retail to Wholesale in Knowledge Exchange

As the GSURR knowledge ecosystem developed, the leadership noticed the growing number and total cost of individual country-to-country knowledge exchanges. Countries like China or Brazil received upwards of 50 delegations a year, burdening the local agencies as well

DOI: 10.4324/9781003199083-15

as the World Bank's own local teams' time and resources. While the impact and benefits from each exchange were enhanced as design of the exchanges improved through adoption of the *Art of Knowledge Exchange* methodology described in Chapter 9, the need to develop a more cost-effective approach became increasingly evident. What was needed was a knowledge-exchange platform incorporating four key features:

- *Global reputation*: Knowledge exchanges would have to be hosted by an organization or institution with demonstrated solutions to critical development challenges relevant to many clients worldwide. The organization would have to recognize the value of sharing its knowledge and development solutions with others. This value could be increased reputation among peers, new business opportunities for the organization and the consulting ecosystem around it, and direct benefits to educational institutions that could partner with the knowledge-providing organization to expand their services and business opportunities, among many others.
- *Pre-event learning opportunities*: The organization hosting the exchanges would have to be able to offer a knowledge-sharing platform that documented successful solutions in order to allow participants in knowledge-sharing events to learn as much as possible in advance through print and online materials.
- *Methodology*: The knowledge exchanges organized would have to follow good practice design consistent with the *Art of Knowledge Exchange* methodology, fostering multidirectional sharing wherein all participants would share their challenges and experiences as part of the overall exchange.
- *New solutions orientation*: The overall approach would have to involve a focus on facilitating active co-creation of solutions, going beyond simply sharing experiences.

Finding a Solution Without Reinventing the Wheel

There had been a number of previous efforts at the World Bank to go beyond one-to-one knowledge exchange. These include, among others, engaging universities to develop customized training courses for clients, group exposure visits to World Bank's headquarters for training, and e-learning courses that showcase client solutions. GSURR leadership determined that, while useful, these approaches did not meet the features noted previously. Another approach was needed. The GSURR knowledge and learning team suggested leveraging an existing and already successful knowledge-sharing partnership with the Government of Japan, recognizing that the Tokyo Development Learning Center (TDLC), established through this partnership, included many of the features needed for the new approach it wished to introduce.

Founded in 2004, TDLC had been set up to serve as a knowledge platform that would share Japan's development experiences with World Bank clients and other interested parties in the developing world. Housed in a state-of-the-art conference center in Tokyo and supported by a dedicated team of knowledge management and learning specialists, TDLC had originally been established as the Japanese node of the World Bank supported Global Development Learning Network (GDLN), a partnership that pioneered videoconference-based learning more than a decade before it became a commonplace tool on every computer. Together with other GDLN affiliates, TDLC disseminated experiences and solutions drawn from various knowledge institutions in Japan to interested parties across East and South Asia and Africa.

GSURR's search for a platform that would allow for a new approach to knowledge exchange came at an opportune time. The Government of Japan had been looking for opportunities to raise the TDLC partnership to new levels of impact by sharpening the sectoral focus of its programs and by focusing more on World Bank projects and clients. The two parties agreed to revamp the TDLC program as it moved to its third 5-year phase. They agreed on the following elements:

- *An urban and resilience focus*: TDLC would work with Japanese cities, agencies, and partners to document and share exciting solutions to urban and resilience challenges applicable to city clients designing or implementing new programs to be financed by the World Bank.
- *Appreciation of global knowledge exchange*: TDLC would collaborate primarily with Japanese cities that saw a strategic value in sharing their knowledge with other cities worldwide. These cities would be selected through a rigorous process to ensure their commitment to the program's principles.
- *Focus on face-to-face, in-person exchanges*: The knowledge-sharing platform of the TDLC would change from distance learning to face-to-face engagements in Japan, with exchanges designed in such a way as to take maximum advantage of the opportunity for experiential learning provided by face-to-face engagement.
- *Publications and materials complementing event-based learning*: The TDLC knowledge exchange program would be complemented by preparation of knowledge publications, extracting the critical lessons from the participating Japanese cities.
- *Methodology for multidimensional knowledge sharing and co-creation*: A new methodology was developed to foster multidirectional knowledge sharing. All participants would learn from each other and co-create solutions for their individual cities.

At the Core of the New Methodology: The Technical Deep Dive

With the new TDLC collaboration came the opportunity to also develop a new knowledge-exchange modality, building on GSURR's and the broader World Bank's experience in knowledge management and learning methodology while also creating space for experimenting with others. The new modality, "baptized" technical deep dives, was based on multicountry, peer-to-peer learning and knowledge co-creation involving teams of World Bank clients from various countries and organizations along with World Bank staff. The technical deep dives involved a weeklong program that combined study tours, workshops, peer exchange, action planning, and co-creation of solutions to challenges faced by the participating World Bank's client teams around a common theme. Typically, client teams from 10–12 countries were invited, based on a careful selection process that looked to bring together professionals from at least 2 countries per geographical region to ensure both global experiences and some element of proximity-based connections. Each participating team consisted of three to four professionals working in a relevant client country organization along with a World Bank specialist, usually the staff member responsible for the project or advisory engagement with which the participating clients was involved.

The participation of country teams composed of both World Bank clients and staff proved to be very powerful. Not only did it ensure that clients and staff were exposed to the same set of learning material, cases, and examples of successful solutions, but it provided a unique opportunity for clients and staff to engage with each other for an extended period in a non-transactional setting. It was a week of brainstorming, discussions, and co-creation, without the pressures of specific deliveries or project preparation deadlines.

Adding to the positive interpersonal dynamic was the inclusion of action planning as an integral part of the technical deep dive methodology. Each team of clients was asked to bring a specific problem linked to the theme of the week. Together, the professionals from a given client country or city and the responsible World Bank specialist would prepare an action plan addressing how they would act on the lessons learned and inspiration gained during the week of learning and knowledge exchange. As these action plans were jointly "owned" by multiple people, the likelihood of acting on them was considered high as compared to those developed by a single individual or organization.

Each technical deep dive also included one or more international resource experts, often from other countries in Asia such as South Korea or Singapore or from the United States and Europe. The purpose of inviting these experts was to ensure that participating clients were exposed to a range of successful solutions, not just those from Japan. To their credit, Japanese counterparts welcomed and appreciated the inclusion of these additional international experts. Furthermore, attention was paid to creating extensive opportunities for peer-to-peer exchange among participants, drawing on the *Art of Knowledge Exchange* methodology described in Chapter 9. In line with the methodology, technical deep dives also included one or more site or field visits, allowing participants to see firsthand how Japan had addressed some of the challenges associated with the topic. The program on urban flood risk management, for example, included visits to a flood control center and to an evacuation center.

The technical deep dives were designed to each focus on a specific topic, ranging from solid waste management to urban flood risk management, transit-oriented development, urban renovation, inclusive cities, and metropolitan management, to name a few. Ahead of each of the programs, the TDLC team in Japan would produce policy notes or case studies illustrating good practices from Japan. The documents were prepared by Japanese resource experts, usually practitioners or researchers from relevant ministries or cities.

Technical deep dives quickly became recognized across the World Bank as an effective instrument for synthesizing, packaging, and offering relevant global and Japanese knowledge to World Bank teams and their clients involved in World Bank–funded projects. Also the various Japanese counterparts learned from and saw the benefits of sharing their experiences and building bridges with professionals hailing from countries from around the world.

An external evaluation conducted in 2018 by a former World Bank regional vice president and former vice president of the Japan International Cooperation Agency (JICA) recognized technical deep dives as an important innovation of the TDLC program and the cornerstone of its knowledge ecosystem. The report noted that

"without exception, World Bank staff found the TDDs of extremely high value. Most important is the learning approach directed at bottom-up problem-solving. Using a team approach bringing together client representatives and World Bank staff from around 12 countries covering all six World Bank regions, the mix of Japanese experience with peer learning across delegations and the combination of different modalities for knowledge sharing such as lectures, workshops, and site visits has resulted in long term development impacts."[1]

Over the period from 2016 to 2020, TDLC organized 25 technical deep dives, influencing more than 300 projects in 80+ countries globally. The programs provided opportunities for knowledge and operational exchanges to more than 280 national-level and 300 city-level participants from around the world. In 2020 alone, TDLC's technical deep dives informed

19 World Bank projects through operational support activities, leveraging investments amounting to nearly US$2.5 billion in lending and advisory engagements.

Finding the Right Partners

Critical to the success of each of the TDLC programs was finding the right partners in Japan. Not every city can share experiential knowledge or is ready to invest the time and resources to do it well. Working in collaboration with the relevant Japanese government agencies, TDLC organized an open call to invite cities around the country to join the program. The factors considered in the selection included:

- *Comparative advantage in a thematic area*: The city had to show the "good practices" it had developed in one or more of the TDLC thematic areas. These practices were evaluated by the World Bank's top technical experts in the area to ensure they were applicable and adaptable to a wide range of World Bank client cities.
- *Capacity to deliver practitioner knowledge*: The city's capacity to engage in productive knowledge exchanges with other cities coming from different regions was a determining factor. Cities with international bureaus and some English-speaking staff were better prepared. Regardless, the TDLC provided training and technical support to the cities to become first-class knowledge providers to other countries and cities. To do so, TDLC translated the *Art of Knowledge Exchange* materials into Japanese and offered workshops for city officials. Interestingly, the Japan International Cooperation Agency (JICA) also requested such training for its staff involved in knowledge-sharing programs.
- *Commitment at the leadership level*: The commitment of the political leadership of a potential partner city was critical. For most partner cities, either the mayor or a deputy mayor has been actively involved in the program.
- *Mutual commitment*: Most of the costs involved in delivering a technical deep dive are financed by the TDLC. However, participating Japanese cities are expected to contribute, primarily on an in-kind basis, to cover local costs such as making venues available, offering meals and refreshments during learning activities, and providing local transportation for site visits. This approach ensured that each partner in Japan had a stake in seeing successful outcomes of the collaboration.

Between 2016 and 2020, six cities—Fukuoka, Kobe, Kitakyushu, Kyoto, Toyama, and Yokohama—were selected as TDLC's city partners. These cities entered into formal agreements with the World Bank, a first for such arrangements with subnational entities in Japan. And although not formally partner cities, the Tokyo Metropolitan Government and city of Osaka have also been actively engaged in a number of technical deep dives and other TDLC programs.

Why Did Cities Invest in International Programs to Share Knowledge?

Working with and through a knowledge-sharing platform like the TDLC and engaging in intensive technical deep dive programs requires a nontrivial financial and human resource commitment. Why did the cities do it? Their reasons included:

- *Attraction of global cooperation*: The opportunity to enter the field of international cooperation through a platform led by the World Bank was attractive. For several of the participating Japanese cities, this was their first global cooperation engagement, and the TDLC gave them a significant opportunity to gain experience in this field. Participation in the TDLC platform gave Japanese cities new linkages with World Bank urban networks such as the Global Platform for Sustainable Cities (see Chapter 5.8) or the Global Resilient Cities Network (see Chapter 5.6). The Japanese cities are also connected to the GSURR communities of practice that organized the technical deep dives, giving them another platform for global connections and exchange.

- *Introducing the Japanese experience internationally*: Participating cities appreciated the opportunity to codify their experiences in global knowledge assets. While many cities in Japan boast a wealth of knowledge and documentation around their urban development experiences, much of it is published by local research centers. These resources are often only available in Japanese and are not well-known globally. By working through TDLC, the development knowledge of Japanese partner cities has been captured, codified, translated, and repackaged into valuable knowledge assets and have become global public goods.

- *Reputation-building as an attractive center of innovation*: The knowledge assets produced based on the participating Japanese city experiences were disseminated globally, far exceeding the distribution channels currently available to most cities in Japan. This dissemination positioned participating cities as attractive destinations and centers of innovation. Indeed, the experiences and solutions documented influenced the design of global development frameworks and toolkits used by the World Bank across the world, showcasing Japanese cities as models to follow.

- *New business opportunities for local entrepreneurs*: The local consulting companies of the cities got exposure to cities from around the world, opening the space for new business opportunities. The roster of experts and practitioners available for engagements with urban centers worldwide has grown considerably.

Innovation Within and Through the Technical Deep Dives

Throughout the years of the TDLC partnership, GSURR looked for opportunities to innovate further. The technical deep dive methodology was continuously refined to test new ways of sharing knowledge. For example, many of the programs incorporated innovative elements such as gamification and customized follow-up support. Other innovations of the methodology included the expansion of one program to take place in two countries (half in Japan, half in Korea) to share two slightly different approaches to metropolitan management. The exchange of experiences between technical deep dive participants has also led to an interest among them to learn more from each other. TDLC facilitated several of these exchanges. The Integrated Urban Water Management Technical Deep Dive led to a visit by three delegations (Indonesia, Ghana, and Ethiopia) to Brazil to review its experience. Innovations in methodology continued as the program faced travel restrictions during the COVID-19 pandemic. TDLC was able to leverage its experience in working *virtually*, gained in more than ten years of offering training programs by videoconference, to deploy a diverse set of remote delivery tools. Taken together, TDLC was able to reproduce—to the extent possible—the original feeling and interactions that would have otherwise characterized a face-to-face technical deep dive.

In addition, new frontier topics were introduced that went beyond the subject areas and set of solutions typically offered by the World Bank. Some examples include technical deep dives on *aging cities* covering the combination of infrastructure and services required to meet the needs of rapidly aging urban populations; on *creative cities* looking at how cities can

Box 6.1 —The TDLC Technical Deep Dive on Aging Cities

The TDLC Technical Deep Dive on Aging Cities is illustrative of how the TDLC program has been used to catalyze the development of new business areas for the World Bank. The topic itself already underscores the importance of exploring the linkages across different sectors: The number of elderly people globally is projected to grow from 900 million in 2015 to 1.4 billion in 2030 and 2.1 billion in 2050.[2] In 2015, 1 in 8 people worldwide was 60 or older; in 2030, this number will be 1 in 6 people, and by 2050, 1 in 5 people. The number of the world's "oldest old," that is, people aged 80 years and over, is growing even faster than the number of older persons overall; they are projected to more than triple between 2015 and 2050, from 125 million to 434 million. In 2015, women accounted for 54 percent of the world's older population and 61 percent of the "oldest old"—a gender disparity that is not always recognized. Aging—and by the same token, aging in cities—is an outcome of increasing longevity and declining birth rates, which are currently more prevalent in high-income countries. Between 2000 and 2015, 6 percent of the world's largest cities saw their populations decline; most were in developed economies. In the next decade, it is expected that 17 percent of large cities across developed regions will see their populations dwindle. Japan is home to the world's most aged population, with seniors aged 65 years or over constituting a third of the population in 2015—attributed to its strict immigration policy, good healthcare, and low fertility rate. Japanese cities had excellent practices on the topic of aging cities. The Aging Cities TDD was developed around four main building blocks:

Urban infrastructure and city planning: Adopting universal design to ensure that infrastructure and services, in particular housing, are accessible to all persons—with special attention to those with limited mobility or visual, hearing, or other impairments—is key to their inclusion in society. Universal accessibility is beneficial to all population segments, not just the elderly and disabled.

Social dimensions: Issues related to the diversity in older age (i.e., differences between 60-year-olds and 80-year-olds)—in addition to intersectionality with other forms of identity or social categorization such as gender, income, or ethnicity—are all important considerations for governments to design innovative and context-specific social policy targeted to older persons. Cities need to consider legislative protections that prevent older adults from unnecessary institutionalization. This requires creating a range of viable eldercare and healthcare options for seniors based on their needs and preferences.

Jobs and economic development: As the population gets older, it will affect the market for service delivery (to cater to an aging population) and the labor market due to the change in dependency ratios and scale of the active labor force. Economic development strategies would accordingly need to be adjusted to ensure that cities with workers—who are fewer and have a different age profile—continue to retain a vibrant economy. Rather than retiring them away, there is now a growing recognition of the need to engage older people and activate their talents through lifelong learning possibilities, the flexibility of work environments for an older workforce, and opportunities for voluntary community work. Aging also leads to shifts in spending patterns: changes in how money is spent are an opportunity for companies to consider jumping into the "longevity economy." The policy could help align the business environment and incentives to make elderly consumers a potentially huge market segment that is as viable, profitable, and attractive as the millennials.

Fiscal implications: Municipal governments will also need to ensure a sustainable fiscal policy in caring for their older citizens. Governments, especially in poorer cities with a low or declining tax base, will need to consider many dimensions of aging that will impact fiscal policy: among them, higher costs of service delivery in some cases (e.g., mobility/public transport, retrofit of service delivery to elders' needs) but also lower expenditures (e.g., less municipal spending on schools due to fewer school-age children), and unclear implications on revenue collection from property taxes. It is critical to make smart choices and prioritize investments for efficient and equitable public expenditure serving the most needy populations and most critical sectors that may be unattractive to the private sector.

Following the successful implementation of the Technical Deep Dive on Aging Cities, the World Bank has embarked on a cross-sector, global analytical program to expand its understanding of the impact of aging on the urban space and how to prepare for the "longevity economy," which will most certainly be centered in urban areas. The work seeks to shift the paradigm of thinking about the elderly as "dependent" and as a "burden" to one that embraces livable cities for aging populations with a renewed understanding of the elderly as active and productive members of the longevity economy.

foster innovation and development of creative industries; and on *healthy cities* drawing lessons from the ongoing management of the COVID-19 pandemic. These frontier topics were chosen based on client interest, practicality, and potential for development impact, and they were areas in which Japanese cities and government agencies had good experiences to share.

Many of these new topics cut across institutional silos. One of the important, though perhaps less apparent, strengths of the TDLC program was how its activities stimulated lateral thinking and built an understanding of the cross-cutting nature of the various topics covered. The discussions in the Healthy Cities Technical Deep Dive, for example, focused on the city's response to the COVID-19 pandemic. However, very quickly, the discussions showed that the health of cities is not only about health care, but it is also related to the quality of housing, access to essential services such as education, and the protection of essential workers, all well beyond those involved directly in the provision of health services.

The technical deep dives served not only to build bridges across technical silos, but they also exposed teams from other World Bank units to the innovative knowledge and learning methodologies promoted by both GSURR and the TDLC, helping to mainstream them more widely across the World Bank. For example, the Transit-Oriented Development Technical

Deep Dive brought together technical specialists from the urban practice with those from the transport and mobility practice (see Chapter 5.5). And the Urban Floods Risk Management Technical Deep Dive was jointly organized by urban and water specialists. In addition to innovating through refining the methodology and through leveraging frontier topics, the technical deep dive approach entered new territory also by being replicated by other partners. Having recognized the attractiveness of hosting such events, based on their cost-effectiveness and benefits, cities like Jakarta (Indonesia), Cape Town (South Africa), Paris (France), and Medellín (Colombia) have hosted technical deep dive–like events on various topics (the case of Medellín is described in more detail in Chapter 10).

Expanding the Technical Deep Dive Concept from Knowledge Sharing to In-City Support

When GSURR and TDLC introduced technical deep dives as a new modality for knowledge exchange, there was a recognition that programs lasting a week—even with innovations in format and methodology—would not be sufficient to help participating clients to fully translate their action plans and insights into new programs and initiatives. Hence, the TDLC program progressively introduced an offer of follow-on support by Japanese experts to selected participating clients. Rather than offering generic support, though, interested clients had to identify specific issues for follow-up engagements in the action plans they presented at the end of a technical deep dive.

The support offered itself was flexible, including knowledge exchanges, capacity building, and advisory services on a just-in-time basis. Depending on the topic and the nature of the request, TDLC mobilized expertise from a range of organizations including private firms, government officials (both national and city), academia, and nonprofit organizations.

Between 2017 and 2020, client organizations (mainly city-level) involved in 39 World Bank projects benefited from 93 individual follow-on engagements with Japanese partners. Of these, about half were knowledge sharing, including case studies, speakers dispatch, study tours, and videoconference dialogues. The rest were technical assistance engagements to support the design of specific investment projects.

Recent cases from Romania and Panamá illustrate the technical depth and impact that this post–technical deep dive operational support provided (see Boxes 6.2 and 6.3).

Box 6.2   —An Example of TDLC Operational Support: Romanian Cities

Following the first Technical Deep Dive on Urban Regeneration, the delegation from Romania requested operational support for the cities of Constanta, Brasov, and Sector 5 of Bucharest, the nation's capital. The Romanian delegation was impressed with Japan's successes in the regeneration of urban areas, both at the neighborhood level and at the macro scale.

Romanian cities, as they continue to transition away from planned economies and embrace integration with the European Union, are struggling to develop new ways to leverage urban assets that make cities attractive places for citizens to live, work, and play, even as populations decline and age—a challenge Japan is familiar with. As a result, the Romanian clients requested Japanese operational support to learn from Japanese experience in:

- More efficient spatial planning, with a focus on land readjustment schemes.
- Urbanism guidelines, with a focus on the Yokohama Urban Design Guide and several Tokyo neighborhoods.
- Integrated approaches for marginalized communities, with a focus on the Osaka example.
- Managing demographic decline and shrinking cities, with a focus on the Toyama example.
- Long-term local strategic planning, with a focus on the Yokohama 6 strategic projects.

A team of four experts from Japan participated in organized workshops in Constanta, Brasov, and Bucharest in July 2018. These experts worked with professionals and leaders from the three cities with very tangible results. The representatives from Constanta, for example, learned from Yokohama how to strategically use underutilized and abandoned port infrastructure for new business activities. In Brasov, the experience from Toyama was taken on board for leveraging strategic urban interventions to serve as magnets for attracting and retaining people in medium-sized cities and compensating the declining and aging populations with the fiscal challenges this poses.

In Sector 5, home to Bucharest's largest marginalized communities, the local authorities learned from the experience of Osaka's Airin district what it takes to achieve inclusive development in areas with a high concentration of marginalized people. The lessons learned have been integrated into the regeneration strategy prepared for the Ferentari neighborhood, a large, poor, marginalized community within Sector 5.

Box 6.3:   An Example of TDLC Operational Support: Panamá

The World Bank supports the Panamá City Waterfront Redevelopment and Resilience Program, which aims to promote a more sustainable and inclusive urban layout, build greater resilience to climate and disaster risks, and strengthen institutional capacity to mobilize different sources of infrastructure financing in Panamá City. As part of this technical assistance, officials of the municipality had the opportunity to participate in two technical deep dives focused respectively on resilient urban planning for safer cities and on solid waste management. During these programs, the participating officials from Panamá requested support on the interplay of solid waste management and urban floods and on urban design guidelines and participatory planning processes for waterfront development.

TDLC coordinated the engagement of officers from the environmental bureau of Kitakyushu City, an expert from the urban design office of Yokohama City, and three experts from the Universities of Waseda and Kanto Gakuin. They traveled to Panamá

City in 2018 and 2019. The Japanese experts supported Panamá City in developing a zero-waste pilot program designed to reduce flood risks in urban water and in community engagement and participatory methodologies for urban planning and design, in the context of the development of the first master plan of the city.

The technical deep dive approach was applied a bit in reverse in Panamá City. The Japanese experts focused on the Yokohama and Kitakyushu experiences on the first trip. They conducted a series of discussions with local government agencies and visits to the Juan Diaz and Tocumen Rivers and the Panamá Waste Landfill. A "Dialogue on the Yokohama and Kitakyushu Approaches in Urban Planning, Waste Management and Flood Risk: Challenges and Options for the City of Panamá " allowed the experiences to be shared with a much broader group, including the national government, civil society organizations, and research institutions involved in urban development and resilience initiatives in Panamá City.

The second trip focused on Yokohama's Cityscape Sketchbook methodology developed by the city's urban design bureau. A total of 12 experts (5 specialists from the World Bank, 4 experts from Japan universities, and 3 local experts from the Urban Risk Center of Panamá) engaged with community leaders, representatives of NGOs, professors, and university students. The interdisciplinary nature of the support, combining Japanese government officials with university specialists, created opportunities for local officials and World Bank teams to learn from each other and gain new insights on addressing technical challenges. The case of Panamá City suggests that the approach was effective in highlighting the urgent need for multidisciplinary approaches to address the problems of urban floods and solid waste in a more holistic manner. The involvement of the university and officers from the municipality of Panamá throughout the preparatory process and during the second trip helped create the local capacity needed to apply the methodology to other neighborhoods in the city.

This methodology was subsequently utilized to support redevelopment of the riverfront area of the city of Barranquilla, Colombia, and was codified in a guidebook for use by other developing country cities.

Lessons Learned

Much of the TDLC experience was driven by the opportunity of the moment in time: the GSURR leadership saw the cooperation with the TDLC as an innovative opportunity to solve the challenges experienced when delivering peer-to-peer knowledge exchange at scale and to put funding, creative energies, and leadership attention to the endeavor. Some of the leadership lessons learned during the five years described in this chapter include:

- *A commitment to continuous innovation and creative combination of tools*: The continuous search for cost-effectiveness and increased impact sometimes require very different solutions. Moving from retail to wholesale led to many more clients accessing this knowledge and as did breaking the North-to-South single provider model into a multidirectional and multi-institutional approach. For example, the TDLC leadership knew that leveraging multiple tools for use as a menu of options (e.g., technical deep dives, operational support, knowledge assets) were far more effective than a single instrument applied to all client segments.

- *A shared vision at the leadership level of key partners*: The leadership of the funding agency (ministry of finance of Japan in this case), the implementing agency (World Bank), and the knowledge provider agencies (cities and ministries) had to come to a shared vision early on in order to create the appropriate space for designing innovative programs through TDLC. The early agreement on the vision allowed for joint solutions to the many challenges encountered along the way.
- *An in-depth understanding of the multidirectional nature of knowledge sharing*: The leadership of knowledge provider organizations (Japanese cities) needed to understand the benefits of these activities well, especially when they are not part of their core mandate. The ancillary benefits to other stakeholders (e.g., research institutes, city promotion agencies, local consultants) were critical factors for the cities to enter this space. The World Bank found new technical staff with specialized skills in Japan that would not have come across the traditional bench of candidates.
- *Investment in methodologies and skills associated with knowledge sharing*: Knowledge sharing requires highly specialized skills. Cities may have excellent lessons of experience, but the way they are shared is as important as the lessons themselves. Knowledge-sharing programs need to invest adequate resources to build that capacity even in sophisticated organizations. For example, the most interesting lessons are not only found in the final solution but also in the development journey. The intermediate challenges and their solutions, the political and community difficulties, and the participatory engagement to find a way forward are not always easy to document in written form. Developing the skills to tell the stories of challenges and intermediate failures is vital for an engaging knowledge-sharing activity. Even sophisticated organization's like Singapore's Center for Liveable Cities and Paris' International Cooperation unit saw benefits in the technical deep dive methodology.
- *A synergistic connection between the technical deep dive events and the ongoing networking in the World Bank's communities of practice*: The communities of practice in the GSURR knowledge ecosystem not only used the TDLC tools to serve their clients, but the technical deep dives served as an opportunity to connect the community members in ways that single events and asynchronous conversations were not able to do (see Chapters 5.1, 5.2, 5.3, 5.5 and 5.6) The connection between TDLC with communities of practice and business lines was continuously reinforced by GSURR leadership who recognized that standalone knowledge activities that are not connected to an organizations' core business are less effective.
- *Careful selection of participants*: The GSURR leadership viewed the TDLC as a "platinum card" service for clients. Rather than leaving the selection of clients to participate in technical deep dives to the TDLC team or even to individual project leads, selection decisions were made by the regional managers in charge of client relations. The clients selected were generally linked to existing or potential investment programs, thereby offering opportunities, respectively, for policy dialogue or business development.
- *Careful selection of topics*: The technical deep dives were focused on the topics seen as most important and/or innovative by the practice's leadership in view of exposing both clients and World Bank team members to the latest thinking and experiences. The engagement with sophisticated cities in Japan allowed the World Bank technical specialists to open entirely new business lines.

- *Leadership commitment*: Direct leadership support to the TDLC was critical to the success. One or more members of the GSURR leadership team attended most technical deep dives. This participation of senior leaders sent signals to team members of the importance of the program while allowing them to learn firsthand about the model and help with replicating the approach in other programs.

Notes

1 Mid-Term Review for World Bank Tokyo Development Learning Center Phase 3, Arthur D. Little, May 2019, page 5.
2 Das, Maitreyi Bordia, Arai Yuko, Terri B. Chapman, and Vibhu Jain. 2022. *Silver Hues: Building Age-Ready Cities*. Washington, DC: World Bank. http://hdl.handle.net/10986/37259 https://openknowledge.worldbank.org/handle/10986/37259

Chapter 7

An Uneasy Marriage

Leveraging Communications and Knowledge Management Skills and Approaches

Ede Ijjasz-Vasquez

Knowledge Is a Critical Input to Several Functions in an Organization

This book explores the role of knowledge and knowledge management tools as an invaluable input for operational teams to improve their services and products to clients, to innovate, and to enhance productivity. For this to work, knowledge management teams are needed for handling the curation and sharing of knowledge. There are, of course, other functions in an organization that depend on that knowledge. For example, sales teams can do a better job when they have stories of success and specific information on the benefits to clients who have used the organization's services and products. The communications and external affairs teams need such examples of success and impact to do their jobs. Even internal strategy teams need to understand the knowledge, new solutions, and the next-generation challenges that operational teams are encountering in their client engagements.

Communications and External Affairs—Working With Operational Teams

As the GSURR leadership team began its journey to establish a vibrant technical practice, innovating and expanding the range of the practice's services, it became necessary to define a role for communications and external affairs staff.

In the World Bank's structure, the communications and external affairs function is provided by a centrally managed team that assigns staff to work with each department. The external and corporate relations team is responsible for building strategic relationships with foundations, parliamentarians, and civil society; undertaking advocacy and corporate communications; and managing external affairs worldwide. The communications staff working with operational teams provide support in the production and dissemination of research and policy reports and in the preparation of general dissemination products (e.g., blogs, op-eds).

The GSURR leadership was interested in leveraging the communications team's expertise to support the department's vision. Specifically, the communications team was seen as a critical resource in two areas:

- The crafting of technically strong stories and narratives of the suite of technical services GSURR teams provide (including results and innovations) for use with potential new clients.

DOI: 10.4324/9781003199083-16

- The development of content-rich communications assets and knowledge dissemination events to strengthen the global recognition of the GSURR team's work among development practitioners.

To make progress in these two areas, the first communications and outreach strategy was based on the following three principles:

- *"We are all communicators"*: The task of developing and communicating technically strong stories and narratives of GSURR suite of services was not the responsibility of the communications team alone. It was defined as everybody's responsibility. The communications team members have unique skills, but they are not tasked to do the work alone. This was an important departure from the traditional approach to developing communications materials.
- *Communications and outreach are an integral part of the bundle of services to clients*: The ultimate goal of the World Bank services is to support changes in government policies, investment decisions, and individual behaviors for the benefit of society and the poor. Helping countries achieve this goal requires more than financing and knowledge. Communicating effectively about new solutions, future trends, global lessons of relevance to a country, and possible policy and program reforms to resolve development challenges is equally important.
- *Consistency in communications is critical*: A strategic, consistent narrative on the World Bank's work, results, and strategy is fundamental to achieving the institutional goals. This consistency requires upskilling of technical teams in communications to allow them to make better presentations; engage with media; and deliver clear, concise, and effective messages. The upskilling began with the leadership team and continued with the leaders of all the communities of practice and other technical leaders in the practice.

Communications and Knowledge Management Teams: Breaking Silos for Better Results

Very soon in the development of work plans and the initial activities, it became clear that communications and knowledge management are two sides of the same coin: their work is based on and leverages similar raw information and knowledge development challenges, solutions, results, failures, and lessons. They bring complementary and, at times, related technical skills and approaches. At the same time, their purpose and objectives, while being somewhat related in terms of information sharing and dissemination, also differ in some respects that are considered essential by team members and can cause friction. Importantly, the two teams have different reporting lines and see their work as perhaps related but completely independent—and, at times, going in opposite directions. Even when—for example, in smaller organizations—the communications and knowledge management functions may have been combined by tasking one professional with both, that person's activities may tend to focus on one rather than on both sets of activities, considering the person's specific skill set or inclination.

The areas of expertise of communications and knowledge management teams are related but distinct and hold the potential for important complementarities.

Box 7.1   —Areas of Expertise of Communications and Knowledge Management

Communications—Areas of Expertise

- Messaging and narratives
- Branding
- Ability to reach large audiences
- Multiple communications and outreach channels, including social media
- Consistency and simplicity of messages
- Document repurposing into communications assets
- Storytelling for engaging communications with large audience

Knowledge Management—Areas of Expertise

- Community building
- Engagement and collaborative learning
- Platform establishment
- Lesson extraction
- Learning, knowledge sharing, and co-creation methodologies
- Document repurposing into knowledge assets
- IT systems for knowledge management
- Storytelling as a knowledge management tool

In the meantime, the differences in culture and approaches between the communications and the knowledge management communities are also substantive.

Box 7.2   —Differences Between Communications and Knowledge Management

Communications

- *Audiences*: in the thousands to hundreds of thousands
- *Top down*: messages are defined at the top of the hierarchy and replicated downwards
- *Corporate image*: protective of corporate image and mostly positive—informally referred to as a "cathedral" of well-crafted messages

Knowledge Management

- *Audiences*: in the hundreds to thousands
- *Bottom up*: knowledge is generated at the team level and aggregated/distilled upwards
- *Lessons from innovation*: adaptation, and experimentation are integral to knowledge—informally referred to as a "bazaar" of knowledge

---

What could bring the teams together, though, was that the communications and knowledge management teams face three common challenges when working with technical teams:

- A general tendency to focus on the "product"—as a knowledge or communication "asset"—at the risk of forgetting at times the "user" or "reader."
- A diverging tendency to get too technical in the knowledge product or too superficial in the communications product.
- A general lack of understanding by technical teams about the skills and expertise that the knowledge management and communications team bring to them when partnering to jointly develop an expanded suite of services for clients.

The Transformation Journey: Common Knowledge Management and Communications Approaches for Better Results

How did the GSURR leadership succeed in breaking down the silos between the knowledge management and communications teams? First, the leaders of both teams were invited to be part of the GSURR extended leadership team, bringing them closer to the core of the business and making them part of one team. Then, three areas of work were launched that were relevant to both teams and required them to collaborate: 1) skills building and incentives, 2) joint product development, and 3) experimentation with new tools.

In the area of skills building, the two teams worked together to develop a structured program covering several areas where the technical teams needed upskilling. The program included training on media engagement, social media platforms (including corporate guidance on engagement), public speaking, design of knowledge-sharing events (including panels and workshops), and delivering presentations, among others.

Many of the training programs were designed as coaching sessions for specific events. For example, if members of a community of practice were going to present in an all-staff townhall, the communications and knowledge management teams would work together and jointly provide feedback and coaching. For the annual global technical gathering of all GSURR staff, the knowledge management team would coach staff in the design of their workshop sessions.

In parallel to skills building, the GSURR leadership team put forward a program of incentives and recognition that would bring communications and knowledge management teams together. First, as specific milestones of outreach and dissemination were met, the leadership team would celebrate the achievements—from the growing number of social media hits around a flagship policy report to the references picked up by global media outlets. Second, some of the all-staff townhalls were designed to give visibility to leaders and members of the various communities of practice. The president and the CEO of the World Bank participated in some of these sessions. The chance to present their work and innovations to top leadership was a strong motivator and a signal of how important knowledge was to the organization.

In the end, the communications and knowledge management team developed several joint products and engagement platforms, bringing to bear their complementary skills. These joint efforts led to higher quality and more targeted communications and knowledge-sharing assets. These assets were designed as "EAST" products—easy, attractive, social, and timely (see also Chapter 3). Some of the joint products and platforms included the revamped GSURR newsletter (see Box 7.3), a new approach to engagement in conferences (see Box 7.4), and a repurposing strategy for policy and research reports.

The World Bank produces many high-quality policy and research reports. Unfortunately, many of them do not have the broad dissemination and outreach they deserve. Online downloads of some of these reports linger in the hundreds. The communications and knowledge management teams developed a new approach to several repurposed assets from flagship reports. These assets ranged from immersive media packages (e.g., infographics, beneficiary stories, photograph exhibits) to online courses (see Chapter 11). By developing a range of assets, the messages of the flagship report could reach different audiences—from investment and donor partners to students worldwide. The audience reach was monitored by numbers and types. This data allowed refinement of the asset repurposing approach, which was recognized as a good practice by other World Bank teams.

Box 7.3   The GSURR Newsletter

Many organizations and teams in the World Bank launch newsletters—internally as well as externally—to communicate and share knowledge. The GSURR newsletter followed a somewhat different path:

- The newsletter was a "repurposed" product in the initial phase—no new material would be produced specifically for the newsletter to keep it agile and with low production costs.
- Communities of practice that wanted to develop their own newsletters were encouraged to use a similar structure and "feel" to facilitate aggregation and reuse.
- The newsletter was designed to encourage recipients to open the knowledge assets being promoted; this action was an important measure of success.
- The GSURR leadership defined a gradual growth strategy from the get-go: first, an internal electronic newsletter designed to foster knowledge sharing across team members located in more than 70 offices worldwide; second, an electronic newsletter designed to break silos with other technical practices and reach a larger World Bank audience; and, third, an electronic and printed periodic publication for clients and partners with an external audience in mind but keeping the knowledge-sharing objective. The first two steps of the growth strategy were achieved with good success. The format and structure of the newsletter was copied by many other teams across the World Bank.
- The newsletter design evolved to emphasize the key objectives of the GSURR global knowledge ecosystem (see Chapter 4), including silo-breaking across technical disciplines, knowledge for action, linkage of communities of practice to business lines, co-creation with clients, and innovation through knowledge.

Box 7.4   Conferences—A New Engagement Approach

The number of national, regional, and global conferences and events in development can be overwhelming. At the same time, they are very important venues to build connections, share knowledge, and learn about new developments in the technical field of the conference. The GSURR leadership worked with the communications and knowledge management teams to develop a new engagement approach to maximize the investment of time and resources in conference participation. This new approach included:

- Early identification of knowledge assets to be promoted, including specific dissemination campaigns prior and during the conference.
- Structured touch points during the conference for the GSURR team to come together and share information on each team members' activities and new connections.

- Development of a communications "message matrix" to help all team members deliver consistent messages from the knowledge assets during workshops, media engagements, and social media postings.
- Early engagement with clients to support their participation and sharing of their experiences and co-produced knowledge products and investments to further leverage the dissemination channels.
- Leveraging the work of communities of practice and showcasing their lessons and innovations reinforced the connections between these communities and business development and the coherence of the global knowledge ecosystem.
- Planning and recording of videoblogs with clients and partners to continue building the knowledge-sharing and communication assets taking advantage of their presence at the conference.
- Consistent debriefing and evaluation for lesson learning and improvement actions for the next conferences.
- Use of conferences as a vehicle to raise the profile and build professional capacity of "rising stars" within the organization. A couple of young staff were invited to join the GSURR delegation (comprising senior leadership and technical staff) at major conferences to gain experience and exposure.

The GSURR leadership encouraged the communications and knowledge management teams to *experiment and innovate* in terms of formats, approaches, and platforms. Some of these innovative approaches led to interesting new products such as videoblogs (vlogs), social media chats, and virtual reality/augmented reality (VR/AR) platforms.

The videoblogs platform was launched well ahead of its common use across development agencies. The vlogs were identified as a channel to share new knowledge in a short visual format that could easily reach larger audiences. They were designed to encourage viewers to access other knowledge assets with more information and lessons. The vlogs were easier to produce and complete than written blogs with their multiple rounds of review and editing. They were also liked by clients who volunteered to participate as a way for them to share their innovations and lessons through a World Bank platform. Production of the vlogs also helped to cement the link between the communications and knowledge management teams, as one of the members of the latter team had unique video production skills. The link was further strengthened as Tokyo Development Learning Center events became platforms for recording vlogs involving both GSURR technical staff and partners and clients.

The AR/VR products brought new technologies to communications, knowledge sharing, and stakeholder engagement. These products were piloted at several of the technical deep dives of the Tokyo Development Learning Center (see Chapter 6). They were effective tools that generated excitement among communities of practice members and clients.

Other experiments did not translate into good results. These failures were supported by the GSURR leadership. They were an opportunity to show that innovation requires a risk-taking attitude and failures are normal and expected. When the return on investment of these experiments did not fare well against other products, the approach taken was to fail fast, learn, and improve or discard. Some of these experiments included podcasts and Facebook Live events that failed because of high production costs and lack of supportive infrastructure in the organization (vlogs and X (formerly Twitter) chats were found to be better products with lower production time and costs, able to leverage existing platforms in the organization, and capable of reaching much larger audiences). The failures were not necessarily due to the tools themselves but a variety of external and internal factors that were reviewed as part of the fail-fast-and-learn approach.

Challenges in the Transformation Journey

An important challenge that both the communications and knowledge management teams faced was the difficulty of sharing stories and knowledge of failure. In the World Bank, like many other organizations, the organizational culture and incentives are not conducive to analyzing and reflecting on failures. Development is a complex undertaking and failures—small and big—are common in the design and trial of new solutions. Development is not a one-lane road with a clear path from design to completion. Sharing the lessons learned in a way that is systematic, understandable, and non-offensive is key to help others avoid similar failures. The only knowledge-sharing tool that allowed sharing of those lessons was the South-South Knowledge Exchange Facility (see Chapter 9). These exchanges created space for informal conversations between practitioners that allowed for effective transfer of knowledge about experiences with failure. The organizational culture and the lack of methodologies for documenting lessons from failures prevented us from solving this challenge.

A second challenge was the difference—at times—between corporate guidance for the communications team and the transformation the GSURR leadership team wanted to push. As discussed earlier in this chapter, corporate communications in the World Bank have a clear mandate and parameters. The communications and knowledge management technical disciplines and teams are seen as separate and independent, with different mandates and audiences. As the communications team had a different reporting line, finding a compromise was sometimes difficult. By finding ways to achieve the objectives and metrics defined by the central communications team, we were able to move forward on the coordinated platforms and integrated products developed by the communications and knowledge management teams.

Leadership Lessons

The success of the change process to break the silos between knowledge management and communications was, in great part, due to the active engagement of the GSURR leadership. This engagement was particularly important in four areas: vision and strategy, metrics, skills building, and incentives.

The definition of a new vision and strategy for the communications and outreach work required intensive leadership engagement. The opportunities for greater impact, enhanced cost effectiveness, and innovation were too great to be missed. The leadership team had to sell this strategy by navigating the corporate communications requirements and finding a common ground to achieve both the organizational and team objectives.

The definition of metrics and the disciplined measurement and course correction were critical to show the importance that the leadership team gave to this area and to prove the benefits of the new way of working. Reporting back to the team and senior leadership opened the space to maneuver, experiment, and innovate.

The building of communications skills for the team could not be done by imposition from the top. It required a combination of leadership by doing and intangible incentives. The

GSURR leadership team was the first to take the communications skills upgrading courses and to share the lessons with the technical teams to encourage them to follow with their own upskilling efforts. Team members that took advantage of the upskilling opportunities were selected for presentations and engagement with senior leadership of the World Bank.

The Unfinished Agenda

Changing a long-standing culture is a continuous process. Managing diverging incentives and interests between the communications and knowledge management teams required continuous engagement by the leadership team. Two areas of this silo-breaking agenda that required further work were the influencing of other units in the organization to replicate the lessons learned and the identification of competencies for team members that could navigate both the communications and the knowledge management areas of expertise. These "integrators" could fulfill the important function of a connecting tissue between the two teams.

Three other areas for further work in the interface between communications and knowledge management are

- *Metrics and indicators*: The metrics GSURR used were simple first-order indicators focused on outreach and audience (by segments when possible). There is a need for more sophisticated metrics on policy influence, targeted segment readership (e.g., how many policymakers are reading policy reports and being influenced), influence in policies and behavior change, and use of knowledge assets by individuals who have been reached through communications channels. These indicators and metrics are fundamental to understand the effectiveness and ROI of different channels, products, and platforms.
- *Client capacity on communications*: GSURR's experiences in breaking silos between communications and knowledge management teams could be of interest to clients. Chapter 10 describes how the World Bank experience in knowledge management was used to support capacity-building efforts for government agencies in countries from Indonesia to Colombia to build their own knowledge management systems. A next possible step would be to work with these knowledge management units and agencies to implement the lessons of our silo-breaking journey with communications.
- *Methodology and incentives to communicate failures*: A methodology to communicate the failures and the challenging road to development solutions is needed in the development community as are incentives to encourage staff to do so. GSURR's initial attempts were not successful to overcome the institutional and individual resistance to share lessons from failure.

Chapter 8

Making Knowledge "Stick"

Journeys Towards a New Knowledge-Sharing Culture

Monika Weber-Fahr[1] *and Philip Karp*

An Opening for Change

In the midst of the World Bank's 2014 reorganization towards Global Practices, the knowledge and learning teams in the Sustainable Development Group set out to capture the moment: they would "ride" on the fact that the hierarchies were busy with the politics of organizational change. No one had the energy to micromanage them and demand specific details as to how the not insubstantial learning and knowledge-sharing budget was being used. The opportunity had opened up for an end-to-end radical shift. The teams' idea was to design an entire week of learning and knowledge-sharing events that would not only bring some 1,500 staff together from across some 100+ country offices and the headquarters teams—but that would also invite everyone to claim their space as "knowledge citizens" in the organization. Simply by participating in the events offered, attendees of "Forum2014" would be able to adopt behaviors and attitudes supportive of active knowledge sharing, good personal knowledge management practices, and a commitment to lifelong learning, all three key elements of knowledge citizenry.

The Journey: An End-to-End User-Centric Knowledge-Sharing Event for 1,500 Staff

What would make "knowledge stick" was the question that the design team put at the heart of its vision and all communications. "Sticky knowledge" as a concept was more intuitive to explain than the somewhat elusive term of knowledge citizenry. And it was easy to use as a litmus test when the team had to check its choices and confirm that it was still on the intended path. Drawing on the three dominant learning theories—behaviorism, cognitivism, and constructivism—the design team invited a user-centric design consultant to work with them in developing ten learning *formats* that would indeed create enough space for knowledge to "stick." Armed with these *formats* and the stories that explained why they would work for everyone, the team then embarked on its journey to create a new knowledge-sharing and learning environment that would also influence the organization's culture more broadly.

The journey to design and deliver a large, end-to-end, reimagined knowledge-sharing event different and impactful enough to shift much of the organizational culture on learning and knowledge sharing involved 11 steps:

1. *A multilevel authorizing environment*: The team reached out across all hierarchies and units to build ownership and mobilize enthusiasm. Key groups targeted included middle

DOI: 10.4324/9781003199083-17

and upper-middle management—since they needed to sponsor staff to attend; knowledge-sharing focal points in thematic departments and communities of practice—since they would mobilize the content to be shared; administrative and logistical staff—since they had to go along with what was a new way of organizing events and activities; and a selected group of change agents across the organization who were enthused by the proposition of "making knowledge stick"—since they would be trained as forum facilitators.

2. *Interaction is king—A fixed set of formats for knowledge sharing*: Based on tried-and-tested learning theories and the experience of the professional learning and knowledge-sharing teams, 11 *formats* were developed and tested for *usefulness* for "making knowledge stick" and for *enjoyment* by the target groups. The idea was that only these—and no other—*formats* would be available when offering a knowledge-sharing activity. Each of the formats was assigned a format coordinator, charged with assisting interested units to shape their knowledge-sharing activity in ways that would take full advantage of a particular format once it was chosen. The beauty of the approach was in the user-centric design of each of the formats: there was little to argue—in terms of "but I always use my PowerPoints this way"—where the engagement and joyful experience of the participant would be at stake. Each of the *formats* was to offer "bite-sized" knowledge appropriate for short attention spans, include collaborative elements, be practice-based, be delivered in peer-to-peer settings and small groups, respond to bottom-up sourced interests, and offer a view towards longer-term learning.

3. *A central design and coordination team*: Staffed with "volunteers" from across all units, Forum2014 was a large knowledge-sharing and learning event that would bring together colleagues from many organizational units—to learn from each other and with each other—across thematic and institutional "silos." Given the institutional insecurities in the middle of a reorganization, it was important that the centrally operating design and coordination team brought together staff delegated for this purpose from across multiple units. Thus, many units had "one of us" in the design team, someone who also—in return—helped "sell" the idea of doing things differently when "back home."

4. *Consistent, focused, and colorful communication*: All communications in regard to Forum2014 had to "model" the approach that was driving the event's design. The user-centric perspective meant that all communications were short, pleasant to look at, clear, easy to recognize as a Forum2014 message, designed on a "need to know basis," facilitating key messages with visualizations, repetition, and choice of appropriate font sizes.

5. *The topics for knowledge sharing were exclusively sourced "bottom up" from staff across all units*: Based on a broadly administered survey ("send in your topics to learn" * "send in your topics to share"), a topic map was created. Regional and sector focal points worked together to translate the topic map into actual session topics and to identify session owners. Also here the design rules were clear: if you are not "on the map," there is no space for your topic. In order to, nevertheless, be able to promote innovative solutions that might not have gotten a lot of votes in the "bottom up" exercise, sector and regional coordinators were given latitude in how and whom to mobilize as session owners.

6. *All "performers"—speakers and session facilitators—were coached individually on applying interactive learning techniques*: Forum2014 involved more than 400 speakers and over 100 facilitators—more than during previous events and mostly driven by

Box 8.1   Formats for Knowledge Exchange That Made Knowledge "Stick"

Genius bar: One-on-one assistance on a come-as-you-go basis by experts on specific questions. The format was used a lot for IT.

Experts on call: One-on-one assistance to staff wanting to learn from a particular and internally well-known expert. A booking system was provided and staff could prearrange 15-minute in-depth conversations about a topic of interest.

Project clinics: Staff would sign up for a "clinic" when they had a project that they would want to have informally "examined" by colleagues who were looking to help the staff to fix or improve on certain dimensions. This one-hour long format was initially undersubscribed—many staff clearly felt concerned about opening themselves up for criticism—but eventually very popular once some well-respected colleagues spoke up on behalf of it.

Hard talks: Leaders in a particular field, both externally and internally to the World Bank, were invited on a "hot seat" from which a moderator asked them a series of fast-firing questions drawn electronically from the audience. Very much a moderated "all you can ask" affair, these sessions invited direct participant engagement by having participants send their questions to the moderator electronically—then to be displayed on a large screen behind the Hard Talk interviewee.

Trade secrets: Smaller informal sessions with 15 or fewer attendees allowed during which specific team leads would offer to talk about their specific "trade secrets" in terms of operational or between-the-lines challenges and how to tackle and resolve them.

Master classes: With attendance restricted to "masters," that is, staff who already had considerable experience in a particular area, the conversations ensuing during Master Classes were very much built around peer-to-peer exchanges stimulated by a prominent or highly respected Master Class lead.

Project expo: Catering to participants with a more visual orientation, the Project Expo featured posters displaying key dimensions and experiences with a variety of projects, inviting visitors to learn from the posters while being *coached* through various dimensions by the project's manager.

Meet the manager: This format was highly popular for knowledge exchange, inspired by the reorganization and the fact that most managers had only recently been appointed to their roles and many staff did not know them. Approximately 10-15 tables were arranged with respectively 1–2 managers at each table. Since the managers were made to rotate every 20 minutes during a single lunch session, staff in attendance would have the opportunity to get to know and exchange knowledge with at least 3–6 of the new managers.

Up close and personal: Set up like a TED-talk, the Up Close and Personal sessions featured one presenter and a storytelling style. Presenting staff had been chosen competitively from younger staff and staff with shorter tenure in the organization. This would offer presenting staff the opportunity for visibility through knowledge exchange while giving participating staff a "tour de force" across multiple new topics in short time. Attention and knowledge retention were built around a voting system that invited staff to participate to nominate the best performing presenters.

the deliberate choice to limit all activities to smaller groups. Without exception, every speaker or content owner was briefed on the intricacies of the *format* chosen for their session—an exercise that mostly went well and was met with great enthusiasm by the "performers". Many arrived in Washington, DC, after a trip from wherever they were working to find that they had to abandon the old and tested set of PowerPoints that they normally used. Most were intrigued by the organizers' insistence that a knowledge-sharing event must primarily serve the participant-learners and not be shaped to fit the preferences of the person sharing their knowledge. There were some notable exceptions—including the odd "renegade" trying to smuggle in a PowerPoint despite all previous coaching—but the strong authorizing environment that the design team had built by then kept the *Luddites* at bay.

7. *Depth in collaborative learning comes with the right people in the room: Picking participants rather than allowing for a free-for-all session attendance*: One of the most uncomfortable—but in the end highly successful—choices made by the Forum2014 design team was the decision to invite all registered staff to seek admission rather than to simply sign up for particular events well ahead of time. Once everyone had submitted their session choices, the team went through the excruciating exercise to ensure appropriate diversity for each session—creating balanced participant groups in terms of location (country office versus headquarters), sector background, tenure, gender, and nationality. For some formats—such as the Master Classes—the participant picks went purposefully the other way: here it was important to ensure a similarity of expertise so that *Masters* could talk to and learn from *Masters*. Interestingly, the positive feedback from the Master Classes was particularly strong in this regard: many of the experienced staff commented that they rarely if ever have been in a room with others bringing similar experiences and how much they felt they benefited from this setup.

8. *Keeping the conversation possible: Small small small session sizes*: The tendency in most large organizations is to try to fill a room with many people. Most speakers, in fact, seem to think that the more participants they attract the more successful their talk should be considered. Not so at Forum2014. While the design team was very much aware that in the literature there is no consistent view as to the number of participants that constitutes "too many," the approach taken here was based on the expectation of knowledge exchange and the need for "air time" for everyone during a 60- or 90-minute session. Most formats did not allow for more than 20 participants; only one format—the Hard Talks—allowed up to 70 but built in interaction via an electronic polling and survey tool. Many formats were based on one-on-one interactions. The feedback in the end proved this choice to have been the right one.

9. *"Bite-sized" knowledge only*: Yes, the world is as complex as it is complicated. And so most definitely the type of knowledge that World Bank clients expect must be substantive, reflected, peer-considered, and, of course, practical and feasible to apply. Nevertheless, when sharing knowledge with others, it's important to keep in mind your counterpart's attention span—and that this attention span is very short. All Forum2014 speakers and facilitators were, therefore, coached to share knowledge only in "bite-sized" formats, limiting individual remarks to just a few minutes, using storytelling formats to engage, and "peppering" everything with interaction between them and the participants. The concept of "bite-sizing" was intuitive to everyone, and it became wildly successful, to the degree that it helped guide the type of knowledge assets shared through the Open Learning Campus (see Chapter 11) and being

featured in other guidance documents such as the *Art of Knowledge Exchange* (see Chapter 9).

10. *Talking about—and modeling—community and joy in learning and knowledge sharing*: Much of the event design aimed at stimulating a sense of community and joy. This included simple elements, such as positivity-oriented messaging throughout all communications, to visual elements, such as the use of primary colors in all displays. The design team had mobilized some 150 volunteers from among junior staff, alumni, and the family network to serve as room minders, registration assistants, and so on; for many, participation in the event was a rare opportunity to learn and interact with frontline World Bank teams, and the joy they brought to their assignments was infectious. The notable absence of director- and vice president–level announcements in all sessions was a strong signal that "this is from you for you" and also contributed to a growing sense of community throughout the five days.

The Results: Did It Work? and What Worked Best?

Contrary to most knowledge-sharing events, Forum2014 had developed right from the start a *theory of change* that described the design team's overall aspiration. The goal was not about "bums on seats" nor (only) about "happy feedback"; the overall goal was to mobilize staff to take on the concept of "knowledge citizenry" and to motivate participants to apply what they saw and experienced to inform and improve the services provided to their clients. A member of the design team with monitoring and evaluation skills was appointed to design a solid *results framework* and to make sure that a system would be in place to collect information appropriate to highlight whether or not and, if so, which results were achieved.

Directly after each session, participant ratings were collected "the old fashioned way": very simple paper-based ratings were collected on three scales. While these provided no good insight on the long-time "stickiness" of knowledge, they were a good indicator to the degree of inspiration that participants walked away with from the sessions they engaged with. Three months after the event, a more detailed survey was sent out. Eighty-five percent of participants confirmed that they attributed a part of the improvement in their job effectiveness to their experience at Forum2014. The percentage of those saying they learned new skills varied quite significantly across formats: Perhaps not surprisingly, the *formats* featuring the least number of participants at a time and the highest possibility for customization, such as the Genius Bar, the Project Clinics, and the Master Classes, got the highest rating.

The Waves: *Knowledge Citizenship* Spreading Across the Organization

Forum2014, in many ways, opened up new spaces for those staff who had—or found newly—an inclination to invest in their knowledge citizenry. Many of the larger groups beyond the Sustainable Development Group began experimenting with *no-PowerPoint, no-talking-down* formats that promoted collaborative learning, co-creation, and innovation. This included the Legal Department, the Environment Department, the Independent Evaluation Group, and the Water Global Practice.

The newly formed Global Practice for Social, Urban, Rural, and Resilience (GSURR) took inspiration from the Forum2014 experience as it set out on its own journey to create a culture of knowledge citizenship. Over the next five years, the GSURR knowledge and learning team used major Practice–wide events to promote this culture, to create a sense of community, and to introduce knowledge-sharing formats and skills that were then carried forward by the Practice's various knowledge communities in their own activities and events.

GSURR Forum 2015—Follow the Sun

For its first Global Practice–wide event, GSURR management elected to focus primarily on community building, recognizing that, at that point in time, this was more important than the content of the program itself. The challenge, however, was how to have an event with small enough groups to allow for effective networking and community building while, at the same time, providing staff with access to and "face time" with senior management of the Practice.

The solution adopted was a decentralized event but with a schedule that allowed for interaction across locations. The event was held, simultaneously, at three locations; Bang-kok (Thailand) (bringing together staff from offices in East and South Asia as well as head-quarters staff who worked on those regions); Istanbul (Turkey) (bringing together staff from offices in Eastern Europe, Central Asia, and Africa); and Washington, DC (United States) (bringing together staff from headquarters and from Latin America).

One of the GSURR directors served as "host" at each location, while the GSURR senior director traveled on a whirlwind itinerary that allowed him to spend at least half a day at each location over the course of the 3-day event. Many of the formats that had been intro-duced during Forum2014 were utilized, with the added dimension of sessions that took advantage of time zone differences to start a discussion at one location, have it picked up at the next, and finalized at the third.

In addition, the GSURR knowledge and learning team took advantage of gamification to jump-start team building and networking among the disparate groups of staff who had been brought together with the creation of the GSURR Global Practice. They engaged a company that specializes in team-building activities at corporate retreats and events, utilizing a place-based, scavenger hunt–type format to force teams to work together. GSURR worked with this company to customize its approach, replacing general trivia games with sector-specific information and incorporating use of public transport to get around the city while carry-ing out the various tasks associated with the game. Teams were put together purposefully, ensuring that no two staff from the same unit or country office would be on the same team. Thus, by the end of the first day of the event, staff had already worked and solved problems with half a dozen staff who they had probably not met prior to the event.

Each morning and evening, videoconference sessions were held connecting the three loca-tions and allowing for sharing of highlights of the respective discussions. Moreover, staff who were leading the various technical sessions had the option of connecting one or more of the other locations. During the event, the organizers also introduced tools for electronic polling; something that would be utilized extensively in GSURR knowledge and learning events going forward. Post-event surveys found that, on average, participating staff had made at least 15 new contacts, exceeding the target of 10 new contacts that had been estab-lished by the organizers.

GSURR Forum 2017—Focus on Content

For its next GSURR-wide Forum, which took place two years later, it was decided to bring all staff to Washington, DC, an opportunity that was of importance in particular to staff based in country offices. The event was held partly at World Bank headquarters and partly at an offsite location. Unlike the first GSURR Forum, where content was secondary to networking, a heavy emphasis was placed on quality and relevance of content of the various sessions, with the various GSURR communities of practice assigned responsibility for defining session topics and selecting speakers and materials. Once again, many of the formats that had been introduced during Forum14 were utilized, and associated coaching was provided to all presenters. Gamification was used once again, this time based on pop culture, with staff assigned to "houses" loosely based on the *Harry Potter* novels.

GSURR Forum 2019—Celebrating Success

Still another GSURR-wide Forum was held about 18 months later, again in Washington, DC. For this third Forum, even more emphasis was put on quality of content. By this time, the GSURR communities of practice were well-established and were in a very good position to plan and organize high-quality sessions incorporating cutting-edge knowledge. Pop culture was again woven into the event, this time using the *Game of Thrones* TV series as the theme and including costume play as well as friendly competition between "houses." A few months prior to the third Forum event, World Bank senior management had announced a new reorganization that would result in the splitting off from GSURR of the Social Development Practice. As such, the Forum event, held just prior to this reorganization taking effect, was used to celebrate successes of the previous five years while seeking to ensure that the culture of knowledge citizenry that had been carefully cultivated would be carried over into both the slimmed down Urban, Land, and Resilience and Social Development Practices.

Lessons for Other Organizations

There are a number of lessons that can be drawn from the experience of the Forum2014 and GSURR Forum events.

First, these experiences demonstrate how "events" can be used as a vehicle to introduce new behaviors and ways of operating, particularly with adequate attention to coaching key participants. By taking staff outside of their usual day-to-day office settings, they become more open to new ideas which, can catalyze change.

Second, the events demonstrate how gamification and use of pop culture can help to develop an *esprit de corps*, which is so important to a newly constituted organization.

Third, culture change can live on—despite multiple organizational changes—where the culture shifts have been grounded in profound and personal experiences. Even now, eight years after the first Forum2014 introduced a massive shift in approaches to learning and knowledge sharing, taking a user-centric rather than a speaker-centric approach, many staff will remember the various Forum2014 and GSURR Forum events and the innovative formats they introduced. And they will look to apply, even if only some of them, where they can. However, as these staff move to other units and eventually leave the organization, the culture of knowledge citizenship will leave with them—unless kept alive through signals and structures offered by the organization and its leadership.

Note

1 The success of the Forum2014 experience described in this chapter is due to an extraordinary team that included an extraordinary team that included, among many others: Vivek Raman, Arno Boersma, Avjeet Singh, Barbara Bitondo, Chana Alfaro, Chirine Alameddine, Helke Waelde, Maria Iturralde MacDicken, Monika Kosior, Neesham Spitzberg, Silpi Chalasani, and Tim Heine.

Chapter 9

The Art of Knowledge Exchange

Spicing Up the Menu of Knowledge-Sharing
Modalities

Shobha Kumar and Yianna Vovides

Introduction

South-South and practitioner-to-practitioner knowledge exchange can—when done well—
be powerful tools for sharing, replicating, scaling up, and adapting successful solutions or
for avoiding repetition of failures. On the other hand, poorly designed exchanges can be
a colossal waste of resources. Recognizing this, the World Bank invested, in conjunction
with the establishment of a trust fund and facility for supporting South-South Knowledge
Exchange, in the development of a methodology for results-focused knowledge sharing.
The methodology, known as the *Art of Knowledge Exchange,*[1] offers a structure to guide
knowledge-exchange activities such that they are uniquely results-focused. These structures
are easy to undestand and apply to the design of knowledge exchanges, even when the
organizing staff have little background or experience in this space. Conceptually based on
the World Bank Institute's Capacity Development Results Framework (CDRF), the *Art of
Knowledge Exchange* methodology allows for both scaling and assuring the quality of a
wide range of knowledge-exchange initiatives.

GSURR Takes Up the Charge

When GSURR was set up, one of the early initiatives of the new leadership was to reach
an agreement with the team responsible for the *Art of Knowledge Exchange* to collaborate on customization of the guidebook and on its use to train all staff within the Global
Practice on how to design results-oriented knowledge exchange activities. The idea was: 1)
GSURR clients should be able to access the most effective combination of instruments to
address their development challenges, inviting them to customize, replicate, and scale up
development solutions in ways that would fit with their needs; and 2) along with using the
process of developing skills on knowledge exchanges with and for clients, to build a spirit of
knowledge citizenry among this very diverse group of staff and a common language for and
understanding of the value of knowledge exchange, collaboration, and co-creation. Since
learning about the *Art of Knowledge Exchange* was built around a purpose and goal that
everyone shared—improving the services to World Bank clients—the rationale for staff to
participate did not need much explaining.

GSURR leadership had been clear to staff: everyone was invited—and encouraged—
to see themselves as and become a "knowledge management agent" or, as it was sometimes called, a "knowledge citizen". The process of customizing the *Art of Knowledge
Exchange* guidebook would offer opportunities for this to happen. Involving staff in the

DOI: 10.4324/9781003199083-18

customization—through integrating case studies, road-testing the methodology, and offering customized and hands-on engagements—would build broader ownership of the product, enabling staff to see themselves in this space. At the very outset, it became clear that it was important to first build and strengthen a GSURR-wide consensus on the power of well-designed knowledge exchanges. Inviting all staff to join *Art of Knowledge Exchange* workshops allowed everyone to experience firsthand the potential available. Deliveries of the workshop were organized during major GSURR-wide learning events and for staff, both in Washington, DC, and in country office locations to make it convenient to join. As a consensus emerged on the value of this methodology, motivation to design knowledge and learning offerings as part of projects grew among staff, and many also went on to inspire their partners and clients to adopt a systematic and results-focused methodology for knowledge exchange.

Box 9.1   The *Art of Knowledge Exchange*: Getting Ready for Broad Delivery

Launched in 2011, the *Art of Knowledge Exchange* methodology has met with enthusiastic responses among Bank staff and their counterparts. Initially, along with developing the methodology, the World Bank Institute invested in associated learning and knowledge-sharing products and activities including guidebooks, workshops, case studies, clinics, e-learning courses, webinars, hands-on clinics, and one-on-one advisory sessions. Jointly they provided a synergistic blend of instruments to meet the needs of different audience groups. Task teams across the World Bank—at times together with their partners and clients—were introduced to the approaches and methods to systematically integrate knowledge exchange as part of a larger change process. "Champions" were recruited, and a cadre of knowledge management facilitators was developed who would be able to design and deliver *Art of Knowledge Exchange* workshops. Through these workshops, an extensive group of sectoral specialists and practitioners was reached, including over 2,500 World Bank staff. Beyond these participants, over 20,000 development practitioners are thought to have been exposed to the *Art of Knowledge Exchange* products and services through workshops and outreach activities, both in person and online. The *Art of Knowledge Exchange* product family now includes four customized guidebooks: *Art of Knowledge Exchange for Social, Urban, Rural, and Resilience Practitioners* (developed for GSURR and the focus of this chapter); *Art of Knowledge Exchange for Water Sector Professionals*; *Art of Knowledge Exchange for the Global Environment Facility and Its Partners*; and *Art of Knowledge Exchange for Climate Change Practitioners*. The basic guidebook is available in nine different languages (Arabic, Bahasa, Chinese, English, French, Japanese, Portuguese, Spanish, and Vietnamese).

The *Art of Knowledge Exchange*, at the time, already had an excellent track record for customization and offered a tried-and-tested methodology ripe for adaptation to GSURR's needs. Methodology and good practice examples would be adjusted to reflect GSURR sectors and context, becoming more directly relatable for staff, partners, and clients. A broadly shared sense of contributing to GSURR's organizational transformation effort emerged from the *process* by which the customization took place. From the outset, it was clear that the GSURR-specific adaptation of the methodology and guidebook would have to maintain the same level of quality as the rest of the suite of *Art of Knowledge Exchange* products while being completed during a very short time frame. The choice was to include some existing cases and examples related to GSURR in the main narrative while also developing new materials on the use of technology and social media to increase engagement, reach, and impact of knowledge-exchange initiatives. Also, the toolbox in the *Art of Knowledge Exchange* guidebook would have to be enhanced to include some new and innovative instruments and activities that had been developed by GSURR teams and were familiar to staff in the Global Practice. These included *technical deep dives, design boards*, and *gap analysis*.

- *Technical deep dives* (TDDs) are an immersive, experiential learning instrument focused on a common thematic challenge faced by stakeholders from several countries or cities who come together in a knowledge provider country to learn from local experts and through peer-to-peer exchange. Pioneered in this format by the Tokyo Development Learning Center (see Chapter 6), the instrument has been used widely in other GSURR programs and by GSURR partners.
- *Design boards* are an activity that incorporates informal, working-level, hands-on sessions conducted in small groups. These were used extensively by the GSURR Social Development teams as a "safe space" for discussions regarding project design and implementation.
- *Gap analysis* is an activity that helps identify the gap(s) between the present state and desired future state, along with the tasks needed to close the gap(s).

Identifying the right case examples and narratives was critical to broaden ownership and sustain interest among GSURR staff in the methodology overall, and so a wide net was cast to identify experiences from as many groups as possible. Further, to make the guide as relevant as possible to GSURR staff, three detailed case examples were integrated throughout the guidebook, illustrating the application of the methodology in exchanges involving countries and sectors in which GSURR was engaged. The case examples chosen included a knowledge-exchange effort between Japan and Vietnam on urban flood risk management; an exchange among Myanmar, Indonesia, and the Philippines on empowering communities for community-driven development; and an exchange among Honduras, Nicaragua, and Colombia on recognition of indigenous land rights. In addition, the guidebook also included a case from one of the GSURR's key external partners, the 100 Resilient Cities Network (see Chapter 5.6) and copies were provided to its members. Once the examples and cases were finalized, workshops were rolled out right away; in the meantime, new teaching cases were developed for subsequent deployment.

For the new GSURR *Art of Knowledge Exchange* guide to remain relevant over time, it was important to open up the possibility of making updated content available—interactively—and to target new audiences in the future. An augmented reality component was, therefore, included as a part of the publication. The augmented reality component involved an interactive cover page that would connect the printed edition to digital resources on the web.

Once completed, the task of making all GSURR staff aware of the new guidebook was half done already—if only because of the broad involvement across the practice. Still, GSURR's leadership wanted to make sure everyone also appreciated the strategic relevance of using the guidebook for active knowledge-sharing work. Printed copies of the guidebook were delivered to all GSURR staff members, and workshops were offered during learning weeks and at other learning events around the world. Also, the *Art of Knowledge Exchange* template and methodology featured systematically wherever South-South funds would be deployed for the design and delivery of GSURR knowledge management and learning initiatives for staff and clients. These included, among others, the use of technical deep dives as standalone knowledge-exchange engagements and a series of peer learning events that were part of a programmatic knowledge-exchange effort.

Box 9.2   Technical Deep Dive: Creative Cities

In 2020, the Tokyo Development Learning Center in collaboration with UNESCO hosted a technical deep dive on the topic of *creative cities* for urban development. Government staff and technical experts from ten countries were invited: Albania, Bolivia, Cameroon, China, Ethiopia, Georgia, Nepal, the Philippines, Saudi Arabia, and Sri Lanka. Japan had already experimented with various models to foster cultural and creative industries with eight Japanese cities registered under the UNESCO Creative Cities Network. The technical deep dive, thus, leveraged the Japanese experience of fostering cultural and creative activities for inclusive economic development to engage participants in discussion and experiential learning activities related to policy, institutional, and cultural conditions necessary to promote creative cities.

Box 9.3   Peer Learning Series: Integrated Urban Transformation

The city of Medellín in Colombia is widely recognized for its remarkable urban transformation. To leverage this experience, a series of knowledge exchanges was arranged in 2018 and 2019 that involved urban practitioners from ten cities in Africa and Asia: Cape Town and Johannesburg (South Africa), Dar es Salaam (Tanzania), Kinshasa (Democratic Republic of Congo), Nairobi (Kenya), and Kigali (Rwanda), Chongqing (China), Ho Chi Minh City (Vietnam), Jakarta (Indonesia), and Mumbai (India). In collaboration with the respective city governments and local organizations, GSURR hosted three formal peer-to-peer knowledge exchange events that included approximately 70 participants each in Medellín, Cape Town, and Jakarta. Participants included city and regional officials; World Bank experts; and members of the private, mobility, nongovernmental, and education sectors as well as other development practitioners. Modeled on the technical deep dive instrument introduced by the Tokyo Development Learning Center (see Chapter 6), the learning series featured site visits and experiential activities, networking sessions with peers, design labs with master practitioners and global experts, and action planning and reflection sessions.

Using a guidebook on knowledge and learning approaches—the *Art of Knowledge Exchange*—to influence staff behaviors vis-à-vis each other and their clients was an innovative and, at that point, an untested approach to organizational change. In fact, choosing the knowledge management arena as a platform to amplify leadership expectations about effective collaboration and innovation had been unheard of at the time in the World Bank. Interestingly, the impact of promoting such approaches as part of good business practice went well beyond the World Bank's organizational borders. Having a common framework for knowledge sharing facilitated things when GSURR staff partnered with other organizations, typically wherever the partnership involved South-South Knowledge Exchange initiatives. Like-minded partners and institutions such as the Global Environment Facility (GEF) and UNESCO came to the fore, opening up their own treasure chests of methodologies. Since the GEF had already created its own adaptation of the *Art of Knowledge Exchange* a year or so earlier, new synergies emerged. More materials became available for sharing, and staff could learn from each other's experience. Every time a partner organization joined the larger *Art of Knowledge Exchange* community, more tools, methods, and experiences emerged. Customization of the main toolbox and guidebook was involved and that provided an even richer set of instruments and activities. The latest adaptation of the guidebook, developed through working with the Climate Investment Funds (CIF), came with a particular focus on climate change practitioners, resulting in multiple enhancements and a further expansion of the toolbox.

The approach taken was successful in instilling a strong sense of collaboration and co-creation among GSURR's staff and partners, and it also served as a catalyst for innovative thinking, connecting clients to new information and shaping new business opportunities across regions and countries. The *Art of Knowledge Exchange*'s wide availability helped clients to customize, replicate, and scale up development solutions they saw working, with their own eyes. The robust design and delivery of the workshops; the interactive facilitation style; a simple and intuitive road map, which resonated with both the "seasoned" and the "newcomers"; and an environment conducive to learning and knowledge sharing drove much of the positive reaction. Staff proactively commented on having learned much and for the long term and gained motivation to apply the methods in ever wider contexts.

Demand soon outstripped the supply that a small core team could provide in terms of one-on-one coaching and design support, and thus opportunities were sought to work with regional knowledge-sharing organizations to set up regional centers of excellence for the *Art of Knowledge Exchange*. A first start was made by working with the Agency for Cooperation and Investment of Medellín (ACI) (see Chapter 10) and the Tokyo Development Learning Center (TDLC) (see Chapter 6). ACI, for example, benefited beyond the work itself, gaining local and national visibility and recognition as a leader in international exchanges and putting Medellín on the international map as a knowledge hub. Other partners and institutions of excellence, such as the Seoul Metropolitan Government and Johns Hopkins University, hosted deliveries of *Art of Knowledge Exchange* workshops and invited other institutions to send their staff to learn the methodology.

Box 9.4   High in Impact—Low in Cost: Changing the Knowledge Exchange Experience

Paving the way for sustainable change in Nairobi Metropolitan Services: Conversation with Mwangi Wamagunda, engineer and project liaison officer, Nairobi Metropolitan Services Improvement Project. Trained as technical engineer but also handling the role of a project liaison officer, Wamagunda's role at the Nairobi Metropolitan Services Improvement Project brings him face to face with nontechnical challenges at every phase of the project cycle. "Just before we went to Jakarta, we had an impasse on planning our railway city. People felt that they were not being listened to," says Wamagunda. His chance to participate in the Jakarta Urban Lab in December 2019 proved to be a rich and timely learning experience. He got to see how Jakarta had used participatory planning processes to: 1) successfully introduce policy initiatives related to integration of land use and transport, 2) manage its disaster response, and 3) successfully implement regulations like Car Free Day. The Jakarta Governor passed the regulation in 2012 officially establishing Car Free Day as a weekly public activity with an objective to reduce pollution and promote public health. Wamagunda remarked:

> Seeing what they have been able to achieve in Jakarta with the Car Free Day gave me motivation and confidence that this can work even in our context if we just listen to the people and take time to prepare for the engagement.

He realizes that the key to achieving sustainable change is carrying along the beneficiaries on this journey of planning and implementation and moving away from the tendency to focus on the politicians. Wamagunda also took the experience from Jakarta to design the technical deep dive in Kenya—a knowledge exchange, capacity development and networking program on urban development issues which brought together local, regional, and international urban practitioners in Nairobi. He said:

> I had a chance to localize this knowledge sharing and learning methodology in our own context and it worked. The urban practitioners from different local counties also saw the value of this knowledge exchange, and we hope to continue using it and improving upon it

At a personal level, Wamagunda says, "After these experiences, I have moved much beyond my field of technical engineering . . . now I am doing social engineering and bringing people together, without it nothing works."

Box 9.5   Understanding the Value of Different Viewpoints

Conversation with Wenchao Jiang, associate professor, water science and engineering, Chongqing University, China.

As an associate professor at Chongqing University in the critical field of water science and engineering, Wenchao straddles the two worlds of academia and expert consulting for the city government. With deep interest in water systems, urban planning, and environmental protection, Wenchao is keen to see the practical application of his research and teaching work and feed that learning back to his students. His visits to Medellín, Cape Town, and Jakarta gave Wenchao a precious opportunity to understand the practical challenges and solutions that other parts of the world are working on.

"I have already taken the learning from the three cities and applied it in my work with the city of Chongqing where my department provides design and consultation services," says Wenchao. Further noting,

With the inspiration I gained from Jakarta on their initiative of vertical planting and use of rainwater resources, I have included vertical plants and rainwater harvesting in my latest plans and advice to the city government. We are a mountain city with narrow roads, so this is a good solution for us to enhance our landscape in a sustainable way and to add greenery to walls.

"I recently also had a chance to apply the learning from the vibrant Victoria and Alfred Waterfront Regeneration project that we saw in Cape Town to our upcoming river front regeneration project," adds Wenchao. He has also taken his learning from the three Urban Labs to his students:

I have already included the Medellín case of urban regeneration in my course. I also teach differently and design my class field trips differently. My classes are more interactive as I have used the knowledge exchange methodology from the Urban Labs and my class field trips are designed using the techniques I experienced in Medellín, Cape Town and Jakarta.

At a personal level, Wenchao truly valued the opportunity to learn alongside practitioners and to see different viewpoints:

I have been trained in the academic world. So, I have a different viewpoint. During the workshop, I had a chance to see practitioner (especially administrator) viewpoints and got to learn together with practitioners instead of academics or solely with engineers. The message I took away is that we must think about practical things as it is the practical things which are the ultimate test of application in the real world, and viewpoints and possibilities from various backgrounds are always important and should be at the core of my thinking and solution seeking.

Box 9.6   Urban Regeneration in Nairobi With Inspiration From Medellín

Survey Feedback from Ruth W. Muroki, Director, Planning, Nairobi City County Government, Kenya

Having seen the street regeneration in Medellín provided the inspiration and confidence to push for the implementation of the Luthuli [Avenue] street regeneration. Luthuli Avenue is a busy street in downtown Nairobi. Prior to the intervention between March to June 2019, the street was very congested due to many buses on the street, and the congestion was further aggravated when buses used the street as a temporary parking facility while waiting for passengers. We initiated a multi-stakeholder process to regenerate Luthuli Avenue. The Urban Planning and Environment Department took the lead, working closely with the Transport, Infrastructure and Public Work departments and the UN-Habitat. We also included the nongovernment actors as well as the community owning businesses on the street. The key interventions included removal of buses from the street, pedestrianization of the street, minimal one-way vehicular traffic, planting of trees and beautification, and waste management and provision of waste bins. An immediate noticeable result of the intervention was that the noise pollution, which was being generated by touts yelling out for customers, banging the sides of the buses to attract their attention, and constant hooting by the drivers, ended instantly. This was much to the relief of the street users—especially the business community. Also, air pollution from the exhaust pipes went down drastically as the buses were no longer there.

Why Did It Work? What Are the Lessons Learned?

Using the *Art of Knowledge Exchange* as a pretext and conduit for leadership messages and expectation on collaboration and co-creation in client services and innovation was made possible by a confluence of five factors:

First, the *Art of Knowledge Exchange* was—at the time the GSURR leadership tasked the team with customizing and rolling out across its 800 staff—an established methodology with a solid toolbox and track record.

Second, the process chosen by the team included a vision for scale-up and outreach. Thinking big right from the start allowed searching for opportunities to scale, partner, collaborate, and bring in champions.

Third, the bottom-up approach chosen for customization proved to be the right approach for creating ownership among staff, a common language, and an appreciation of the methodology. Casting a wide net to include stories and showcase examples can be a tightrope to walk, but it elevates the product's appeal, provides space for innovation, and builds staff's personal connection with the product. The decision to customize the *Art of Knowledge Exchange* by inviting GSURR staff to submit case stories and case examples from their work gave broader ownership of the product across the Global Practice and enabled the staff to see themselves as knowledge management agents while, at the same time, giving them a common approach and vocabulary.

Fourth, a significant effort was made to offer learning products and methodology to each staff member, finding ways to reach diverse groups and learning preferences. Buy-in from skeptical stakeholders came with opportunities for experiential learning. Instead of explaining the benefits of a well-designed knowledge exchange to external partners, the team offered opportunities to join one of GSURR's programs as a resource expert or participant so they could experience the power and impact of peer-to-peer learning firsthand. Importantly, the principles promoted by the *Art of Knowledge Exchange*, namely, the principles of peer-to-peer learning, were adopted in the development of the roll-out activities themselves. UNESCO, the Korea Research Institute on Human Settlements, Singapore's Center for Liveable Cities, and the United States National Oceanic and Atmospheric Administration are among the organizations that adopted elements of the *Art of Knowledge Exchange* principles and methodology after participating in GSURR-organized programs.

Fifth and finally, just as for all successful organizational change initiatives, strong leadership buy-in at the highest level and a broad enabling environment were critical. Support from GSURR's top leadership enabled champions at different levels to develop momentum and share their enthusiasm with staff across the practice.

Note

1 The Capacity Development Results Framework: A Strategic and Results-Oriented Approach to Learning for Capacity Development, The World Bank Group, Washington, DC. (See http://siteresources.worldbank.org/CSO/Resources/228716-1369241545034/The_Capacity_ Development_ Results_Framework.pdf

Chapter 10

It Takes Two to Tango

Organizational Capacity for Knowledge Sharing

Steffen Soulejman Janus

The Context: Why Country Capacity for Knowledge Sharing?

At 7:58 a.m. on Boxing Day (December 26) 2004, a 9.1 magnitude quake struck the northern coast of Sumatra in Indonesia. This set off what would become the deadliest tsunami ever recorded, killing over 230,000 people across 14 countries. The province of Aceh in Indonesia was particularly affected by the disaster. Confronted with a challenge of unimaginable proportions, the Indonesian government responded swiftly. Officials in central, regional, and local governments mobilized support to vast numbers of populations in dire need of help with medical treatment, shelter, sanitation, food, and other basic needs.

In 2011, several years after the tragic event, the Government of Indonesia reached out to the World Bank to request support with capturing and sharing its knowledge on disaster risk management (DRM). Many officials directly involved in the 2004 disaster response had already retired or were about to retire. Critical knowledge was about to get lost for disaster management authorities in Indonesia. At the same time, Indonesia received numerous requests to share its experience with large scale DRM. The challenge was clear: how could Indonesia retain its tacit knowledge from managing disasters to inform national and subnational disaster mitigation efforts and responses while also sharing the vast set of experiences with other countries who are facing similar risks?

Fast forward to March 2013 in a different continent. Following the national elections, Kenya embarked on an ambitious journey of decentralizing its governance, with the national government shifting significant powers to 47 counties. The idea of Kenya's devolution is simple: local governments are closer to the people they serve and can, thus, deliver selected services to local citizens more effectively. They can allow for more equitable allocation of resources and facilitate more meaningful participation of citizens in decision-making on matters that impact them directly. But the challenge was enormous. Establishing 47 governments with legislative and executive functions, building on previous institutional arrangements with insufficient capacity to take over the delivery of critical services required leadership, agility, and—lots of learning.

In 2017, Kenya's Council of Governors (CoG) approached the World Bank to get help with establishing a peer-learning and knowledge-sharing mechanism for and between counties. The CoG, itself a new institution that brings together the 47 county governors to facilitate policymaking and learning on devolution, required a practical platform that would allow policymakers and technical practitioners in counties to learn from experiences, good and bad ones, with devolved service delivery. How did a county achieve impressive targets on participatory budgeting? Which measures were taken by another county on improving

DOI: 10.4324/9781003199083-19

universal access to healthcare? What did a county do to increase its own source revenue? Champion counties quickly emerged in many different sectors and from all parts of the country. The idea was to develop a knowledge center that was able to identify, document, and facilitate the sharing of devolution experiences on a just-in-time basis.

A third example, in Latin America, had different circumstances but similar needs. With about 2.5 million people, Medellín is the second largest city in Colombia, after the capital Bogota. In 1990, Medellín was mainly known for its drug cartels and held the undesirable title of "most dangerous city in the world.,". Fast forward to 2014. Medellín's extreme poverty rate was reduced by 66 percent and its homicide rate slashed by a whopping 95 percent. The city had just been awarded the title of "most innovative city in the world" by the Urban Land Institute and had been tapped to host UN-Habitat's renowned World Urban Forum. How did a failed city transform itself into a model for cities around the world? The Medellín urban development experience is without a doubt inspiring, and many mayors and city administrations from Latin America and other regions wanted to learn about Medellín's success story. Faced with much demand, the city authorities, led by Medellín's international cooperation agency, ACI,[1] requested the World Bank to assist with strengthening institutional capacities to meaningfully share its experience with visitors. The goal was to move the knowledge-sharing efforts from an ad hoc model to a more systematic and results-oriented model. Where delegations had initially been put on a standardized tour, ACI wanted to facilitate a more individualized learning experience for selected delegations that were ready to affect change back home. In addition, ACI aimed to improve Medellín's external image as part of the city's efforts to increase foreign direct investments. Knowing that it is difficult to attract investors to put their money in a city with a reputation for crime and drugs, it was important for ACI to show the impressive transformation of Medellín to a city worth living and investing in.

These three examples from different sectors and geographic locations may, at first, not seem to have much in common. But upon closer examination, striking similarities emerge. Three commonalities particularly stand out: First, they all value local experience and solutions as an important source of innovation and development solutions. Second, all three recognized that peer learning can effectively complement structured learning, helping to strengthen public service capacities. And third, they all had the goal and strategic vision to tackle knowledge not as an ad hoc afterthought but to build or strengthen institutionalized knowledge functions. Let's look at these drivers for action more closely:

1. *The value of local experience and solutions*: Whether it is a local response to a tragic tsunami or earthquake or a quest to implement meaningful citizen engagement, often the most compelling solutions come from experiences that local stakeholders can relate to. Government officials and decision-makers in local institutions use peer institutions as benchmarks to measure performance. They get inspired by success stories and suboptimal outcomes inform their policy reform and implementation decisions. It is often easier to understand why a solution was effective and which steps had to be taken for it to work when one can relate to the local context in which it happened. While the idea is simple, development practitioners unfortunately often look for global good practice before making the effort to see what indigenous or local knowledge is already available. At the same time, this local knowledge can also inspire South-South learning between countries that grapple with similar development challenges.

2. *A recognition that peer learning can effectively complement structured learning: How do people learn?*: Most people will be influenced by their experience moving through the educational system from primary school up to a university degree. Much of this experience is part of a well-calibrated structured learning approach where one listens to and engages with a lecturer, teacher, and, in an ideal situation, with classmates. Effective adult learning relies heavily on the experience of peers. In fact, in many cases, they heavily complement or even replace the experience of a teacher. When policymakers meet for knowledge sharing, they tend to be practical and laser-focused on workable solutions. They want to learn to solve a problem quickly and effectively, ideally with the bonus of working with an approach that their neighbors have already successfully implemented.

3. *The goal to institutionalize knowledge functions:* Knowledge sharing is happening all the time. When someone discusses their experiences with colleagues or brainstorms on a solution with professional partners, they effectively share knowledge. Much of it is ad hoc and isn't something on which one focuses. Some development initiatives and projects use knowledge sharing strategically at the project level. They strengthen capacity of project teams to deliver on a task at hand, sending technical staff to participate in study tours and other peer-learning activities. But often, those capacities fade as project teams get dissolved once the project is finished. Governments, thus, increasingly aim to develop institutional capacities to document and share knowledge, to build resilience against brain drain from retiring or exiting staff, and to help take successful solutions to scale. The former is a matter of fostering sustainability, while the latter makes good sense economically and politically. Why reinvent the wheel and take the risk of a failure when a tried solution has better chances in succeeding?

This chapter discusses what it takes to get started and what implementation of a dedicated knowledge-sharing initiative can look like, building on the examples of Indonesia, Kenya, and Colombia. And while all three examples come from the public sector, it is noteworthy that most of the challenges, processes, and methodologies are applicable in the private sector as well.

Getting Ready to Support Organizational Knowledge Sharing

Investing in strengthening of organizational capacities for systematic capturing and sharing of experience is increasingly becoming an important strategic objective for organizations and country institutions around the world. On the other hand, many organizations are still struggling with setting up knowledge initiatives. Organizational change is difficult, knowledge often elusive, and progress notoriously difficult to measure. To further complicate matters, successful knowledge initiatives all have in common that they are based on strong ownership and participation of their constituents. In other words, one cannot buy a successful organizational change by just bringing in a competent external advisor or vendor.

With this discouraging backdrop, why did the World Bank invest in the knowledge and learning capacity of its clients? For the World Bank and particularly the GSURR Global Practice, this made good sense for three reasons: first, the World Bank's role as a convener and broker of knowledge across countries and regions requires strong counterparts at both the demand and supply side of the knowledge-sharing equation. GSURR, wanted to build networks of partners with several knowledge hubs as internationally recognized go-to places for practical peer learning. The example of TDLC in Japan, covered in Chapter 6, showcases the significant benefits of systematic peer learning. But for this to work across regions, inspiring and well-equipped partners are needed as sources of knowledge and solutions as are well-prepared knowledge-seeking organizations that understand what they want to learn. Second, the World Bank strives to strengthen country institutions as part of its operational work. The stronger the institution, the more likely a reform effort will succeed, no matter in what sector. In many developing countries, institutions and organizational capacities are weak. Moving beyond the traditional approach of building technical capacities on urban or social matters without addressing organizational culture and behavior change has proven insufficient. Organizations that are not making use of the collective brain power of their staff and constituents will be less likely to deliver programs and services effectively. Third, and maybe most importantly, there is a desire to ensure that organizational change is sustainable. Short-term successes of projects are nice, but the goal of any World Bank operation will always be a more long-term sustainability of the reform effort. This requires a solid foundation built on trust and partnership within and among partnering organizations. It requires culture change, ownership, and dedication.

The genesis of organizational knowledge sharing (OKS) was a response to the country-led efforts to establish South-South cooperation (SSC) as an important complementary approach to development effectiveness. In the late 2000s, the World Bank actively supported the desire, particularly of middle-income countries, like China, Brazil, India, Indonesia, Colombia, and Mexico, to facilitate more horizontal partnerships and triangular cooperation with traditional development partners. Working with the international Task Team on South-South Cooperation (TTSSC), the World Bank contributed to the successful establishment of SSC as a vital part of development effectiveness at the Busan High-Level Forum in 2011 and its inclusion in the G20 declaration shortly after. While these were tremendous political achievements, it was less clear how countries would go about institutionalizing South-South knowledge exchange (SSKE) in concrete terms.

The idea of client-driven organizational change was at the core of the World Bank's OKS program. Initially started at the World Bank Institute, OKS initiatives have been successfully implemented in many countries over the years. The objective at the time was twofold: strengthen country capacity for systematic knowledge sharing towards strong and independent knowledge hubs that can facilitate meaningful peer learning at scale and increase organizational performance and learning through better knowledge and learning systems. The former intended for the World Bank to gradually move towards a more wholesale model for SSKE as an alternative to the costly and time-consuming organization of bilateral one-off exchanges. The latter aimed to equip country institutions with knowledge and learning capacities that enable more effective delivery on their respective core mandates, usually service delivery to their citizens.

OKS engagements have proven a valuable resource as they decidedly don't focus on technical skills building alone but rather on developing a knowledge culture with strong incentives based on mutual trust among staff and management at all levels.

This is usually also the interest of top management of any organization. Therefore, and not surprisingly, the requests for assistance came from inspiring leaders who wanted to see transformational change in their organization and field of work. In Indonesia, the request to the World Bank for support to their newly created national disaster risk management agency BNPB[2] came directly from the head of the agency and cabinet minister, Pak Willem Rampangilei. The objective of BNPB's top management was to change the way learning on disaster happens in Indonesia. The agency invested in an impressive new training campus outside of Jakarta but felt the need for more transformative culture change in the organization. In Kenya, Jacqueline Mogeni, CEO of the Council of Governors, saw the need for the CoG to build institutional capacities to deliver on the council's mandate to facilitate peer learning among Kenya's 47 counties. A top-level vision and continuous support from senior management are vital for the success of any institution-wide knowledge initiative. They are also the starting point of the World Bank's support of organizational knowledge sharing.

Implementing an Organizational Knowledge Sharing Initiative

Developing knowledge-sharing capacities in an organization naturally requires more than just technical skills and systems. It is foremost a culture change process. The Organizational Knowledge Sharing Capacity Development Framework[3] (see Figure 10.1) includes both measures that address the enabling environment for knowledge sharing and learning and the technical competences needed to do it well. A total of eight pillars allow for a 360°-perspective of what organizations must think about when embarking on a change process to foster knowledge sharing, collaboration, and continuous learning from experiences. The first four pillars address the enabling environment for knowledge sharing, arguably the more difficult part to implement.

While there is not necessarily a fixed sequence at which to tackle these pillars, it is useful to start out with the leadership and organizational culture dimension. As a first pillar, it is critical to get a good understanding how motivated people are to document and share their tacit knowledge, how much it is valued and celebrated in the organization, and to what extent top- and mid-management role models transparent knowledge-sharing behavior. The second pillar focuses on the governance arrangements for knowledge and learning. It seeks to establish clear roles and responsibilities for knowledge- and learning-related activities and tasks. This pillar also covers the systems and platforms needed to support knowledge management. The third pillar looks at the critical dimension of funding. It is one thing for organizations to say they value knowledge sharing and learning but not all follow through and make it an investment priority as part of budget planning. The last pillar under the enabling environment dimension seeks to understand and build on internal and external knowledge partnerships. Knowledge sharing inherently requires at least two parties. Organizations can tremendously benefit from partnering with like-minded peers that can complement the existing knowledge pool. While issues of property rights and competition can hamper open sharing of selected knowledge between partners, this tends to be less of an issue in the public sector.

The second set of pillars focuses on technical skills, starting with building expertise on how to identify experiences that are worth sharing and documenting them in such a way that they become accessible for a future knowledge-sharing activity. Knowledge capture is somewhat of an art and the World Bank OKS program has developed a simple, yet effective methodology[4] to document tacit knowledge and experiences for sharing and scale up. The second technical pillar seeks to facilitate the packaging of knowledge into digestible and targeted learning objects which can be used for peer learning and in structured learning programs. This can be particularly useful for learning offerings that would benefit from more local examples to increase relevance for a particular audience. The third pillar in the technical skills category helps organizations and teams to both broaden and deepen their expertise on knowledge sharing itself, offering a wide array of instruments and tools

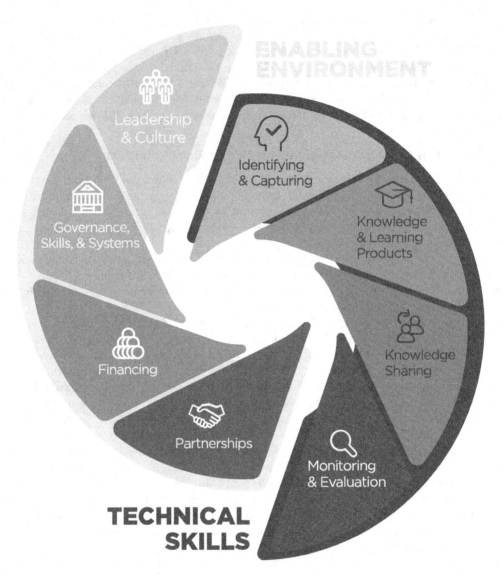

Figure 10.1 The Organizational Knowledge Sharing Capacity Development Framework

that facilitate knowledge sharing and peer learning in different circumstances. These are covered in some detail in Chapter 9 on 'The Art of Knowledge Exchange'. Lastly, a monitoring and evaluation pillar rounds off the framework with capacities and approaches to measuring progress towards becoming a knowledge-sharing organization.

So much for the theory. But how is this framework being applied in practice? Let's look at program implementation using the examples from Kenya, Indonesia, and Colombia. In all three cases, the engagement started with a multi-stakeholder assessment and visioning workshop where representatives from all departments and levels of seniority came together to develop a joint understanding of the current knowledge and learning performance of the organization. The self-assessment process took participants through a series of reflection exercises in different performance areas, followed by individual rating of a set of standardized indicators. This allows for surfacing of perceptions from different vantage points in the organization and to stimulate discussion on what works well already and where change is needed. It also initiates a first discussion across departments on knowledge sharing and learning as a strategic performance area. At Colombia's ACI, the assessment revealed the lack of a systematic approach and theory of change for documenting tacit knowledge as well as deficits in facilitating more outcome-based learning with visiting delegations as part of South-South knowledge exchanges. In Kenya, the participants from the Council of Governors secretariat recognized the lack of a clear governance function and lack of resources to facilitate knowledge sharing. Furthermore, the self-assessment revealed that staff were generally not motivated to share knowledge. Similarly, at Indonesia's BNPB, management realized the lack of interest and incentives to share knowledge with peers. A culture change was needed. Following the assessment and analysis of the status quo, the participants developed a joint vision of what the organization would become within three years. In the workshop in Kenya, the participants came up with the creation of a dedicated knowledge center. They even had a name for it: "Maarifa Centre"—the Swahili term for knowledge from experience and wisdom. The vision for Maarifa Centre was "to Be Kenya's Premier Devolution Knowledge Sharing and Learning Platform for Effective Governance and Service Delivery."

The agreement on current gaps and a future vision is critical as it allows the organization to set markers in a timeline for a change process. The logical next step is to fill this timeline with activities to address the deficits. Using an approach borrowed from rapid results initiatives, the participants agree on priority gaps and actions to be addressed in consecutive 100-day windows.

The most common gaps fall into four categories: culture, governance, systems, and competences. At Kenya's CoG, this led to the drafting of a knowledge management strategy, which became the overall strategic guideline for Maarifa Centre. It included guidance on incentive mechanisms and laid out the roles and responsibilities of the future knowledge team. It also defined the need for an online repository and a rich mix of knowledge-sharing activities. In 2017, Maarifa Centre made its first appearance with a flagship Innovation Forum on Kenya Devolution, bringing together participants from across the country to share their innovations in agribusiness, health care, youth employment, and last-mile service delivery. Participants were not only able to learn from peers about their solutions to common challenges but were also invited to sign up for bilateral follow-up meetings. The forum sparked numerous collaborations across the country, building on Maarifa Centre's ability to convene actors that shared innovations and those in need of solutions. As one participant put it:

"This Forum is an eye-opener for me. I had no idea there were so many of my colleagues working on solutions to some of the problems I have in my county. I am very inspired to use these innovations back home".

Another significant gap that exists in many organizations is a lack of technical capacity to design the appropriate platforms and systems that meet the needs of the organization, identify and capture relevant experiences, and select appropriate knowledge-sharing activities and instruments to facilitate outcome-oriented peer learning. In Colombia, the World

Bank team supported ACI with the development of a structured approach and templates to document experiences. This was complemented with the design of an in-depth peer learning program for international delegations interested in learning from Medellín's transformative urban development experience. This approach, dubbed the "Medellín Lab," brought together delegations from multiple cities for an exciting interactive learning program. The weeklong endeavor included experiential learning in an urban scavenger hunt through the city, small group sharing sessions, and a multitude of fun and creative exploration and learning activities. The goal: inspiring the participants with solutions that can inform decision-making back home.

Together with the World Bank, ACI organized two Medellín Lab programs, one on urban crime and violence prevention and one on integrated urban transformation. The second Medellín Lab was part of a programmatic initiative involving ten cities from Latin America, Africa, and East Asia. Following their learning journey in Medellín, the participating city officials came together again at learning lab events in Cape Town and Jakarta, while the city of Nairobi used its experience from these three learning labs to organize its own lab for cities from across Kenya (See Box 9.3 for more detail).

BNPB's top management was keen to identify the many relevant and innovative approaches to mitigating and responding to disasters across a vast country with densely populated cities and hard-to-reach remote areas. To document local solutions, the BNPB team used the OKS approach to documenting experiences. The 5-step process consisted of 1) identification, 2) capturing, 3) validation, 4) formatting, and 5) learning. For the identification and capturing steps, the World Bank trained a team of knowledge capturers that scouted and crowdsourced promising and successful solutions from across the country in various priority areas and documented them using standardized templates. A committee of experts was responsible for the validation of knowledge assets and to ensure quality control. The documented experiences were subsequently formatted and prepared for use as learning materials.

The length of the support engagements under the OKS program vary. But the examples from Kenya, Indonesia, and Colombia all benefited from an understanding that culture and behavior change will not come overnight. The collaboration with ACI in Colombia went over the course of three years, while, with BNPB in Indonesia, it was delivered over four years. In Kenya, the World Bank is now entering its fifth year of partnership with the Council of Governors on knowledge sharing.

Progress and Results

Results of organizational culture change programs and knowledge-sharing activities are notoriously difficult to measure, and attribution tends to be a challenge. But a few indicators can shed light on meaningful change that was inspired by peers who engaged in mutual learning. The following describes some examples of success stories, with an understanding that these are mere highlights as part of a long journey to becoming a knowledge-sharing organization.

Perhaps the most inspiring story of change at Indonesia's BNPB came from a shift in how the organization dealt with internal knowledge sharing and staff learning. Traditionally, this was exclusively done through classroom-based training that staff had to complete on a regular basis. As part of the OKS initiative, top management introduced a strong incentive for staff to regularly share their tacit knowledge and experience with peers. To collect necessary points to manifest readiness for career advancement, all staff had to share a relevant recent experience once a month with peers. For this, dedicated knowledge café rooms were established at BNPB's newly built headquarters. Knowledge-sharing sessions were organized almost daily, and staff invited to volunteer their experiences. Retirees, former high-ranking officers in the organization, joined the sessions as facilitators and provided feedback and reflections. The sessions were regularly frequented by top management, which provided an additional incentive for staff to be present. Over time, these knowledge-sharing sessions became an important mechanism to complement structured learning offerings with tacit knowledge from practical real-life experiences. Furthermore, BNPB has designed and implemented numerous knowledge-sharing programs with countries such as Myanmar, the Philippines, and Haiti, firmly establishing Indonesia as an important place for learning on effective DRM. Experiences such as emergency protocols for schools and factoring in indigenous knowledge and local wisdom in disaster preparedness plans have been successfully adopted in other countries.

In Kenya, the Maarifa Centre has become a recognized platform and go-to place for knowledge on the country's devolution journey. Its unique role as a knowledge and experience broker between counties has enabled the organization of numerous peer-learning programs and activities in various areas of devolved service delivery. Hundreds of inspiring solutions from all over Kenya have been documented and shared on its online platform.[5] While this is already quite an achievement, perhaps the most exciting success lies in the change these solutions have sparked in county governments. Whether it's an adoption of a new approach to solid waste management with inclusion of local micro-entrepreneurs or the use of participatory budgeting methodologies in previously skeptical county governments, knowledge shared by peers has sparked and informed development initiatives and programs across the country. In another example, the Maarifa Centre team has put together a compendium of local solutions to addressing the COVID-19 pandemic. Counties have access to practical approaches their peer counties have taken to get personal protective equipment, solidify local health care capacities, improve public information, and manage more equitable access to vaccines.

At ACI Medellín in Colombia, knowledge sharing continues to be an important pillar of the organization's partnership work with cities from around the world. Through the investment in further strengthening its knowledge-sharing capacity, ACI has delivered two high-profile Medellín Lab programs, which have sparked exciting replication efforts in the participating cities. City officials of Kinshasa have, for example, adopted the Medellín approach to participatory urban design and community engagement to ongoing urban renewal efforts as part of a World Bank–funded US$0.5 billion operation. In Nairobi, the learnings from the Medellín Labs have influenced the design of inner-city renewal activities. For ACI, the efforts have also paid off as they have solidified Medellín's ties with international partners outside of Latin America.

These are just some examples of how knowledge sharing, if done right, can result in meaningful change. What should we be looking for? The most optimal outcome is a replication or adaptation from a shared experience somewhere else. Other examples of successful sharing of experiences can be policymakers getting inspired to undertake reform efforts, the speeding up of decision-making processes, or implementation progress due to use of more effective tools or approaches. Organizational culture change indicators can include improved access to information and perception of transparency in decision-making processes, increased readiness to share knowledge with others because of more trust, and overall workplace satisfaction.

Lessons Learned

As any organizational change process, OKS engagements come with challenges that need to be carefully managed. Perhaps the most important one being the need to integrate knowledge and learning as part of the day-to-day work processes of management and staff. How can you create an entire knowledge ecosystem without it not adding to the existing workload? While knowledge and learning systems are not necessarily very budget intensive, OKS engagements do require investment of staff time. In environments where time is a scarce commodity, some department heads, managers, and staff push back on added responsibilities. Developing sound incentives for knowledge sharing is thus critical for success. In addition, knowledge and learning need to be firmly embedded in existing workflows.

To create buy-in across the organization, the OKS imitative team needs to work with all parts of the organization in a holistic manner to affect change. While top management tends to be on board rather quickly, seeing the opportunity for transformative change, middle management at times tends to be more resistant to change. It is, therefore, critical to get clarity on a shared problem and build ownership of the potential solutions first. This only works if all critical actors are part of the change process from the get-go.

For the success of knowledge initiatives in organizations, it has been very helpful to identify respected internal champions to take the lead in the change process of the organization. These champions don't necessarily have to come from top management although that is certainly helpful too. Ideally, knowledge champions are opinion leaders in the organization that build their reputation on informal leadership. They lead by example and inspire colleagues with their openness to share information and knowledge on relevant experiences and learnings.

Another lesson is to carefully weigh what can and should be outsourced and which capacities should be built in-house. While it may be, at times, easier and faster to hire external specialists to get the "knowledge-sharing job" done, this will likely not result in any sustainable institutional capacities. It is, therefore, advisable to map out key knowledge processes and tasks and make an informed decision on which of them should be staffed internally and which can be covered by external vendors. This is particularly relevant in the context of development projects, which tend to heavily rely on project management units that are assembled for a particular task and dissolved upon project completion. Unfortunately, this practice builds little institutional memory and much of the experiential knowledge acquired gets lost once project team members move on to new positions. Anchoring core knowledge functions institutionally tends to be more sustainable.

A related lesson learned is that knowledge management and learning require strong governance in the organization. This function should be centrally anchored with a direct line of sight to senior management and hands-on nodes in the operational departments. Building on a strong organizational knowledge-sharing culture where sharing and learning is everybody's business, dedicated staff and teams can provide an important guidance and support function.

This leads to the next lesson learned which emphasizes the need for adequate resources and funding. The work with country partners in Kenya, Indonesia, and Colombia was built on a strong commitment to funding of knowledge and learning activities. This facilitated investments in staff, platforms, and systems and made it much easier to plan for longer-term knowledge programs and activities and strategic planning of activities. If knowledge sharing remains an unfunded mandate that is nebulously mainstreamed in everyone's work programs without clear accountability and a budget commitment, it will likely fail. Knowledge and learning should be a fixture in yearly budget planning.

Lastly, an organizational change process takes time, and some of the investments in culture change and the setting up of organizational knowledge-sharing systems and processes require patience. Organizational knowledge-sharing capacity development is a marathon, not a sprint and, as development practitioners, we know that behavior change won't come over night. Firmly embedding knowledge and learning in long-term initiatives and partnerships with governments is both strategic—and increasingly welcome—by clients.

When getting started, the challenge may appear unsurmountable. As mentioned earlier, the OKS framework helped to provide a road map of priority areas to tackle. It is useful to work on achievable milestones and bring people along the journey of change. To keep the momentum over time, it is important to celebrate successes. As one example for recognition, the Maarifa Centre team in Kenya won second place at the 2018 Public Service Innovation Awards. Its work was showcased at different occasions internationally, for example, the fourth High-Level Meeting for Country-Led Knowledge Sharing in Bali (Indonesia). BNPB built in regular recognition by top management who joined knowledge-sharing events and activities and celebrated the knowledge-sharing work in internal communications.

What Is Next?

The important work on organizational knowledge sharing continues to exist at the World Bank. While there is currently no dedicated team for OKS work, the World Bank's support to country clients continues selectively as part of the World Bank's operational portfolio. For example, in an exciting engagement in Saudi Arabia, the team has just finished its support to the General Authority for Real Estate (REGA) with a strategic organizational knowledge-sharing program, and in Kenya, the work with Maarifa Centre is now being scaled up in counties. But more needs to be done. As many development projects nowadays include South-South knowledge exchange and offer bilateral peer-learning opportunities for policymakers and technical specialists, those activities tend to be isolated, project specific, and resource intensive. As more and more countries invest in the development of strategic knowledge capturing and sharing capabilities, development project teams will benefit from more streamlined, programmatic, cost-effective, and well-designed knowledge-sharing efforts. Development partners such as the World Bank will need to continue to lead the way to not treat OKS as an afterthought or "nice-to-have" but as a critical investment in the long-term performance improvement of country institutions.

The field of organizational knowledge sharing continues to bear tremendous opportunities, with multiple areas in need of further innovation. One of the big frontiers remains the development of effective knowledge hub entities in various development fields, building thriving and sustainable communities of practice across regional boundaries. Such knowledge hubs should ideally be country-led and supported by a wider coalition of partners. Furthermore, the COVID-19 pandemic has shown the tremendous scope with using the latest technologies and systems to facilitate knowledge sharing in a cost-effective and meaningful way. It will be exciting to see how these experiences can evolve into a future mix of blended knowledge-sharing programs. Lastly, more work needs to be done on monitoring and evaluation. Strengthening measurement of robust indicators and getting better data on the direct linkages of knowledge, performance, and results will be critical to convince some of the remaining skeptics.

Weak capacity of country institutions and private sector companies continues to be one of the major impediments to development. As more and more country partners embark on the rewarding journey of becoming knowledge-sharing organizations, we continue to learn more about how organizations learn and what makes them perform better. This is not only important domestically but can also have tremendous impact on peers in other countries. As one of the participants at the Medellín Lab in Colombia put it:

> *"It is so inspiring to see the city of Medellín thrive nowadays. I would not have thought such change was possible in such a short time. I go back home invigorated and ready to propose some of these innovative solutions to my teams. There is much to be done, but I know we can change our city too!"*

Notes

1 Agency for Cooperation and Investment of Medellín: www.acimedellin.org
2 BNPB: Badan Nasional Penanggulangan Bencana: www.bnpb.go.id
3 Janus, Steffen Soulejman. 2016. *Becoming a Knowledge-Sharing Organization: A Handbook for Scaling Up Solutions Through Knowledge Capturing and Sharing*. Washington, DC: World Bank.
4 Janus, Steffen Soulejman. 2017. *Capturing Solutions for Learning and Scaling Up: Documenting Operational Experiences for Organizational Learning and Knowledge Sharing*. Washington, DC: World Bank.
5 https://maarifa.cog.go.ke/

Chapter 11

Anywhere, Anytime

The Open Learning Campus

Sheila Jagannathan

Introduction

The World Bank's *Open Learning Campus* (OLC) plays a central role in fostering innovation and building capabilities suitable to assist World Bank staff and clients in accelerating the deployment of effective development solutions. It consists of three elements: a specialized team of learning science and technology specialists, a highly versatile online platform combined with multiple tools, and a virtual learning ecosystem that includes not only the OLC's own staff but also the decentralized learning and knowledge management teams that support each of the World Bank's Global Practices and other departments. For simplicity, these three elements will be referred to collectively as the OLC over the remainder of this chapter.

The OLC played an essential and supportive role for the World Bank's Social, Urban, Rural, and Resilience Global Practice (GSURR) during and after the reorganization into Global Practices that took place in 2014. Fitting with the mandate to facilitate cross-regional knowledge flows, the OLC offered geographically distributed staff and clients multiple and convenient opportunities to refresh skills and learn about innovations in various sectors on a continuous basis. Learning offerings channeled through the OLC allow staff and clients to jointly bridge knowledge gaps and to co-create integrated solutions to address complex development issues. Since its launch, more than 7 million learners from 190 countries have accessed the OLC, and approximately 6,000 digital learning activities have been designed and curated, gradually starting to realize the vision of the OLC as a destination of choice for development learning. In seven years, the face of client learning in the World Bank has completely "flipped," going from 95 percent face-to-face and 5 percent blended learning offerings to 95 percent digital and blended offerings combined with less than 5 percent face-to-face delivery.

Right from the beginning, the OLC was designed as a single destination for staff and client learning, taking a unique learner-centric approach. This decision had been foreshadowed by other developments, both inside and external to the World Bank, resulting in a setup that was rather distinct from that found in many other organizations where virtual learning tends to be limited to staff-only offerings, typically built on a learning management system that focuses on managing learning rather than on creating a positive user experience for the learner. The developments leading to the OLC's unique design included the continuing relocation of World Bank staff positions to country offices where staff could be closer to clients and more able to provide hands-on support for project implementation. The downside of decentralization was, however, that staff would have fewer face-to-face interactions with their peers at the World Bank headquarters in Washington, DC, missing the opportunity to benefit from learning from more experienced colleagues in other fields or listening to the insights offered by those working in different countries. At the same time, new approaches

DOI: 10.4324/9781003199083-20

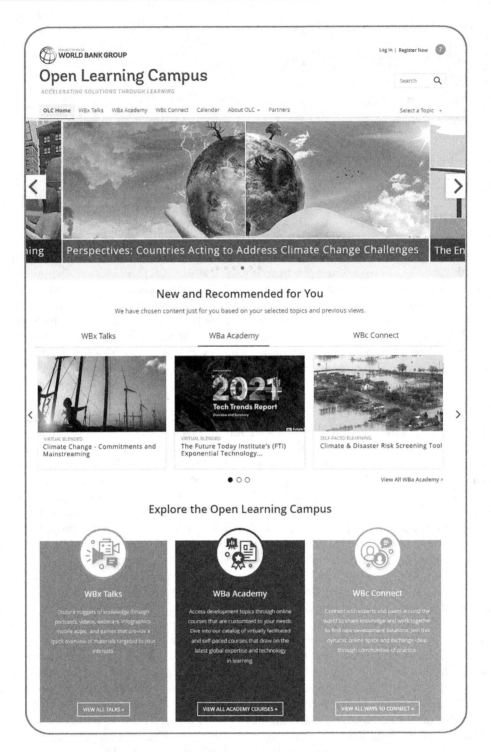

Figure 11.1 World Bank Group's Open Learning Campus Website

Source: Author generated

to innovation brought more interest in structuring staff-client collaboration in developing new solutions. Also, advances in technology resulted in improved internet access and in the availability of flexible choices for learners and more mobile devices made it convenient to use multiple formats of virtual learning—text, video, quizzes, online interaction, dialogue, and so on. Last but not least, innovations in pedagogical design and emerging educational technologies helped the OLC to emerge as a facilitator of continuous learning rather than offering the "document dump" that web-based learning had hitherto often come to be used as. The new designs took a learner-centric approach, offering attractive avenues for blended learning, including interactivity and learner engagement while also tracking outcomes

Offering Multiple Entry Points: The OLC's Three Schools

In catering to different learning needs and styles, the OLC, right from the start, created opportunities for staff and clients to participate through one of three "schools." This allowed moving away from weeklong courses of formal learning to flexible learning pathways more fitting for the busy practitioner:

1. *WB Talks (WBx)*: This school enables busy professionals to explore nuggets of knowledge through micro-learning in the form of video talks, podcasts, videos, knowledge notes, games, and apps. In compiling the WBx offerings, the OLC team curates knowledge products focused on capturing tacit knowledge such as Independent Evaluation Group lessons or the International Finance Corporation's SMARTLessons.
2. *WB Academy (WBa)*: This school helps learners unpack deep learning related to development challenges and solutions through virtually facilitated or self-directed e-courses, massive open online courses (MOOCs), and blended learning.
3. *WB Connect (WBc)*: This school enables learners to engage with others to find crowdsourced solutions to development challenges. Using a range of tools, from social media to mobile texts, knowledge exchange can be promoted between clients, partners, and global citizens. Examples of such topical communities include urban floods, smart cities, integrated water management, and land and house thematic groups.

For example, a city planner can access bite-sized learning modules on energy efficiency through WBTalks (WBx), learn more about the relationship between energy policies and climate participate in a massive open online course (MOOC) through the WBAcademy (WBa), and thereafter engage with colleagues in a related community of practice through WBConnect (WBc).

Working With Technical Teams to Leverage Dynamic and Innovative Pedagogical Approaches

The OLC's team of learning specialists worked intensively with World Bank technical teams to facilitate adoption of some of the best ideas from advances in science, pedagogy, and technology for adult learning. Over time, the experience in developing and offering learning opportunities was translated into a series of simple OLC methods or practices (Figure 11.3), applied uniformly across most offerings. In essence, learning programs developed for busy development practitioners must focus on *practical solutions* to complex development challenges (as opposed to theoretical or conceptual); offer *experiential and project-based* learning approaches; include opportunities for *peer-to-peer exchanges* on challenges; and be characterized by *interactivity* in terms of engaging with content, experts, and peers. Tools often used to translate these methods into an actual learning offering include but are not limited to gamification, mobile telephony, engaging virtual classrooms, social collaboration, and virtual and augmented reality.

As a result of OLC offerings deploying innovation in learning methods and tools, using mobile, social media channels, and classrooms on the cloud, continuous learning has been made possible based on flexible timing and personalization that no longer require waiting for periodic training events. Allowing for *just-in-time* and *just-enough learning*, World Bank staff and clients now can learn on-the-go; recommend and rate learning; embed learning in the flow of their work so it is available at the exact point of need; access personalized learning pathways that balance formal, informal, macro, micro, and on-the-job learning experiences; and connect to peers across the globe who face similar challenges.

The OLC team invested, in particular, in promoting collaborative learning as studies have shown that where virtual courses include team collaboration components, participants are 5 times more likely to sign on more frequently, 2 times more likely to remain active on the site, and 3 times more likely to contribute to discussions, according to internal participant evaluations. Virtual learning can be a lonely experience, so introducing a cohort-based, facilitated learning environment, where learners interact for four to six weeks, leads to more benefits than learning alone in a purely self-paced setting.

Box 11.1 Open Learning Campus Examples for Leveraging Collaborative Settings in Online Learning

Share peer group good practices: An urban planning course discussed how to make roads that are currently dominated by cars accessible to pedestrians. Inviting practitioners from New York City (US), which has pedestrianized parts of the city (such as Broadway), into a virtual conversation via webinars to discuss the technical, political, and social aspects of bringing about the change made a huge difference. A follow-up e-discussion with planners from cities in World Bank client countries (such as Mumbai, India) resulted in designs of own action plans for implementing these ideas in local contexts.

Crowdsource solutions through e-discussions: E-discussions can help identify solutions for local problems, such as littering of streets. The e-discussions could generate innovative ideas of how to combine community engagement with enforcing regulations and securing political support from local leadership. Participants in the course use the ideas to develop their own local solutions.

Co-create policy solutions via small group collaboration: In a municipal finance course, small groups were asked to develop a policy framework based on what they learned as well as their own experiences on how to raise local revenues to support municipal services. The results were then shared with the plenary for feedback, leading to improvements and more learning.

Provide mentoring and coaching by experts: In a smart city–planning course, an expert on big data and the Internet of Things guided participants to discover the benefits of building a digital platform for city governance. Through demonstrations of practical applications and virtual site visits, participants were introduced to the digital tools and then given an opportunity to discuss the extent to which these tools apply in their contexts and how they can be customized.

The OLC has also successfully blended e-learning modules with face-to-face sessions. For example, under a program financed by Korea, lending and learning have been synergized through blended learning programs that bring together World Bank project task teams with their client counterparts. For example, the OLC and GSURR teams collaborated for delivery of a blended learning program on solid waste management under this modality, partnering with the Korea Research Institute on Human Settlements.

Integrating Different Sources of Knowledge and Enhancing Access: Benefits for Staff and Clients

Internally, the shift in the learning approach created key benefits for staff. The OLC offers a unified calendar and a one-stop shop for learning products services, overcoming earlier fragmentation. World Bank staff, 50 percent of whom operate out of country offices, are provided opportunities for continuous upskilling to facilitate growth and career mobility. A standardized suite of learning services is offered to all major learning providers across the World Bank, International Finance Corporation, and Multilateral Investment Guarantee Agency, providing consistent learner experiences and the opportunity to learn together with many others from across the organizations. Centralized monitoring of all learning data, including expenditures and learning effectiveness, allows for continuous improvements for learners and the OLC.

Externally, the shift created key benefits for clients' learning, massively enhancing accessibility of World Bank knowledge. In collaboration with Global Practices and the regional departments, the OLC team systematically converts World Bank Group flagship

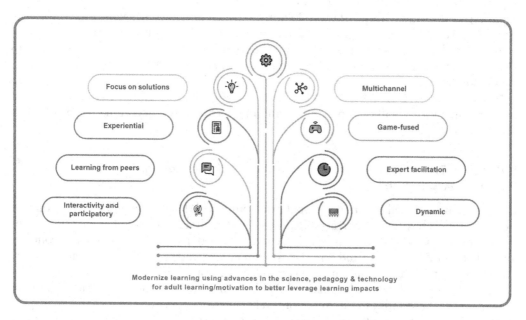

Figure 11.2 Open Learning Campus Methods for Learning to Leverage Impact
Source: Author generated.

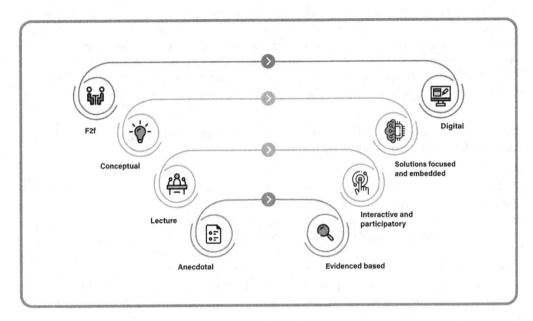

Figure 11.3 Shifts in Learning Methods Through the Open Learning Campus
Source: Author generated.

reports into actionable learning products for broader audiences. For example, the OLC repackaged the *World Development Report 2020 Trading for Development in the Age of Global Value Chains* as a MOOC, mobilizing some 35,000 learners from 192 countries; similarly, solid waste management e-courses based on the World Bank Flagship *Waste 2.0* engaged 100 policymakers and practitioners globally, according to internal OLC statistics.

Not surprisingly, learner feedback has been overwhelmingly positive: over 95 percent of learners rated the overall quality of OLC offerings as favorable, according to participant's evaluations.

Balancing Global Access With Local Specificities: Learning Partners Around the World

In recognizing the need to balance global availability with local or country-specific dimensions, the OLC has forged partnerships with select regional and country partner institutions. The partners work on customizing content to better meet local needs and contexts and deliver products locally and often by combining face-to-face settings with virtual tools. For example, the OLC maintains a successful partnership with the Chinese Academy of Governance to translate and localize a global learning program on sustainable urban land use planning. Thousands of mid- to senior-level Chinese civil servants participate in the program annually, benefiting from both the World Bank Group's knowledge and connections and the Academy's expertise as well as from the peer-to-peer learning experience facilitated by the latter. Interestingly, this partnership goes back several decades and has evolved over the years from distance learning via CD-ROM to live videoconferencing and, finally, to blended learning.

Putting the Open Learning Campus to the Test: Learning in Times of COVID-19

The COVID-19 pandemic abruptly pivoted the entire learning community worldwide from in-person to virtual learning. In March 2020, the OLC also moved to 100 percent virtual learning programs for staff and clients. Years of investment in learning infrastructure and learning services paid off, including the state-of-the art technical infrastructure to host and deliver virtual programs, the ability to offer 24/7 support services for learners, combined with an in-house pedagogical design team, and a supporting network of e-learning vendors that enabled the creation of high-quality learning products.

Beyond the OLC, many operational teams also began offering learning virtually, mostly based on videoconferencing and not benefiting from the pedagogical experiences and tools that had come to characterize OLC offerings. Initially, the quality of digital learning was variable, with long videoconferencing sessions being a common criticism. Gradually, the OLC team started supporting the World Bank Group learning community with clinics, one-on-one coaching, templates, and a knowledge resource hub to improve the engagement and interactivity of virtual programs.

Feedback during this abrupt transition indicated that learners' expectations had changed—they were no longer willing to passively sit through seemingly endless presentations. Instead, presentations were scheduled for pre-watching and then introduced through live sessions, followed by group discussions and collaboration. In addition, to avoid "video conference fatigue" and to engage global learners, the OLC implemented new and innovative delivery modes, combining live webinars with asynchronous learning bundles, virtual field visits, e-discussion forums, active assignments, and interactive e-books. Post-COVID, the impact of these innovations is being evaluated, with more experimentation and research to improve active learning within fully digital spaces, optimize engagement in small groups, and encourage social connections.

Good learning design overcomes distraction and digital exhaustion, engages learners, and leads to successful outcomes. COVID-19 demonstrated how replicating in-person learning experiences is more than organizing Zoom sessions: it requires an artful blend of two design approaches, both *synchronous* (in real-time, fixed times both in-person or online) and *asynchronous* (any time, any place, at the learner's convenience).

Understanding the Effectiveness of Open Learning Campus Offerings: Overwhelmingly Positive

In its simplest form, learning effectiveness refers to the quality of the learning experience, and measuring seeks to assess whether the learning program met its intended goals and objectives. Typically, career progression, professional interest, or performance enhancement are primary motivators for staff and clients to participate in learning programs.

The OLC uses three questions to understand how far the overall learning objectives are achieved.

1. *Overall quality*: How would you rate the overall quality of the program?
2. *Skills gained*: Did your knowledge or skills increase as a result of participating in this program?
3. *Job impact*: How would you rate the relevance of the program as it relates to your work or job responsibilities?

Feedback received from participants between July 2017 through May 2021, totaling over 2,500 responses across 40 learning programs, has been overwhelmingly positive, according to internal OLC statistics. While over 90 percent of respondents had confirmed their professional- or performance-related interest as a reason to participate, over 96 percent of respondents rated the overall quality of the learning program at 5 or higher (out of a 1–7 scale), over 94 percent rated the job impact 5 or higher, and over 97 percent rated skills gained 5 or higher. Among participating staff, respondents rated the overall quality of the World Bank Group staff learning program at 95 percent; participating clients rated the overall quality of client learning even slightly higher. The comments left by respondents as part of the internal OLC feedback survey are illuminating and show, in particular, for participating clients, how valuable insights gained from and connections made through OLC courses can be for policymakers at all levels in World Bank client countries.

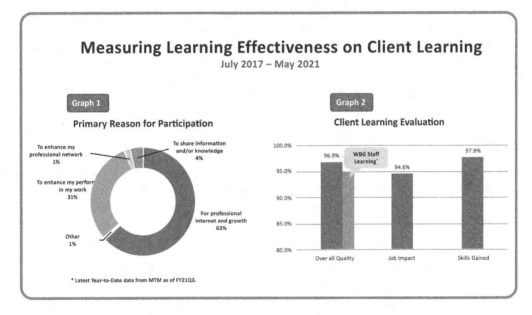

Figure 11.4 Feedback on the Effectiveness of Staff and Client Learning (July 2017–May 2021)
Source: World Bank OLC data.

Box 11.2   Respondents' Anecdotal Feedback on Plans to Apply Their Learning

Smart Cities for Sustainable Development (Virtual Knowledge Exchange)

- Being a policeman, it helps me to secure my area in a better manner with new tools available for evidence gathering and for better police services delivery.
- I would share my knowledge and skills gained through the course within the ministry and projects undertaken here in Tonga. Further, I would contribute on town planning being conducted on relocation and planning for suitable sites to establish the government's development initiatives.
- I plan to apply the knowledge I gained from this course on smart cities to develop myself professionally, so as to achieve a safer environment and sustainable development in Africa and worldwide.
- I work as a city planner; therefore, I will draft strategies learned in this course to place my city on the way to become a smart city. I know there will be challenges to implementation, but a start needs to be made as the city is growing at a fast pace.

Urban Upgrading for Inclusion, Sustainability, and Resilience in a Time of Global Pandemics

- Coming from a more technical (GIS) background, it is critical to have this knowledge when applying GIS to upgrading projects. I am working on two World Bank–financed lending projects that have upgrading components, so the materials, case studies, and sources presented in this course serve as good references as we move forward to implementation.
- I used the knowledge to prepare a new operation on urban upgrading for the north of Mozambique that will benefit informal settlements.

Strengthening Geospatial Information Management: Using the Integrated Geospatial Information Framework

- The course enhanced my conceptual understanding about geospatial information and equipped me with various implementation tools and ideas. I found it practical and the knowledge and skills can be applied in disaster risk management and resilience building efforts.
- I used the knowledge I gained to implement a strengthened geospatial data infrastructure in my country to help achieve an integrated decision-making solution for sustainable development.
- I used the knowledge and understanding gained from this course to modify our country-level action plan, aligned to our national priorities.

Offering Monitoring and Evaluation of Learning: Campus Services for the World Bank Teams

Apart from annual reports on learning, the OLC also provides monitoring and evaluation services to the World Bank Group's learning community, including coordinators and their managers and directors—essentially to anyone interested in better understanding learning uptake, delivery quality, and expenditure.

- *Corporate evaluations* measure inputs, outputs, and outcomes of learning, which allow senior management to forecast human capital investments while optimally prioritizing scarce resources. The latter involves predicting future performance and identifying scrap learning (no longer relevant modules) to better manage learning investments.
- *Self-service reporting dashboards* allow for on-demand generation of corporate reporting and indicators at the Vice Presidential Unit (VPU) and GP levels. These include:

  - Corporate quarterly reports and data on key performance indicators, such as quality, relevance, and impact.
  - Participation and activity reports.
  - Monthly raw data distribution to learning coordinators and designated contacts.

- *On-demand data* is provided as customized Excel reports to help with data needs when developing learning programs or reporting on staff learning for VPUs or units.
- *Clinics and coaching services* are offered to build capacity on how to analyze, use, and detect trends from available reports and analytics.

Lessons From the Open Learning Campus Experience: What Worked Well?

Shifting from a fragmented learning landscape to a single destination for development learning—Prior to the OLC, most World Bank Group departments had ad hoc approaches to staff and client learning. Even during the times of the World Bank Institute (WBI)—the World Bank's own client learning department—there was no single platform for learning, no central calendar that would summarize all World Bank Group learning activities, therefore not allowing for consistent learning experiences and forgoing the opportunity for organization-wide tracking and managing learning usage, participation, and expenditures. The OLC successfully instituted an ecosystem approach to learning and addressed several concerns that had been raised by the Staff Engagement Survey and World Bank Group International Evaluation Group review on learning participation and expenditures. A notable internal concern was prioritizing career development opportunities for staff, many of whom were located in geographically dispersed time zones. Externally, World Bank Group client and partners were interested in learning and co-creating solutions from the vast repository of knowledge within the World Bank Group on what worked and what did not work.

Modernizing learning by leveraging lessons from the global revolution in learning—Technology is changing the learning landscape, and the OLC represents the World Bank Group's commitment to harnessing the global revolution in learning in support of efforts to lift people out of poverty and promote shared prosperity. Inspired by the success and credibility of proven approaches to online learning, the OLC has facilitated a fundamental shift from traditional learning to an open, interactive, and networked learning ecosystem. Through its offerings, the OLC makes much of the World Bank Group's vast knowledge accessible, often transforming tough-to-digest reports into learning that is actionable. OLC offerings provide dynamic learning opportunities where diverse audiences can learn at their own pace and access the knowledge they need.

Building bridges between people to learn and connect—Apart from the challenges of decentralization, staff across the World Bank face complex development obstacles that require them to upskill and reskill on an ongoing basis. Staff interactions with clients increasingly require the co-creation of knowledge, development of collective vision, and ability to work across sectors in teams rather than just relying on domain knowledge and experience. OLC programs have contributed to building and nurturing these connections. Such programs help build bridges between new and more experienced staff and among people across physical distances, allowing decentralized teams to engage in joint staff and client learning.

Transforming global knowledge into actionable learning—In collaboration with units across the World Bank, the OLC designs and disseminates cross-sectoral learning on emerging World Bank priorities as accessible insights and lessons to World Bank Group clients, partners, donors, and staff. One to two flagship reports from almost all Global Practices were packaged into interactive learning modules to broader audiences as global public goods. Equally significant is the unpacking of deep learning related to development challenges and solutions through virtually facilitated or self-directed e-courses, MOOCs, and materials from face-to-face courses. Client learning curricula are continuously updated with insights on how changes in the external environment or through policy innovations are influencing development outcomes. The OLC's differentiated learning instruments and engagement models are available through a digital platform for flexible access.

Being recognized by external clients, partners, and donors—The OLC has received widespread recognition as a leader for disseminating actionable, flexible learning packaged in digital and blended formats to worldwide audiences as global public goods. Its role as an innovator and leader in the development learning space attracts donor funding for the design and dissemination of client capacity development programs. In addition, it enjoys a partnership with a network of national and regional institutions to help achieve scale and impact by promoting shared value propositions, bridging cultural and geographical gaps, and disseminating customized learning through existing infrastructures. The benefits to development learning through the OLC have been widely appreciated by donors. During the COVID-19 pandemic, the OLC's contributions became particularly evident: The World Bank Group was able to pivot 100 percent to virtual learning for staff and clients almost at the start of the pandemic.

Lessons From the Open Learning Campus Experience: What Can Be Improved

The World Bank's organizational culture must not prioritize operational delivery over learning—World Bank staff are often overworked and operate under intense pressure from multiple stakeholders, including their clients and superiors. As a result, the ability to allocate the time they would need to learn and keep up-to-date professionally is often crowded out. This also plays out throughout the project cycle: once a project design is agreed upon with a client and internally with World Bank management, incentives to revisit the design based on either new evidence or fresh learning insights diminish. The reason: both the client and World Bank management recognize and reward teams that successfully deliver projects within an agreed time frame. New learning insights could potentially disrupt project preparation processes because they call for reworking solutions and even re-engineering designs. A culture of learning is organically created only when staff receive recognition, career growth, or other benefits through continuous learning.

Teams and individuals need to go beyond siloed knowledge—Many of today's most pressing development challenges—such as climate change, pandemics, and the fragility of institutions—call for working across sectors and thematic disciplines. However, professionals with years of operational experience and impressive technical credentials often do not have the opportunity—or sometimes the inclination—to listen to new ideas and adopt them when they come from clients, external sources, or from team members who bring other sectoral perspectives. Digital information easily integrates diverse sectoral datasets, and big data analytics offer insights and possible solutions to multisectoral development challenges in relation to climate, pandemics, or poverty alleviation. Such datasets should become the foundation for cross-sectoral learning programs that combine topics such as energy, water, transport, health, and education.

Incentives for unlearning, reskilling, and upskilling should be set clearly and strongly— Digital applications through machine learning and AI improve our understanding of how and why intended and unintended consequences of policies and investments take place. Staff and clients could benefit by diffusing an organizational culture that recognizes that learning does not end with academic and professional degrees but, rather, is a continuous process that may require *unlearning* long-held beliefs and practices and periodic reskilling and upskilling. For example, an urban planner designing a smart city project today needs to appreciate how energy, water, and mobility systems design are integrated to achieve low-carbon outcomes. The digital tools to achieve these cross-sectoral themes were not available 10 or 15 years ago when perhaps the person had graduated from a university. Organizational incentives need to signal that continuous learning by staff is required for a successful career.

Innovative learning tools and techniques would work miracles when used as part of operational projects—Leveraging modern learning tools and techniques could substantially enhance World Bank operational projects, such as through gaining insights in real time that could improve ongoing processes and inform future projects. Such systematic capture of learning during implementation was impossible in the past, but this is now feasible as a result of rapid digitalization and tools to strengthen feedback loops in real time. These value-added tools and services could be leveraged by operations staff at critical points in the project cycle, such as preparation, implementation, and completion. For example, at the project preparation stage, tools are available to diagnose individual and project team learning needs; at the implementation stage, the OLC's WBx and WBc schools provide 24/7 access to just-in-time micro-learning and communities of practice. At the project completion stage, tools can distill and share lessons learned to improve the design of future projects and provide insights for other GPs.

Technical teams should consider adopting an integrated, programmatic, and curricular approach to capacity building—Many well-designed courses are available on priority topics, such as solid waste management or smart cities. Excellent quality of content, design, and the participation of world-class facilitators lead to great demand from staff and clients alike. However, often absent is the availability of intermediate and advanced courses on the same topics. What is needed is a curricular approach to high-priority topics that goes beyond basics and builds out a learning path. Learning programs need to transition from one-off courses to a learning journey (over a 3- to 6-month time frame) that includes learning modules to raise awareness and provide opportunities to apply and transfer the learning through on-the-job experiences, continuous feedback, and follow-up. This integrated, curricular approach to capacity building can lead to improved performance outcomes aligned closely with the business goals of the organization.

The Future of Learning for Development Professionals: Leadership Matters

However pressing the needs for reskilling may be and however impressive educational technologies, immersive techniques, or new design approaches might be considered, the uptake of learning innovation depends entirely on the leadership of and across an organization. Managers and leaders, including clients, have an important advocacy role to play in this regard.

The OLC's virtual learning ecosystem offers an impressive and wide-ranging set of learning opportunities. Through its three "schools," the OLC enables development lessons to be available to learners adjusted to their needs—just-in-time and versatile in formats, using innovations in technology, neuroscience, and pedagogy. The technology is available, and teams are skilled in deploying pedagogical innovations. What is now needed is for organizations to encourage a culture of continuous learning. Blended and collaborative learning opportunities are indispensable to better understand and co-create solutions to urgent development problems, including climate change, pandemics, fragility and conflict, and urban planning.

Box 11.3   Today's Learning Ecosystems Offers the Flexibility to Continuously Learn or Unlearn

Traffic congestion and air pollution are chronic issues for developing countries that are designing urban spaces centered on vehicles and workplaces. Repurposing public thoroughfares for pedestrians and encouraging workplace and leisure commuters to use public transit instead of individualized transportation have the potential of improving the quality of life for all citizens under specific conditions. For example, digital apps can ensure that timely public transportation is available for both work and leisure. Amenities, such as water fountains, street lighting, and waste removal, provide comfort to shoppers. Tax collections from consumer spending in the city are instantly credited to the municipality to boost revenues. Hundreds of such innovations are taking place in cities around the world. More importantly, this knowledge is digitally available, so it can be packaged into accessible learning modules for individuals and organizations to learn, customize, and apply just-in-time to address local priorities. Many of these involve South-South learning in the sense that relevant innovations take place in similar socioeconomic contexts. Furthermore, the combination of digital availability of knowledge and enhanced communications technologies and platforms provides unique opportunities for co-creation of solutions to shared problems. edX and other online learning platforms have played a critical role in just-in-time access. For example, when the pandemic struck in March 2020, about 50,000 persons enrolled in edX courses and learned how to intubate and safely treat COVID-19 patients while protecting themselves from contracting the virus.

References

Agarwal, A. (2020, June). Blended learning is the "new normal" and here's why. *edX Blog*. Retrieved from https://blog.edx.org/blended-learning-new-normal

Arisona, S. (2018, July). The cityengine VR experience for unreal engine: A virtual reality experience for urban planning applications. *ArcGIS blog*. Retrieved from www.esri.com/arcgis-blog/products/city-engine/design-planning/ce-ue4-vr-experience

Berge, Z. L. (1995). *The Role of the Online Instructor/Facilitator*. Retrieved from https://courses.dcs.wisc.edu/design-teaching/FacilitationManagement_Spring2016/facilitation-module/1_Online_Instructor_Roles/resources/roi_Berge-Role%20of%20the%20Online%20Instructorr.pdf

Caro, R. (1975). *The Power Broker: Robert Moses and the Fall of New York* (Robert A. Caro). Retrieved from www.robertcaro.com/the-books/the-power-broker/

Eesley, C. (2014). Online learning is most effective in teams. *NovoEd*. Retrieved from www.novoed.com/resources/insights/stanford-chuck-eesley-study-shows-efficacy-of-team-based-online-learning/

Hiipakka, J., and Chelsey, T. (2019). Four practices to embed learning in the flow of work. *Deloitte Research Article, Deloitte Consulting*. Retrieved from https://www2.deloitte.com/content/dam/Deloitte/us/Documents/human-capital/us-human-capital-bersin-lt-litfow-embed-learning_05–2019.pdf

Jagannathan, S. (2021). *Reimagining Digital Learning for Sustainable Development: How Upskilling, Data Analytics, and Educational Technologies Close the Skills Gap*. Routledge (ISBN 9780367545604).

Jamei, E., Mortimer, M., Seyedmahmoudian, M., Horan, B., and Stojcevski, A. (2017). *Investigating the Role of Virtual Reality in Planning for Sustainable Smart Cities*. Basel: MDPI. Retrieved from www.mdpi.com/2071-1050/9/11/2006

Kirkpatrick, J. D., and Kirkpatrick, W. K. (2016, October). *Kirkpatrick's Four Levels of Training Evaluation*. ATD Press (ISBN 9781607280088).

WEF (World Economic Forum). (2020, October). *The Future of Jobs Report 2020*. World Economic Forum. Retrieved from www.weforum.org/reports/the-future-of-jobs-report-2020

Chapter 12

Low Tech for High Stakes

Service Desks

Pascal Saura

Background—Help Desks and Service Desks

Service desks—an important tool in the organizational knowledge management treasure chest—deliver more than meets the eye, putting a veil over the complex systems that enforce a virtuous cycle of knowledge. Hardworking service desks both leverage and enable a robust architecture of people (e.g., experts, communities of practice, partnership platforms); processes (e.g., knowledge capture, curation and codification, content management, knowledge sharing, dissemination, performance tracking); and resources (e.g., funding, knowledge systems). The optimal configuration for a service desk operating at the scale of an entire organization offers an interesting combination of narrow verticals and broad horizontals, relying on a fine network of communities of practice that are deeply connected to specific topics but also interacting across a corporate architecture and common processes.

History of Help and Service Desks at the World Bank

Many, if not most, thematic departments in the World Bank have operated a help desk at some point in their organizational history, including the Water, Social Development, Governance, and Transport departments. A help desk is focused on a "break-fix" model—what the information technology infrastructure library calls "incident management"—whereas a service desk is there to assist with not only break-fix but also with requests for contextualized advice and new services (IBM IT Infrastructure Library ITIL).[1]

The help desks operated by various departments in the World Bank have varied greatly, in shape and resources and in value delivered, and, at times, were stripped to the bones, down to minimalistic designs that involved nothing but an email distribution list used to circulate questions and hope for answers. Some did not last long or did not go beyond offering one-off answers that would be volunteered by whoever the expert was that happened to be available when questions arose. Experience shows that the more complex the topic, the more one must invest in maintaining a credible service—not just in terms of funding but also in terms of enterprise-wide knowledge systems, information management standards, and knowledge management and learning processes. Whereas cross-cutting functional areas such as accounting, information technology and operational procedures effortlessly maintain long-lasting and well-structured help desks, thematic and sectoral business units typically have had mixed results. Some have staying power; others never really take off. What makes these help desks different from an information technology hotline? Why do they tend to fail and how can they succeed?

DOI: 10.4324/9781003199083-21

Beyond handing over information or data to a client, the service desk should answer four-dimensional questions, that is, *knowledge* questions. Knowledge questions are four-dimensional in the sense that they probe for answers relevant to a place (geography, political economy, culture), a topic (sector, expertise, theme), an activity (advising, preparing, implementing, lending, assessing) and a time (yesterday, 10 years ago, right now, tomorrow, in 6 months). Across these four dimensions, a knowledge question may involve many people, such as beneficiaries, policymakers, experts, and development practitioners, which is one reason why people rather than machines often answer knowledge questions. There is an obvious difference between a question that reads: "Where can I find the latest report on flood management techniques?," which looks for a simple piece of information that an information bot could pull, and one that asks: "What can be done in the future to better prevent floods in the state of Assam?," which is a four-dimensional *knowledge* question. The second question also commands an entirely different response if any aspect of it changes, be it localization, topic, activity, or time. Traditional help desks—with tools such as knowledge systems, online libraries, and lists of frequently asked questions (FAQs)—have limits in answering knowledge questions. Service desks, however, are specifically designed to provide the additional layer that will address the four dimensions of any knowledge question.

What happens when someone sends a question? To the requester, it should feel like the best available knowledge and the most relevant contacts just fell into their lap in a matter of hours. To the team in charge, the process can be roughly outlined as a set of activities comprising analysis and triage, information gathering, expert consultation, consolidation of answers, communication, capture and codification of solutions, case filing, and evaluation. Beyond providing codified information, service desks deliver knowledge solutions, which can only be achieved with the full commitment of management and the participation of thriving communities of practice, as evidenced in the case of *Ask Water*, the World Bank Water Department's service desk.

AskWater

The World Bank's Water Global Practice has been operating a service desk named AskWater since 2016. Introduced in the aftermath of the 2014 reorganization of the World Bank Group, *Ask Water* has managed close to 1,500 cases with user satisfaction rates hovering around 90 percent approval and a user base covering 70 percent of its target population. An internal service open to all staff, *Ask Water* was awarded a prize in 2021 by the World Bank's management team, and it is still in operation.

Ask Water's knowledge services cover country-specific questions and directly benefit World Bank client countries. For example, *Ask Water* accompanied the creation of the first National Water Institution in Papua New Guinea, informed the dialogue with Cape Town through the "Day Zero" crisis, and helped deploy water information systems in Nicaragua, Dominican Republic, the Lake Victoria basin countries, and Moldova to name a few. It provided benchmarking and lessons learned for the establishment of countless water supply and sanitation national strategies. Connecting challenges and solutions around the world, the *Ask Water* service desk linked a project on urban stormwater management in Djibouti with findings from Brazil and approached fecal sludge management challenges in Lusaka using past successes in Sri Lanka, where it also helped pilot payments for ecosystem services. Beyond answering questions, the service desk supports experimentation: engagement with private sector operators in Bangladesh, involvement of women in water resources management bodies in Peru, wastewater surveillance methodologies to detect new waves of COVID-19 infections in Ecuador and Uruguay, and hotspots in Kenya, among many others.

Box 12.1   *AskWater* in action

In May 2021, a World Bank manager contacted the service desk for an urgent briefing with UNICEF about providing refugees with water sanitation and hygiene services (WASH). Questions included main challenges faced by countries when extending existing WASH services, alternative channels governments could explore to attract more funding, and the observed cost of inaction in countries that hosted Venezuelan refugees.

Recognizing a complex request, the case manager initiated a search across analytical works, on one hand, and recent talking points and presentations, on the other hand, so as to align the response to the available knowledge as well as to the most recent official positions on the topic. In parallel, three task team leaders working in Uganda, Yemen, and across the Mashreq were personally consulted on their experience in supporting the deployment of WASH services in refugee camps. In their response, they included reactions from a manager working across East Africa; from a senior economist who helped assess the cost of inaction; and a colleague who specialized in fragile and conflict-affected situations.

One day after the request was made, the response included background from 21 sources. The service desk narrowed this initial response to seven immediately relevant assets offering a combination of ready-made slides, talking points, in-depth reports, and a recent speech, along with an offer to consult directly with any of the six staff who were involved in the answer.

Offering service desk functions had been a World Bank–wide ambition but only took hold for the long term in some departments. Originally, setting up service desks across the entire organization had been part of the 2014 reorganization's plans, covering all development topics, streamlining parts of the work for communities of practice. It had become clear that search engines are severely limited in delivering context-rich and politically sensitive answers. At the same time, communities of practice, while answering four-dimensional questions regularly, had focused on member-specific services and did not have the capacity to capture, re-apply, and expand on answer-services provided. Service desks were to go one step further by sharing questions and answers in plain sight. The attempt to build an organization-wide platform was short-lived, but a few departments managed to make the project stick and thrive. The Water Global Practice was one of them.

Four Principles for Success: Win Support, Remain Light, Collaborate, Recognize

Considering why and how *AskWater* persisted as a successful service desk offers a glimpse at how service desks should be built more generally. Almost from the get-go, the Water Global Practice's knowledge and learning team developed processes to tackle questions

Figure 12.1 AskWater Service Desk Process Flow

from the client-facing teams, as described in Figure 12.1. But beyond running a sound and sustainable process, and among the many lessons that emerged over five years of implementation, four basic principles of success stand out: strong managerial endorsement, a light and nimble structure, a deep culture of collaboration, and a keen attention to individual recognition.

First, win support from management—Convincing management that a service desk was a good idea was relatively easy. Because it proposed a simple protocol to link people, processes, and systems, the service desk was an adequate response to the overall aspiration of facilitating the linkage between global knowledge and local operations, between research and implementation, and between lessons learned and new initiatives. Because the solution proposed leveraging an array of existing tools and would rely on a division of labor among hundreds of staff in order to benefit from the corresponding network effect, it didn't require significant startup investments. Only later was a grant facility added, once the service desk had already shown promise. Finally, in the simple and effective branding of the solution (*AskWater*), departmental management saw a shorthand for its entire value proposition and a neat summary of the otherwise fragmented services it was offering across the organization. Promoting *AskWater* became a recurring talking point in all internal communications. The performance of the service desk was also integrated in the broader departmental monitoring and evaluation framework. Regular check-ins from management assessed the effectiveness of the service and prompted scope and capacity adjustments. Box 12.2 provides an overview of key performance indicators and of the overall monitoring and evaluation (M&E) framework for *AskWater*.

Box 12.2   Monitoring and Evaluation Framework

Most performance indicators for service desks involve specific and granular measures. But the key to operating a successful service desk is also to make its performance integral to the overall monitoring and evaluation (M&E) framework of the department it serves.

Key Performance Indicators Include:

- *Demand*: number of requests; evolution of traffic over time; percentage of target audience using the service.
- *Coverage*: geographic distribution of requests; distribution of questions across areas of focus.
- *Quality*: variety of results produced in response to complex requests. Answers should cover examples across geographic areas and a variety of outputs: customized advice, reports, contacts, etc.
- *Satisfaction*: requestors' verbatim reactions to responses; number of repeat "customers" (same people, different questions); occurrence of follow-up questions.
- *Knowledge mapping*: Where are the knowledge gaps? On the flip side, what common knowledge still triggers recurring questions (same questions, different people)? If not satisfactory, the answers to these questions should result in knowledge creation/acquisition and the development of new training.
- *Strategic alignment*: Given the strategic objectives of the department, are you getting the right questions? On the flip side, are the high-level objectives of the department reflecting the questions coming from the client-facing teams? If not satisfactory, the answers to these questions should result in an effort to strengthen the communication of strategic objectives or to adjust them to the new demands from operational units.

Collection Methods Include:

- Analysis of email traffic and responses.
- Statistics derived from the case-tracking database.
- Comments and ratings from target audience, either spontaneous or as triggered by satisfaction surveys.
- Analysis of the annual corporate-wide staff engagement survey about the efficacy of knowledge and learning programs.

Although the service desk monitors its performance on an ongoing basis, a biannual report to management provides the opportunity to recommend formal adjustments.

Second, remain light and nimble—In setting up the *Ask Water* service, every decision was carefully assessed in terms of its cost-benefit profile. For example, it might be tempting to capture every single aspect of a knowledge exchange to better understand needs and capacity: Who's the requestor? Are they senior or junior in the organization? Where are they based? Since when? Where else did they work before? What other projects are they working on? What is their specialization? And what about the people who answered, can we track the same data about them? Given the capability to harvest these data points seamlessly, and with an artificial intelligence function plugged into other systems, one could have embraced the opportunity to create a deeper understanding of the service desk's user profiles over time, perhaps being able to improve, target, and accelerate the knowledge service provided. But the cost of thorough data monitoring would have been a long-winded intake form and cumbersome cross-referencing, and so the cost-benefit profile suggested to not go down this route.

Third, make it understood that everybody works for the service desk—Although a few people are personally responsible for handling the logistics of case management and answering basic questions with codified knowledge, the service desk must include all the experts and practitioners assigned to the target topic area. The sum being greater than its parts, all the contributors play to their strengths while patching their weaknesses: the same person who asked a question today will be answering one tomorrow on a different topic. At the same time, network effects can begin taking hold: the more people are involved, the richer the answer. The service desk should never be a small unit of people trusted to have all the answers, an unrealistic goal anyway. Instead, it should rely on a large expert network that can be activated at any time.

Fourth, good service desks make their services personal—Most help desks offer an example of what *not* to do by providing an impersonal interface with too many automated emails either absurdly acknowledging receipt (who acknowledged but an algorithm?) or asking for instant feedback through template-based (dead) communication. Whenever possible, triage should instead be managed by identifiable and "real" people. Ideally, they should be junior but as widely connected and appreciated in the unit as possible. Their status and facilitation skills will enhance the speed, comprehensiveness, and quality of the answer curated for the requestor. In the same spirit, the final answer provided to the requestor should always recognize the people who contributed to the solution as will be discussed later.

Adherence to these four guiding principles is what made the *Ask Water* service desk work while others failed. Weak managerial endorsement, overambitious or clunky case-handling processes, and the temptation to have a small team of consultants run the service, instead of a broad network of staff, led to constructs that were disconnected from the natural flows of knowledge. Instead of tapping into the many rivers of data, information, and knowledge that flow across the organization, failed attempts were building standalone research units, remote pools of resources that staff would neither trust nor care to join. But the benefits of strong buy-in from management and staff, coupled with a light and collaborative architecture, must also be preserved and expanded over time.

In the Long Run: Accruing Benefits and Avoiding Pitfalls

A well-designed service desk enables and enriches the entire knowledge management life cycle: it helps unpack tacit knowledge and codify lessons learned, and it provides an "always-on," living connection between those who know and those who use knowledge for implementation, closing what is at times called the "knowing-doing gap." A good service desk should strengthen the expert community and build bridges between users and knowledge systems.

Unpacking tacit knowledge, codifying good practices, and curating critical information—The answer to a complex question is a powerful driver for institutional knowledge and performance: it comes with data, information, lessons learned, and an expert point of view that tailors the answer to its context, potentially alerting the requestor to sensitivities created by context while echoing strategic directions critical to the organization. When engaging with a government, it can be crucially important to gain access not only to reports and statistics but also to the team lead who was there before or to the people who have been following the evolution of the country for 30 years; only in this combination, key elements of the political economy and other surroundings can be understood well. However, the benefit conferred by the ability to tap into rich expertise hides a few pitfalls. One of them is the temptation to systematically consult experts rather than the knowledge base, no matter how simple the question. The availability and willingness of experts may also lead the organization to neglect knowledge codification, which quickly makes people the only source of guidance and can create bottlenecks, a systemic issue for knowledge transfer and often a waste of resources. If constantly pulled in to provide basic answers that should have been codified and served by a search engine in the first place, rare experts soon become unable to focus on the highly technical issues for which their knowledge is most valuable. Beyond making sure that business units remain engaged in proper curation and codification of basic knowledge and processes, the service desk should, in fact, keep razor-focused on accelerating the capture and tagging of solutions for future reuse. In the case of *Ask Water*, the case manager takes great care to assess the complexity and difficulty of each question at hand. The decision to turn to experts or to rely solely on codified knowledge may at first seem like a minor decision, but, in fact, it is a crucial one for the sustainability of the service.

Linking knowledge to action—There is a classic and irritating gap between what an organization knows and what it does. Research and development units and client-facing teams tend to operate in disconnected spaces and easily fall out of sync. Service desks activate a dialogue between knowledge and implementation. By exposing needs from the operational teams, service desk questions reveal recurring issues and opportunities, offer continuous feedback from project implementation, highlight knowledge gaps, and trigger new knowledge creation or curation. In addressing needs from the operational teams, research departments may recommend new approaches and push for cutting-edge solutions as described in a later section. The collective and open resolution of challenges ultimately becomes a formidable learning machine, anchored in praxis and just-in-time problem-solving. It also originates from an immediate and present need, if not desire, for learning, which brings the finishing touch to a convenient alignment with the principles of effective adult learning.

Building an expert community—Successful service desks develop a symbiotic relationship with communities of practice. To create all the value it is capable of, the service desk cannot be a black box. By being very deliberate about attributing answers to the people who contributed their expertise, it recognizes experts, incentivizes knowledge sharing, and helps build a knowledge community. This is not without potential pitfalls. Once the experts are well-known to all, requesters take shortcuts and contact them directly. Experts may be solicited to answer basic questions that will take them away from more strategic pursuits as noted previously, which is already an issue, but the direct exchange between requestor and solution providers will also happen offline, in a parallel space to that where the service desk operates. As a result, the exchange cannot be recorded, tagged, and stored for reuse. As they accumulate, these missed opportunities slowly but surely erode the knowledge collections and deteriorate the value of the public good created by shared questions and answers.

A good way to avoid this potential pitfall is to go all out on branding and communication, ensuring that the service desk is more visible or attractive than any individual expert. Concurrently, management must strongly support the approach and promote the service desk. Light gamification (e.g., *Who raised the best question? Who provided the most actionable solution? Who reacts the fastest?*) and other community management tactics can also help to counteract a natural tendency to bypass virtuous processes. Finally, the service desk will also assign a notetaker in discussions that sometimes unfold over a longer period, for example, in "safe space" meetings—technical discussions outside of the formal review process. It will also coordinate webinars that help scale the benefits of collaborative learning in a formal and open event.

Bridging the gap between users and knowledge systems—Many technology-based solutions for accessing knowledge have been customized by organizations for their internal use and can turn out to be poorly designed and badly integrated with the overall technology stack. The result is an array of clunky user interfaces and a confusing proliferation of overlapping tools. Frustrated users ignore resources that could, in fact, prove useful if only they were more approachable. To mitigate this issue, the service desk coordination provides a human interface that shields the user from the inner workings of the knowledge systems. By navigating the complexity of tools on behalf of the user, the service desk effectively ensures that no existing resource will remain untapped. However, while fighting its way through the tech mess, the service desk should be careful not to add to it. Although a dedicated case tracking system and an interface on which to publish the answers are a must, they should remain simple and integrated. *AskWater* leveraged the capabilities of the World Bank intranet to build its tracking database and host a publishing channel. The features remained few and simple so that they could be configured and maintained by almost any member of the team. While ensuring the sustainability of the service, the low-tech approach doesn't preclude the pursuit of high stakes.

Go-To Knowledge vs. Knowledge to Go Further

Channeled through identifiable people and a visible product, the knowledge management function becomes the result of a strong *pull* (a practice activated by daily questions from the frontline) rather than a tedious *push* ("*Will you please consider using this library of lessons we've learned so far?*"). Funding, behaviors, and support for knowledge activities follow this pull for the same reason that adoption follows satisfaction. Such positive feedback also helps to secure managerial support for knowledge management—needed, after all, to facilitate the coordination and enforcement of standard processes. Endowed with strong uptake, knowledge management can go beyond serving immediate needs and move on to drive the agenda and lead the charge.

Service desks take advantage of the pull of questions in order to push good practices and new priorities—Beyond becoming the go-to resource for knowledge needs, service desks can amplify strategic priorities, promote fresh ideas, and introduce new approaches. A good answer not only addresses the question at hand but also elevates it, and the best answer may lead to reshaping the initial thinking and changing the conversation. It can also recognize that the question is new and that the search for a solution will lead to experimentation. In transitioning from providing "*go-to knowledge*" to leveraging "*knowledge to go further,*" the *AskWater* service desk was paired with a small grant facility that sources external expertise, funds innovative pilots, and provides additional support to initiatives closely aligned with strategic priorities. Traditionally, management and client-facing teams seek identical goals through conflicting tendencies: management tends to push down strategic priorities and not-so-convenient practices that will steer the organization towards where it needs to be in a few months or years. The client-facing team, on the other hand, tends to focus on day-to-day delivery needs. They look for tried-and-true solutions and plug-and-play schemes delivered just in time. While relentlessly addressing the needs of the client-facing teams, a great service desk also promotes the more forward-looking organizational goals, ideally helping to solve today's emergencies in light of tomorrow's directions.

Box 12.3   From Go-To Knowledge to Knowledge to Go Further

In February 2016, a staff member from the Latin America and the Caribbean region asked for examples of lending operations making the disbursement of funds conditional to the attainment of certain milestones by the beneficiary. The idea was to incorporate new incentives (called disbursement linked indicators) into a classic lending instrument (investment policy financing). The service desk identified a few cases experimenting with the approach for the provision of water services in Brazil and Mexico. The Global Lead consulted on this question was familiar with the status of these efforts and, having provided justifications, advised against the approach.

Versions of this question kept reappearing in 2017 and 2018, triggering the same response every time, along with the increasingly detailed recommendation for task teams to consider changing their approach altogether. Whereas task teams kept trying to fit new incentive systems into an old lending instrument, experts kept pushing for them to consider a different lending instrument altogether called Program for Results (PforR). While it had the reputation of being ill-adapted to the water sector, it was, in fact, well-aligned with the needs that the task teams repeatedly expressed in their questions to the service desk. Could *AskWater* respond to the *pull* of a recurring request with a *push* for a better solution—albeit unpopular—that would eventually allow everyone to go further?

The scope of the discussion extended to other sectors and enlisted the help of corporate units. The same team that runs the service desk supported workshops dedicated to this topic in 2017, 2019, and 2021. The workshops included discussions of ongoing pilots, case studies across countries displaying diverse implementation capacity, and testimonies from beneficiaries and process clarifications, which, taken altogether, eventually changed peoples' minds. Water operations are now including more and more PforRs, with projects in Argentina, Benin, Burkina Faso, China, Egypt, India, Nigeria, Tanzania, and Vietnam.

Into the Maelstrom: *Mobilis in Mobile*

Soon, service desks will have more data, better answers, and faster responses, sometimes "spit out" by search engines without much need for curation. Manned help desks may disappear. But the people who run service desks and orchestrate the answers to knowledge questions should remain. They will see their own intelligence augmented by technology and find themselves with more time to distill nuanced answers to complex development challenges. The World Bank is investing steadily in data management and search capabilities. It already leverages advanced text analytics, machine learning, and A.I. (used here to stand for "artificial intelligence" as much as for "augmented intelligence") to make sense of over 70 years of development including millions of analytical pieces, billions of data points, and an overall information landscape going through exponential growth. Through interdependent economies, far-reaching supply chains, and mass migrations, we see development challenges, climate-related disasters, and health emergencies reaching a global scale at an increasingly fast pace. Good service desks must have eyes everywhere and connect experts around the word at a moment's notice, making everyone smarter and reducing seemingly undecipherable complexities. Embracing knowledge for development is learning how to move within a moving environment. What is required to navigate this maelstrom of questions and answers are steady, ingenious, and intelligent captains who know something about knowledge management.

Note

1 See: IBM IT Infrastructure Library (ITIL), notably distinction between Problem Management and Incident Management *www.ibm.com/cloud/learn/it-infrastructure-library#toc-incident-m-dGrGd0XU*

Chapter 13

All Aboard

Pathways for Mobilizing Staff and Leadership at the International Finance Corporation

Kelly Widelska, Daniel de la Morena and Alvaro Garcia Barba

Introduction

The International Finance Corporation (IFC)'s journey in building a knowledge ecosystem began with the establishment of a global knowledge office (GKO)[1] in 2009, charged with formulating a knowledge management strategy and implementation plan, leading corporate knowledge management initiatives, and supporting the organization as a center of excellence for knowledge management. Simultaneously a Knowledge Strategy Committee was established that included at least three vice presidents "from the business," in addition to IFC's chief information officer, the director of communications, and the global head of knowledge. The committee was well-designed: engaging senior leadership and including both the communications and the information technology function proved to be a formula for success. The committee's responsibilities included a seemingly standard set of strategic tasks for a knowledge management function, but as they were integrated into the formal IFC committee structure of governance, tone and ambition were set in ways that would signal the leadership's commitment to using knowledge management as a strategic business lever.

Box 13.1 —Knowledge Strategy Committee Strategic Tasks

- To set knowledge strategy and monitor the performance of knowledge management–related programs and investments across IFC.
- To approve corporate-wide knowledge management investments, standards, and activities.
- To resolve escalated issues and decision gridlocks.
- To steer integration with the different parts of the World Bank Group.
- To direct the communication of all aspects of IFC's knowledge strategy to IFC staff, board, clients, and other stakeholders.

The Strategy: Anchoring Knowledge Management Both on the Top and on the Bottom

Establishing the Knowledge Strategy Committee, with members hailing from the organization's leadership levels, allowed for engagement across IFC in a language that it understood while embarking on its knowledge management journey. Signaling leadership commitment,

DOI: 10.4324/9781003199083-22

both to staff and to other members of the leadership, was a critical step right at the beginning. The rotating membership structure of the committee meant that over time all members of the senior leadership team were able to learn firsthand more about knowledge management and its business value, which was useful for creating greater buy-in across the organization. In addition, the committee assumed a resource allocation role that allowed championing organization-wide innovations, such as establishing the first electronic collaboration platform (SPARK — see Box 13.2), which was a key part of the engagement and democratization process.

Box 13.2 —SPARK

IFC's leadership understood early on that a technology solution was needed to connect staff across its many decentralized teams to IFC's knowledge, its experts, and each other. In 2009, IFC introduced its first corporate collaboration platform—provisionally called iCollaborate—to allow staff to work together on documents, identify experts, coordinate work programs, access key content, and share insights and ideas. A comprehensive change management approach, support structure, and governance led to a successful uptake. Subsequently, the World Bank adopted IFC's technology choice as well as the associated governance approach, paving the way for a World Bank Group–wide platform—SPARK—launched in 2014. In its first year alone, according to internal statistics, SPARK attracted 12,000 active users (from a total workforce of ca. 18,000), hosted 1,500 communities, and sparked 14,000 discussions and 10,000 blog posts.

Knowledge management as a discipline was in its infancy in multilateral development banks in the 2000s. Staff involved in knowledge management had often evolved out of roles with an administrative background, with little, if any, formal or even informal training in the field and little opportunity to learn from each other. To address this challenge, in 2009, the Global Knowledge Office established a community of practice for staff in knowledge management roles. The community encouraged staff to develop their knowledge management skills and to create knowledge themselves. One good example is the process that the community took in creating a guidebook—"A Gardeners Guide to Communities of Practice."[2] Taking a collective learning approach, the process introduced structures which were to become the backbone of knowledge management activities at the department level; the guide was used widely internally (both within IFC and other parts of the World Bank Group) but also was published externally as a global public good.

When launched, the community of practice included some 40 active members and decided to pursue several objectives, including to support IFC's corporate knowledge management agenda, to promote enhanced client responsiveness, and to develop capacity among its members. Membership was open to anyone working on knowledge management tasks, both full-time and in addition to their "day-jobs." While sponsored by the Global Knowledge Office, the community was empowered from day one to collectively define its mission, governance, and operating model. In defining its mission, it committed to become an agent for knowledge-sharing, learning, capacity building, career development, and networking. Other goals included improving staff productivity by facilitating access to content and people; cultivating knowledge and talent to grow the business; strengthening IFC's brand as a global thought leader in private sector development; and creating and sustaining a knowledge and learning culture at IFC. In figuring out how to manage itself, the community decided on an annually rotating leadership drawn from its own ranks, regular biweekly meetings, and an annual two-day Forum for strategy setting, team building, and learning. The community, in its early days, was a critical feature in building IFC's knowledge management muscles and in disseminating the idea that knowledge management could be a value driver for individuals, departments, and the organization at large. Since its inception, it has helped create standards for the career framework for knowledge management staff in IFC, for knowledge continuity ("offboarding"), for intranet and collaboration sites' templates, and for metrics, to name a few. It also played a critical role in rolling out IFC's collaboration platform and the lessons learned program.

The Global Knowledge Office had determined early on that for knowledge management efforts at IFC to succeed, everyone had to play a role. The real challenge was going to be the cultural shift required to motivate staff to move from being passive consumers of knowledge in a silo to full participants in the knowledge life cycle, with additional roles for everyone. Improved technology literacy and skills brought in by information technology innovations and successive younger generations entering the workplace also contributed to this shift. This "democratization" of the knowledge management process has driven the ethos and efforts of the knowledge management teams over the last decade.

In 2012, IFC brought a knowledge management professional with extensive experience from a global consulting firm on board to lead the core knowledge team. In taking on the new assignment, her first action was to undertake a knowledge current state assessment. The assessment identified both critical issues and opportunities—many of which were known but had not been collectively articulated through a governance body to the IFC management team. Specifically, the assessment found that knowledge programs and processes at the time were fragmented and did not reach across regions and departments and that critical knowledge was difficult to find for staff without personal connections. It also noted that even though the "new language of knowledge management" was increasingly being used by IFC's leadership, staff needed better awareness of what managing knowledge meant—how it can drive effective business results—and what their respective roles should be in the process. Finally, the assessment highlighted the growing need for consistent support to extract, capture, and apply lessons learned, including lessons of failure and the need for IFC culture and incentive structure to reward knowledge management activities.

SCORE

Across IFC, the current state assessment had identified a gap between the rhetoric and the reality of knowledge management. The team decided to design a behavioral framework along which a change program could be run that would invite all staff and managers across the organization to integrate knowledge management activities into their day-to-day work processes and behaviors. The trick would be to have the organization's leadership endorse and promote this approach. In developing the framework, the Global Knowledge Office collated examples of existing knowledge management activities from across the organization. Based on the examples, five distinct and specific knowledge behaviors were identified that both responded to challenges identified in the knowledge assessment and demystified knowledge management jargon: "SCORE" was born, an acronym referencing four verbs:

Share, Create, cOnnect, Reflect, and Explore. As a framework of behaviors, SCORE stood out for finding simple and intuitive language that described actionable knowledge behaviors rather than sounding like an amorphous knowledge management lexicon.

Box 13.3 —SCORE

- Share: Proactively share my expertise.
- Create: Contribute to our body of knowledge.
- cOnnect: Build my network.
- Reflect: Draw lessons from past performance.
- Explore: Innovate, grow, and learn.

The SCORE program was launched by IFC's leadership at the IFC Knowledge Sharing Week in 2013 and is still in use today as a backbone for knowledge management measurement and awards. It came with a series of tools for staff and managers: a guide (co-created with the IFC Human Resources team) with a set of common language descriptions and examples of knowledge management activities by grade level that could be used across the organization to help with the integration of consistent metrics in performance conversations and yearly plans. Also, a separate guide was added that would help with developing knowledge objectives and priorities at departmental retreats, meetings, and brainstorming sessions. This was complemented by a series of materials with tips and tricks to support individual SCORE behaviors and with tools for building a communications campaign to increase awareness of knowledge behaviors and to showcase their business value. The program was utilized by managers and teams who were engaged and interested in knowledge management; it was attractive for them because it demystified abstract concepts and translated jargon into tangible actions, providing a framework for thinking about specific behaviors, making things manageable for the audience.

KNOWbel

The KNOWbel Award is IFC's flagship program for recognizing and incentivizing a knowledge management culture across the organization. The awards recognize teams that deliver high-impact services to clients using behaviors outlined through the SCORE program (Share, Create, cOnnect, Reflect, and Explore). Since their inception the KNOWbel Awards have recognized hundreds of projects and staff at IFC. For example, the KNOWbel Awards 2021 highlighted the work of more than 110 colleagues. The KNOWbel Awards have consistently included three main categories: Client Solutions, Increased Efficiency, and Learning From the Past, all of them linked directly to IFC's interpretation of the value of knowledge management for the organization. In addition, there are always annual special categories, driven by imminent and strategic priorities (e.g., COVID-19, climate). The awards recognize teams and individuals, and colleagues receive a monetary incentive, an electronic badge on the World Bank Group directory profile page that features them, and recognition from senior leadership in an awards ceremony. The winning submissions are disseminated across IFC using different communications channels, such as the "Knowledge

Flash" (IFC's monthly knowledge management newsletter) in addition to intranet stories featuring winners. The KNOWbel Awards remain highly sought after across the organization, creating an enabling environment that fosters knowledge management behaviors at IFC and surfaces examples of knowledge behaviors that have translated into concrete business results, thus visibly establishing the connection between knowledge management and business value.

The SCORE-focused KNOWbel Awards have been an effective vehicle in building the understanding of the expected behaviors at IFC while also signaling the importance attached to knowledge management activities as part of everyone's projects and programs. The Global Knowledge Office has worked on adding elements to the SCORE framework, which include an approach to turn the framework into a set of numbers (Core IFC language) to create individual and unit knowledge SCORE cards, thus laying the foundation for a gamification program. The hypothesis is that these sorts of resources will help drive competition between individuals and departments and could be used effectively as a change enabler. As is the case with all good knowledge management programs, KNOWbel continues to evolve.

KNovember

One of the key drivers of the democratization of knowledge management at IFC was the formalization of IFC-wide knowledge-sharing program "KNovember."[3] The program began as a knowledge-sharing day in 2012 and has constantly evolved. It became a weeklong event in 2013, and, finally, a knowledge month in 2014. This evolution was due to the appetite and engagement of staff across the organization, IFC senior leadership's continued sponsorship, and the growing understanding of the importance of sharing knowledge across silos. Each year the KNovember Team builds a useful content-oriented agenda to ensure that there is a good mix of sessions to cover both basic knowledge management skills training (e.g., how to use tools and external databases) as well as overviews of strategic priorities and projects. The sessions are held in person and streamed via video conference for all relevant time zones. All content is recorded and saved on the KNovember website, which makes it easy for individuals to catch up on sessions. Additionally, the team prepares summary notes and animated infographic videos to offer staff with little time a "bite-sized" way to review an hour-long recording. This repository is also a contribution to IFC's operational history, part of the archival program across the World Bank Group (see Chapter 14). The entire KNovember effort is supported by a solid communications campaign not only to create awareness of the program offering and mobilize participants but also to disseminate the knowledge captured during the sessions.

Staff and departments across the corporation can submit session proposals to the KNovember design committee, and based on the session's relevance, the committee forms the final program. These two processes ensure that all staff can contribute while keeping a systematic approach to knowledge sharing in place for each KNovember edition. The event is anchored by an external macroeconomic landscape review, which always draws in the crowds and starts a lively discussion. To give an example of the scale and success of the program, according to event records, KNovember in 2014 hosted 74 sessions reaching 2,700 participants, whereas, in 2019, it hosted 103 sessions and attracted 4,250 participants. Since its inception, KNovember has hosted almost 650 sessions and reached more than 23,000 participants.

Box 13.4   —Examples of Metrics

The KNovember 2019 key performance indicators (KPIs) included the number of participants, number of sessions, breakdown by staff seniority and region, number of country offices participating, number of presenters, number of knowledge quiz respondents, number of special series, and top five most attended sessions.

Well before the COVID-19 pandemic hit in 2020 and many organizations began using online tools for learning and knowledge exchange, KNovember sessions were always available as a streamed resource with interaction via WebEx. The team was cognizant of the shift to virtual global working and the "Zoom fatigue" becoming a challenge to online engagement. Nevertheless, when KNovember 2020 sessions were held—entirely virtually and stretched across November and December—the 25 streamed sessions were brought to 1,827 participants from 76 locations and received an overall rating of 4.53 out of 5 on the usefulness of sessions.

The team has closely collaborated with subject-matter experts to design more engaging, effective, and fun sessions. For example, the team designed gamified learning experiences via Microsoft Yammer using scavenger hunts to find critical pieces of knowledge on the intranet. The use of Yammer and other collaborative technologies has supported the learning experience of regions. Piloting innovative ideas in KNovember has served as a safe experimental environment for other knowledge management teams to learn and replicate successful approaches (e.g., knowledge-based gamification quizzes). The team also adopted instructional design practices to enrich the audience participation and spark relevant knowledge-sharing conversations between senior colleagues and newly onboarded staff. Innovations like these continue to advance the knowledge management culture at IFC.

Knowledge Flash

Every organization that aspires to embed an impactful knowledge management program needs to invest in a solid communications strategy to drive adoption and buy-in. In this context, IFC's Global Knowledge and Learning Office developed "Knowledge Flash," a monthly newsletter putting a spotlight on critical knowledge products and services for internal audiences. It provides a platform that allows different departments to showcase their resources and improve their use, leading to improved performance and value for the client.

Each "Knowledge Flash" issue is created in partnership with the communications team and internal subject-matter experts from the respective departments (e.g., credit, portfolio, climate, gender, and inclusion). The collaboration itself is already a powerful example of how IFC is democratizing knowledge and fostering a knowledge management culture. The newsletter's content is structured in different knowledge-depth levels, ranging from foundational resources to the more advanced ones. It also includes multimedia elements such as videos or images and quotes from a diverse selection of colleagues that create a sense of authenticity as the value of knowledge products is considered.

So far, the first 15 "Knowledge Flash" newsletters reached 7,000 colleagues monthly. The team uses Adobe Campaigns Analytics to track the open and clickthrough rates. Until now, the average open rate is 50 percent, meaning that more than 3,500 colleagues access the newsletter monthly.

What's Next and Reflections

As IFC evolves to support the green-resilient, inclusive recovery in the aftermath of the COVID-19 pandemic with a greater focus on country-level programming, the staffing dynamics are shifting again in terms of geography. Operating in a more and more decentralized format, together with the continuing generational changes to the workforce, now encompassing five "generations,"[4] enhances the need to enable self-service platforms where staff can capture, create, and share knowledge. Related digitization efforts will leverage new technologies and methodologies. IFC's team has already begun to deploy artificial intelligence and machine learning tools to aggregate information and generate relevant knowledge for operational staff. Now, further exploration of more interactive multimedia content and gamification solutions are being considered to foster motivation and engagement through games and competitions that connect staff to experts and to relevant content— a new knowledge management strategy in the making. Once approved, this strategy will strengthen current knowledge capture and sharing programs and champion new initiatives on incentives and collaboration.

Encouraging the right knowledge management behaviors to drive business value and embedding a knowledge management approach in operational and corporate processes are not easy in any organization, and IFC is no exception. During the last decade, IFC has made significant progress in establishing a program that made knowledge management "everyone's business." Beyond the many innovative initiatives, one of the key success factors for IFC has been the consistency of managerial support for knowledge management and the engagement of senior leadership across the organization. They have modeled and promoted a greater understanding of the value that knowledge management can bring to units, departments, and our clients, an iterative process that is constantly evolving.

Notes

1 The GKO become the GKLO in 2015 when it integrated operational learning to its mandate.
2 www.fsnnetwork.org/sites/default/files/A%20Gardeners%20Guide%20to%20Communities%20 of%20Practice%20-%20World%20Bank.pdf
3 Rebranded to KNOWvember in 2021.
4 At present, the five generations in the workplace include:

  • Traditionalists—born 1927–1946
  • Baby Boomers—born 1947–1964
  • Generation X—born 1965–1980
  • Millennials—born 1981–2000
  • Generation Z—born 2001–2020

  www.hrexchangenetwork.com/employee-engagement/articles/generations-in-the-workplace#

Chapter 14

Fighting Organizational Amnesia

The Evolving Role of the World Bank Group Archives

Elisa Liberatori Prati

The Context

The World Bank Group, early on in its genesis, took the decision to afford itself what some may consider a luxury: a dedicated Archives team—a diverse group of professionals who care deeply about preserving and making accessible documentary heritage in whichever format and media it may come, analog and digital, printed, visual, or oral.[1] These holdings are made accessible to anyone inside and outside the organization as a global public good, considered the foundation for shared history and credible memory in building even stronger multilateral efforts for economic development and prosperity worldwide. The team includes 30 archivists, records, and information management professionals serving over 20,000 internal users and the general public. They encourage and facilitate research into the history of what is the oldest and largest among the multiregional development banks, and to this end, they work to preserve, protect, and provide access to one of the world's largest collections of records related to international development, going back to 1946. The team's work is a living testament that innovation, decision-making, and change can benefit from the knowledge of the past.

Mantra, Vision, Goal

The World Bank Group Archives team's mantra is straightforward: just as much as memory is an important asset for an individual—so much that its loss is considered a painful condition to be prevented; for an organization, its *institutional* memory is a key asset. Without institutional memory, it is hard, if not impossible, to take evidence-based strategic decisions that draw on an organization's wealth of experiences. Yet, as staff retire or otherwise leave organizations, taking their experiences and knowledge with them, it is up to professionals like an archives team to establish mechanisms that will commit knowledge to institutional memory and help the organization retrieve it later. It is in this context that the World Bank Group Archives team has developed its vision to *unlock the vault of our Archives and give voice to the documentary heritage of previous generations of development workers as a valuable public good that illuminates the past to address today's challenges in our development work*. Wherever organizations take a longer-term view when providing services, also having a longer-term memory is critical for success—and the "development industry" is no exception. When it comes to promoting economic development and supporting governments in implementing institutional and policy changes, progress is rarely immediate and impact is measurable often not only over the next few years or so but also across future generations. The Archives team has, therefore, dedicated its efforts to making institutional memory usable, building on years of strategic work to not only provide access to but also discovery of

DOI: 10.4324/9781003199083-23

the lessons of the past. Innovative archival methods and practices have been deployed to facilitate as much online access as possible. By leveraging technology and through strong partnerships across the organization and beyond—including with academia—the Archives' holdings and historical resources are brought to the attention of users. The digitization of fragile historical analog holdings and the creation of quality metadata have been keys to this endeavor but so were the creation and maintenance of innovative and intuitive discovery platforms that engage the public to find, explore, and learn from the World Bank Group's rich history. In pursuing these goals, the Archives team has taken full use of—and added to—the organization's strong and reliable information technology landscape. Merging skills and knowledge of the archivists with the power of technology has opened avenues for documentary evidence to translate into influence and impact.

Box 14.1   Fighting Institutional Amnesia: Online Platforms

- *The Archives Holdings*: The Archives Holdings website, at archivesholdings.worldbank.org, serves as the catalog for the World Bank Group Archive. The user can browse and search descriptions of records and, in some cases, access digitized copies of the records immediately. The catalog also gives context about where the records originated and how they were used when they were created as active records.

- *The Historical Timeline*: With hundreds of key events, the timeline—available at timeline.worldbank.org—tells the story of how the World Bank Group evolved from a facilitator of reconstruction and development following the Second World War to its present-day mandate of alleviating poverty and promoting shared prosperity. Each event is illuminated by archival records, photographs, audio/video recordings, reports, oral history transcripts, project information, online exhibits, presidential profiles, and more. Metadata is available via API.

- *Documents and Reports*: The full collection of over 300,000 operational documents is available in *Documents and Reports* at https://documents.worldbank.org/en/publication/documents-reports.

- *World Bank Projects and Operations*: Through projects.worldbank.org users can find information about thousands of World Bank projects and operations in all sectors dating back to the first loan to France in 1947. Each project page provides information that places the project in the context of the overall work of the World Bank.

- *The Historic Photographic Collection*: Thousands of historical pictures are available in the *Photo Catalog* at archivesphotos.worldbank.org/en/about/archives/photo-gallery. Over 500,000 photographs document project work in member countries, official signings, and other historic events and personalities. The photographic holdings are made up of transfers from administrative and operational units in the Bank Group, including two large transfers from External Affairs and the Office of the President, which include photos of Bank presidents, annual meetings, project (country)-related, senior staff, Bank Group membership, loan and credit signings, and promotional/public relations photos. It's a work in progress: new digitized photos are added to the site monthly.

The Archives: A Function Between Knowledge Management and Learning

Fighting institutional amnesia: The 4-D approach—As the Archives team shaped its approach—from preserving information for fiduciary purposes to enabling access to and use of information—the "4 Ds approach" (describing, declassifying, digitizing holdings, and ensuring their discoverability) was developed. Gradually, the WBG Archives transformed into an engaging and relevant source of documentary evidence and experience and a source of more easily accessible knowledge. Doing so included the development of a number of custom-made open knowledge platforms; all of them are accessible from the World Bank's external website[2] that easily guides the user through the unfolding of 75 years of development history.

Building community and attachment: A user-centric approach—In the Archives team's work to preserve and make accessible the documentary heritage of the World Bank Group, much consideration is given to the users of historical knowledge, their needs, interests, and behaviors. To this end, the Archives team continuously innovates in creating opportunities for discovery, innovation, and learning. Users can be anyone across the World Bank Group as well as its clients' organizations in addition to the generic public and its many civil society groups, academia, and private companies. In attracting its current and potential users, the Archives team has taken an event-based approach and invested in a number of initiatives to create physical space for people to connect both with the Archives and with others using it.

Box 14.2   Inviting Everyone to Come Along: People, Activities, Spaces

- *Personal attachment through an engaging physical space*: Anyone visiting the World Bank's Archives and Library today may be confused: instead of a somewhat stale place with files in shelves—the way an archive tends to normally look—they will find a colorful brainstorming-type space, giving the impression of a truly vibrant hub for exchanging ideas. Aware of their mandate to open up and create accessibility, the Archives' team has invested in a layout and furniture more akin to creative brainstorming and suitable to hosting a variety of social and learning events including happy hours, coffees, open houses with internal and external partners, panel discussions, and author talks. There are armchairs with colorful pillows, seating cubes for visitors to easily move and reconfigure for different activities; dry-erase walls for brainstorming session; computers and iPads for in-house use by clients; a designated virtual conference area; a fully equipped presentation space for blended learning; and a World Bank publication wall to attract passersby to take a look at the latest reports and flagship works, using a shared iPad for exploring the full Bank eLibrary collection. Just a few steps further, there is the Archives' secure reading room, where researchers can access analog materials in an ideal preservation environment.[3]

- *Attraction across sectors through conferences, workshops, and events*: Drawing on its most valuable resource—knowledge of the World Bank's history—the Archives team has developed an outreach strategy built on events that explore specific aspects of the history of the World Bank Group and their impact on development, as well as topics related to the theory and practice of the Archives themselves. These events—conferences, brown bag lunches, or other formal or informal activities—are typically put on together with other units across the World Bank Group, including the Library—a most instrumental partner—the research department, sector or regional units, and corporate teams, such as the Legal team and the 1818 Society of World Bank retirees. A good example is the 2012 workshop on *Using History to Inform Development Policy: The Role of Archives.*[4]

- *Staff engagement through participatory research*: With its focus on users, the Archives team has begun to open up new routes for its user community to participate in research. A good example is the genesis of the study *The World Bank's Engagement With Transport in Cities: The Early Years* by Slobodan Mitric.[5] A World Bank retiree and former urban transport expert, Mitric had extensively researched the archival collections. The Archives new online platforms allowed him to run his work by other former and active Bank staff before publishing: seasoned experts who were on the front lines of the Bank's expanding engagement with the sector were able to share their tacit knowledge with current Bank staff, and Mitric harvested what was said, thereby finding entry points to further uncover additional knowledge that would have otherwise remained hidden in the historical records.

- *Visibility through rewards for fighting institutional memory loss*: Like any Archives team, the World Bank's team relies heavily on the support of staff across the entire organization—the often unsung heroes of information management that identify, file, and pass on information they or the staff they work with produce in their daily business activities. An annual and festive awards ceremony is put up every year, since 2013, to recognize whoever has made outstanding contributions to the management of information. The ceremony gives broad internal recognition to the winners, bringing attention to what they have done—but shining light on the topic itself, a helpful side-effect for activities that are still considered by too many to be a "backroom" or "just tedious" work. The awards are part of a small series of formal World-Bank–internal awards designated to recognize outstanding contributions. Staff compete across the whole World Bank Group; anyone can be nominated across all organizational units, grades, and physical locations. Senior management is also mobilized by the Archives team: they act as organizational sponsors and, importantly, take turns in recognizing the awardees with great fanfare.

- *A sense for history through taking a "trip to the Mine"*: When dealing with something abstract such as history and information management, there is nothing quite like a moment of "personal touch" to build a positive relationship. This is what the Archives team had in mind when, in 2007, it began offering a bus trip ("Training on Wheels!") for selected staff and managers to come and see for themselves what is in "the Mine." "The Mine"—a former limestone mine in Pennsylvania—is one of the largest and safest underground repositories in the United States for the preservation of paper documents, photographic materials, and films. The World Bank leases four secure vaults as large as football fields filled up with stacks 15 ft. high. The archival boxes, if piled up one on top of the other, would rise seven times as high as Mount Everest. The underground tour around the stacks takes visitors through "history stops" in chronological order with exhibits of original documents and the explanation of their context. The visit is an impressive, motivational, and perspective-changing experience for every participant; for some, it offers a new and deeper understanding of information management, for others the opportunity to build friendships with colleagues from across the organization, and again, for others, it provides a glimpse into history they did not know existed. Everyone returns inspired and with a sense of community and purpose.

Strengthening organizational culture: History "alive"—An organization's history can play a very specific role in offering staff a sense of togetherness and appreciation, a sense of belonging to the organization they work for. The World Bank Group has long been astute in leveraging their historical assets in this way—and the Archives team has played quite a central role in this. Routinely, the Archives team contributes to staff onboarding activities, such as through the new staff orientation workshops. The team also contributes to chronologies and historical documents, to celebrations of anniversaries that matter in organizational history, such as country membership anniversaries, first projects in specific sectors, founding of different institutional branches, etc.

Box 14.3   Celebrating Organizational History: The Shoulders We Stand On

- *Celebration of Life for Jim Wolfensohn*: James D. Wolfensohn had been one of the longest serving World Bank presidents, a shaper on many critical fronts throughout his tenure between 1995 and 2005. With his death on November 25, 2020, the World Bank Group and the international development community lost an influential leader. Having reinvigorated staff and development partners, many of the initiatives, projects, and reforms implemented under his leadership continue to inform the Bank Group's development priorities and practices today. His passing created an important moment for staff to rally around a shared history of how they saw the institution evolve during Wolfensohn's tenure. The Archives team was at the core of this outreach—providing digitized historical audiovisual items related to Wolfensohn as the backbone for several events, products, and communications to and with staff and the public.

- *Living Black History*: Black History Month is celebrated every year in the United States, and as an organization hailing diverse staff right from its inception, the World Bank Group has unique perspectives to contribute. More recently, archivist Bertha Wilson has begun to translate these perspectives into a series of profiles of African American World Bank staff. Published at www.worldbank.org/archives, the series has so far featured Dr. Frederick Douglass Patterson, invited by the World Bank to join its first mission to an African country; William Kelly, Jr., one of the first 26 staff members already in place when the World Bank opened for business in 1946; and Thelma D. Jones, who led much of the community outreach over many years.

- *McNamara Years Oral History Project*: Robert S. McNamara was the longest serving World Bank president, at its helm for 13 years between 1968 and 1981, leading a sharp pivot to development and tackling the challenge of poverty and laying the basis for the outlook and role the World Bank Group takes today. Between 2016 and 2018, the Archives team hosted John Heath, a sociologist and former Bank staff, now professor at the American University School of International Service in Washington, DC, who undertook a special project for which he conducted a series of over 60 interviews. The oral history project aimed to delve into the individual experiences of staff who worked with the World Bank during those years to illuminate strategic priorities, ways of working, sequence of innovations, and evolving organizational culture. Staff memories add important details and vibrancy to understanding the Group's history and how that history resonates today, particularly in areas where the written documentary evidence leaves gaps. In addition, a 2021 *book written by the six personal assistants of President McNamara*[6] complements the insights into many pivotal moments.

- *Presidents' Speeches Collection*: In 2018, the Archives team realized it was missing a great resource from its online collections: presidential speeches had been saved throughout the organization and archives but never centrally collected or included in an easily accessible central repository. The value of the speeches is that they reflect the evolution of the organization: strategies, shifts in development policies, major achievements, and milestones in a very clear language, easily understandable by nonspecialized/technical audiences. In addition, since the 1940s, twice a year—during their annual meeting and their spring meeting—the presidents formally address the World Bank Group's constituencies of member countries and take stock of progress and setbacks in a highly structured way. Hence the value of this collection. The Archives team succeeded in locating the speeches, digitized, and catalogued them. By now, transcripts of more than 1,000 speeches from 1946 to present are browsable and searchable and accompanied by some fascinating audio selections.[7]

Creatively managing outreach: Strategies to serve new audiences—The World Bank Group Archives team benefits from a strong culture of service and client-orientation that comes with the territory—its organizational placement within the information technology group. The team's deep knowledge of the Archives' holdings give rise to a unique ability to find creative connections between the current work of the Group and the lessons of the past. On top of these two assets, the Archives team also brings unique "customer rela-tions": many of the Archives' users spend significant time with the archivists—typically on location but also through the online resources—and this gives the archivists a unique opportunity to listen to and learn from their audiences, identifying new needs and oppor-tunities to devise ways of solving their clients' challenges and addressing their needs.

Box 14.4   Setting Strategic Priorities: Outreach and Engagement

- *Digitizing all key holdings*: The Archives team has digitized more than 1.4 mil-lion pages of archival records that had been declassified in accordance with the World Bank's Policy on Access to Information. These records were made available through the World Bank Group Archives Holdings site (*archivesholdings.world-bank.org*) and the Bank's Projects and Operations database (*projects.worldbank.org*). They chronicle the thoughts, experience, expertise, and applied solutions of generations of dedicated World Bank development workers, partners, and mem-ber countries. Access to these records allows researchers, development practition-ers, and Bank staff to draw upon lessons learned and prior successes to improve the design and implementation of current Bank work and inform the decisions of today's development community in pursuit of the Bank's Open Agenda.

- *Segmenting and targeting audiences "upon arrival"*: The World Bank Group Archives' holdings are vast and the online historical resources and tools availa-ble are abundant. To welcome, inspire, and orient new users, in particular online users, the Archives created three short videos. The first focuses on the "Treasures of the Archives" and describes the possibilities available when researchers "jump in and explore" its holdings. The second video invites the public to "Explore the Archives" and the many resources that may answer or further refine your research question, while the third video provides guidance to those ready to "Dig Deeper Into the Archives" and submit an Access to Information request. All three videos are available from www.worldbank.org/archives. In addition, there is a "welcome desk"—both in the physical area and virtually—with a "live person" who helps users of the Archive orient themselves.

- *Packaging and curating content: Oral histories and un-podcasts*: The oral history site at oralhistory.worldbank.org gives a voice to hundreds of development practi-tioners of the past since the birth of the organization in the late 1940s. The interviews are accessible by interviewee, country, or chronologically by presidential tenure. In addition, the team is now testing the podcast format and just produced the first in a new series of *Development Reflections*. These products are called "un-podcasts," since the team is not made up of communication professionals but archivists. The first documents the work of Scott Guggenheim, a founding father of community-driven development at the World Bank. His personal history and perspective set out how he came to apply core concepts from anthropology to one of the big chal-lenges of the 20th century, the role that poor people could and should be playing in modern development. Using his involvement in the Kecamatan Development

Project in Indonesia, Guggenheim described his journey to developing an approach using core concepts from anthropology and sociology to develop a model that the World Bank could work with using its own comparative advantages and skills. Bringing this rich history to life demonstrates the impact of the past on the present and contextualizes the ongoing criticality of involving the poor and disadvantaged in development.

- *Creating "experiences" to have history come alive: Beyond books and papers*: More recently, as the World Bank Group itself aged and celebrated its anniversaries more consciously, new opportunities for outreach to current and potential Archives' users emerged. One such opportunity was the 2019 *Annual Bank Conference on Development Economics (ABCDE)*[8] that took place during the 75th anniversary year of the Bretton Woods conference, which in 1944 had led to the establishment of the World Bank and the International Monetary Fund. The Archives' team supported the conference with an exhibit in the atrium of the Bank's main building in Washington, DC: seven large panels were prepared to tell conference participants and other interested parties about the history of the Group, accompanying information banners, document displays, and a digital timeline via interactive iPads. Exhibits and history engagement events have impact: during this time, visits to the Archives' website and timeline numbered over 11,000 unique visitors. The Archives also created a toolkit of products, all available digitally, for communications officers across the Bank to deploy in their units or country offices. To complement the experience of the exhibit, a unique full-immersion cultural experience was created with the *Bretton Woods @ 75 at the Dining Rooms initiative:* in the main dining room in Washington, the Archives team hosted Bank staff, top management, and conference participants to celebrate the anniversary. A unique experience had been concocted, including a menu inspired by the Bretton Woods Conference's farewell dinner, 1940s music performed live, and archival artifacts on display. Guests were given individual Bretton Woods Conference delegation cards, with biographical information and stories concerning the original Bretton Woods participants and the opportunity to take pictures with two key players of the 1944 Conference, John Maynard Keynes of the UK and Henry Morgenthau of the US in life-size black-and-white cut-outs. This engaging way to bring history to life prompted a collective reflection on seven decades of multilateral work—successes and failures—in informal settings.

The Foundations: Drivers and Enablers

Less visible than the history and knowledge function but with just as much relevance, the Archives also have fiduciary responsibilities for current records management and for information governance within the organization. Both, in turn, feed into the knowledge services provision. The Archives team's responsibilities cover the entire life cycle of information: from creation to final disposition—including either destruction of information in accordance with the World Bank Group's rules or preservation of and access to information that has enduring archival value. It is worth noting that even destruction has value in knowledge management as it ensures that only the most valuable information is kept by discarding information with only transactional or temporary value. By "destroying" selected records, the team enables easier search, access, and use of others.

The question though is: how can a team of 30 cover—with these responsibilities—an organization of 20,000+ staff? Just like any other knowledge function, the Archives team invested in a number of dimensions to be able to respond to this tall order, including gradually professionalizing the team over 20 years to smoothly operate in the digital age; taking a strategic focus on communicating the value of two foundational policies to leverage support and convince staff of the long-term impact of their active contribution; establishing partnerships inside and outside the organization to reach wider audiences, test innovation, and expand one's own capacities; and establishing and leveraging strong relationships with the IT colleagues to effectively embed the Archives team's products and services into the World Bank Group's technology platforms.

Box 14.5 Responding to Growing Demand: Choices Made and Partnerships Built

- *Professionalizing the Archives team*: In the early 2020s, there are excellent graduate programs for archival science offered by universities around the world producing a pipeline of strong professionals ready to tackle the challenges of today's information ecosystem. What they have been trained to do had to be "learned by doing" not long ago. The discipline understands the inherent nature of records and archives and their value to an organization and society at-large; it can expertly manage records throughout the life cycle from creation to preservation or destruction; it knows how to configure and implement records systems and archival systems for maximum information governance benefit; it makes careful and defensible selection of records for acquisition, performs intellectual control for archival holdings according to applicable standards, and has nuanced understanding of the juridical relationship that records and archives have with the law, ethics, and professional responsibilities. Aware of these competencies, the World Bank Group's chief archivist has long and carefully invested in workforce planning, selecting and hiring top professionals within headcount and budget constraints. The investment in professionalizing the team has enabled it to continuously enhance its impact and to address the increasing complexity of responsibilities as the organization grows and evolves in the digital age.

- *Leveraging institutional policies on information management*: The authority of the Archives relies on two major policies that are binding across the entire World Bank Group: The *Policy on Records Management* endows the Archives with clear responsibilities and authorities, and the *Access to Information Policy* is the basis for the vision to make the Archives' holdings accessible and transparent. The *Records Management Policy* is as old as the organization and dates back to the 1940s. It sets the responsibilities of staff—at all levels—to take care of records and information (the future archives!) and endows the Archives team with the authority to establish and implement retention schedules of records in close consultation with the business, the legal department, and the audit and investigative functions.

This policy supports creation, capture, and disposal of records and is the foundation of the existence of the Archives. The *Access to Information Policy* came into effect in 2010 and is the "transparency" policy of the organization. It regulates how information can be released to the public, either on a proactive and systematic way or reactively in response to public requests. For proactive declassification, the Archives team relies on processes and tools to declassify final operational reports and for posting them in two public collections, *Documents and Reports* and *Open Knowledge Repository* respectively.[9] For reactive declassification, prompted by Access to Information requests, the Archives team works in partnership with external relations colleagues. In addressing requests for information older than 20 years, the Archives team has been entrusted by the organization with the responsibility to implement declassification and disclosure according to well-defined criteria. This policy, in addition to the hundreds of individual requests received since the policy's release, and in addition to the millions of self-service–based downloads from the public collections every year, has been a major driver behind the Archives team's work in curating and ensuring accessibility of key records. The demand for these records and the associated information confirms the value of the public good that the Archives have been mandated to provide.

- *Building partnerships across the information management community*: Keeping records well is a task for everyone, and so in 2011 the Archives team set up a World Bank Group–wide network of *Focal Points*—information management professionals hailing from about 30 major functions, encompassing operational, corporate, and financial units. The network was set up at the time when the software that had long been supporting records management was replaced with a new tool, so there was an immediate need for Focal Points to assist with the change management processes this new system required. Within the network of Focal Points, the Archives team took the role of the secretariat. Over time, the network evolved into a community of practice, meeting monthly; discussing information management issues, projects, and technical solutions; collecting requirements for the technical teams from the various areas of the organization; and disseminating back information, strategic directions, and change-management instructions in a consultative and coordinated way across the organization. Participation is voluntary, yet this community is one of the longest lasting informal advisory bodies on information in the organization. Why do staff truly like this forum and continue to contribute actively? Much will have to do with the human touch and the sense of community that have been key ingredients in building the network: this is a community of users who feel listened to, appreciated, and engaged—*friends* of information management. At the same time, there is impact through numbers: the Archives team is able to reach, through this network, groups of staff that would be out of reach for any particular unit, ensuring compliance with policies and adoption of systems. However, the Focal Points network operates only at the World Bank Group's headquarter offices in Washington, DC. To reach information management colleagues in the country offices, the Archives team has invested separately, taking into account these staff's specific situations. Every other year, regional Learning Hub events are organized that offer the opportunity for training in new developments in records and information management but that also create space to establish personal relationships and to form a community of friends across geographical areas. Thus forming a high-impact partnership in a collaborative way, the Archives team is not only able to get to know its colleagues around the globe personally but also build the basis for everyone's future contributions for knowledge access purposes. The Archives team's partnership approach extends also to external partners such as academia and the archives teams of other international organizations, here mostly to test innovative approaches to managing the holdings. An example is the partnership with the Columbia University History Lab[10] to test the use of artificial intelligence on historical holdings and the annual exchange with the International Council on Archives' Section of International Organizations (ICA SIO) colleagues to discuss pressing technical issues such as long-term preservation of digital holdings and exchange hands-on experience on emerging IT solutions.

- *Nurturing relationships with the Information & Technology Solutions group (ITS):* Within the World Bank Group, the Archives team is administratively part of ITS. Endearingly calling themselves "the I in I&T," the team finds the "&" to be a meaningful recognition of the value of what information managers and knowledge services providers do and how important the partnership with their technology colleagues is. Being placed within ITS offers an organizational positioning right at a powerful nexus where technology, information governance, and current records meet the Archives. Technology develops at a fast pace, and this impacts current records creation and the archives of tomorrow. Not by coincidence has the World Bank Group early on made decisions that embedded functions allowing access to the Archives into the broader systems architecture. Such decisions make organizational sense since they contain costs, enhance information management, and create space for innovation. There is only one system that is independent from the organizational suite—the Archives' long-term digital preservation solution for born-digital records with enduring value. This system "stands alone" simply because the big tech firms have not yet focused on ensuring availability of electronic records in the long term. For the World Bank Group, on the contrary, it matters that its electronic records are available to researchers 500 years from now to tell the story of economic development!

The Indicators: "Flows" of Information and People

Understanding the impact of the Archives' work is a difficult endeavor—if only because insights based on the historical records often unfold far away and across the development community at large. One way to judge "success" is to take note of the attention the Archives team has received over the past years, well beyond the typical history buffs that might have visited. One such recognition of value is the growing number of requests from the World Bank Group's own senior management who frequently seeks out the Archives' expertise to curate historical information to prepare events, anniversaries, commemorations, and even communications and video messages to staff. These are hundreds of such engagements, such as the in-depth historical timeline of the Bank's engagement with Indonesia to mark the 2018 World Bank/International Monetary Fund Annual Meetings in Bali. Also external researchers and academia have become more recurrent users of the Archives, helping to prioritize the digitization of key holdings via an ongoing "dialog." One example of this is the digitization of the collection of records of President McNamara (1968–81), which has eliminated wait times and enabled true "self-service" by researchers, in addition to making the *corpus* available to data scientists to test artificial intelligence tools.

On a regular basis, the Archives team measures the flow of knowledge and information as well as people proxies for the desired impact.

- *Website hits and document downloads*: Figure 14.1 shows the indicators of usage tracked quarterly. The key performance indicators (KPIs) and reporting dashboards shared with management serve as indicators of transparency and accountability and as a proxy for the impact of knowledge sharing with the development community. All three are key dimensions for information managers and provide the input required for management decision-making and support.
- *Skilled staff and retention levels*: Another way to measure the value of the Archives is the professionalism, quality, and skills of the staff the team is able to attract and retain in a job market that is getting more and more sophisticated and competitive. Top-notch professionals have joined the team in recent years proving how appealing the approach to knowledge is that is now complementing the more traditional fiduciary role. Internally, the team's contribution has been recognized in 2018 by the creation of a full-fledged department, composed of archivists, records managers, librarians, and publishing professionals, led by the director and chief archivist, and reporting directly to the World Bank Group's chief information officer. This has further enhanced the opportunity to contribute to strategic decisions more broadly across the Information & Technology Solutions group.

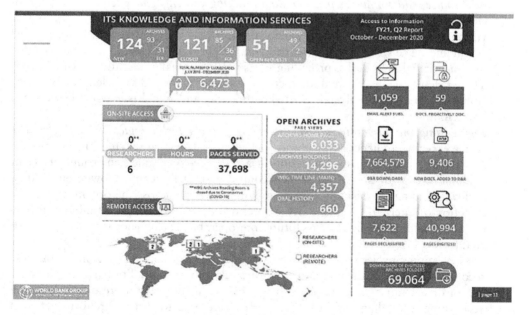

Figure 14.1 Key Performance Indicators Measuring the Performance of the Archives

Lessons Learned: What Worked

What worked: The road to effective knowledge sharing: In looking back on the Archives' journey towards unprecedented accessibility and a broad group of users across the World Bank Group and beyond, the team has identified a number of key steps that contributed to their success.

- *Socializing the Archives' value—Fighting institutional amnesia and access to information as a global public good*: The team's approach helped introduce a longer timeline into the thinking about knowledge management—a timeline that is critical for learning in the development field. The outreach to staff across the organization, through events and contributions to historical moments, made the Archives known. These days, staff reach out proactively to the Archives with ideas for oral histories and for knowledge and learning events, which show it has become known as the engaging knowledge memory function of the organization. Retired staff reach out to return records to the Archive as they now have a better appreciation of the "common good" value of their records. They see how the Archives team makes the records "alive" and accessible for knowledge-sharing purposes. In the past, it was not uncommon for retirees to take home boxes of the files they had worked on during their careers, preventing the organization from capturing and managing knowledge and information.
- *Professionalizing the Archives team*: Investing in and professionalizing the Archives team has been a multiyear effort, and individual elements of this effort run the whole gamut, from selection and onboarding through creating a conducive and empowering work environment to retention. A carefully devised selection process is part of this as much as the involvement of partner units in the selection, onboarding, and eventual performance appraisal of staff.
- *Turning the Archives' physical location into a welcoming space, open for staff and visitors to use, and conducive to both quiet thinking and engaging exchange of ideas*: In close collaboration with the Library, the Archives team took the unusual step to host vibrant retreats and to organize panels, debates, and social events, including award ceremonies. The strategy of *humanizing our physical and virtual space* also included offering virtual help desks, providing users with personal access to the whole team. These face-to-face-just-virtual interactions with a friendly and knowledgeable professional have been especially appreciated in times of pandemic-driven home-based work and remote visits.
- *Segmenting and targeting audiences and leveraging technologies accordingly*: The Archives team's audience segmentation helped prioritize what was most in demand for digitization, creating space for action in a resource-constrained environment. Tight collaboration with the World Bank Group's internal IT teams allowed embedding archival holdings in desktop applications used by staff across the organization. The adoption of international standards of archival description allowed building discovery layers and paved the way to future interoperability. Audience segmentation also enabled creative solutions for the resource-intensive archival description needed for the operational project records of the World Bank. Considering the volume of these records—counting in the hundreds of thousands of boxes—traditional archival methods of description would not have been possible within existing resources. Instead, an existing technology platform and portal were used to surface archival metadata related to these holdings in an online site where the public already visits,[11] providing

this particular audience with the necessary contextual data that would enable the archival records to be understood.

- *Nurturing an open dialogue with all partners*: The Archives team had early on and consistently invested in an ongoing dialogue with knowledge management colleagues within the World Bank Group and with counterparts in other multilateral organizations. This dialog and partnership has been foundational to the team's work and informed much of the work described in this chapter.

What Did Not Work Quite So Well: Challenges Along the Way

Many of the Archives' pathways were dotted with difficult challenges, and many of them were resolved. In retrospect, they all hold lessons—if only how to avoid them or resolve them faster or better. Most notably, progress did not come fast! It took 20 years to demonstrate the value of the Archives to the internal audiences busy with going about their day-to-day business. The support of senior management was crucial, and only twice during these 20 years did that support come in a sustained fashion; when the support came, having a clear strategy and objectives lined up helped in capitalizing on the moment. All along, though, the Archives team always had invested in robust and frequent communications to positively influence views and build understanding of the value of its work. Communications took multiple paths and included relentless outreach, knowledge sharing, and the nurturing of an open partnership-based approach to reach across the organization, including but not limited to powerful enablers in senior management. Attention was given to occasionally insert some fun into the communications tools—such as through an annual calendar that shares pictures of "the way we were" while reminding everyone of the relevance of taking a long-term view. On the other hand, when circumstances turned challenging, the team applied a "turtle strategy," lowering the intensity of outreach, keeping heads down and excellence high.

Among the important lessons learned, the Archives team counts the advice to always engage with clients, partners, and counterparts as early as possible to enable collective ownership of an idea and improve the odds of success. The team also learned that it is possible to achieve great things if one does not worry whether one is "given credit" or not—but instead feeds critical information where it makes the most impact. Appreciation always came, even if late, and with it the familiarity with and the reliance on the Archives' function.

Another lesson concerns the external affairs function—a crucial ally in a large international and multicultural organization. The communications teams have extensive knowledge and experience of political sensitivities that historical knowledge and information can also carry. Therefore, its needs and wants can make or break projects and initiatives. Including the external affairs teams' perspective in archival projects is a wise choice, and doing so from conception even wiser, even with projects that are deemed low-risk by Archives staff. It is useful to be inquisitive and ask the questions that lead to participation and discovery. This is an approach used when teaching—as part of staff onboarding—the history of the World Bank, and it has served the Archives team well beyond such occasions.

Where to Go From Here: Continuity and Innovation

The World Bank's Archives team is committed to always strive to do more and better, following its road map and building on the foundations laid over the last years. The democratization of the access to knowledge, information, and evidence base is an ongoing and large project, involving further digitization and work to enhance online accessibility of holdings. The production of user-friendly knowledge products such as timelines, virtual exhibits, videos, oral histories, and *Development Reflections* complements this work, including, in the future, some of the fruits of adopting artificial intelligence solutions. Knowledge based on evidence from the Archives must continue to circulate as a public good inside the World Bank Group and among the general public. In parallel, the collaboration with the information technology teams will continue, finding new ways to capture current born-digital records within systems that ensure the integrity, reliability, and authenticity of the information and that are seamless and easy for staff to use. Reliable and trustworthy information remains the foundation of knowledge and the antidote to institutional amnesia. The Archives team will also continue to invest in its ability to be a skilled and friendly counterpart to researchers interested in development history, to World Bank Group staff, and to senior management. Only through continued outreach and curation can institutional memory be translated into knowledge and the evidentiary base used to create a world free of poverty—on a livable planet.

Notes

1 The author recognizes the contribution of April Miller, Archives Manager, and the whole World Bank Group Archives team to this chapter, as well as to the progress made over the past 20 years of work in support of the Archives. Robert Malloy, Katie Bannon, Eliza McLeod, and Vlada Alekankina have also contributed to this chapter and continue to lead innovation in the Knowledge & Information Services Department. Much gratitude goes to them too and to Patricia Seabolt, invaluable advisor and editor. Warmest thanks go to our Vice President and World Bank Group Chief Information Officer Denis Robitaille, who has been such a strong and inspirational enabler of the Archives' mission and to Shaolin Yang, our Managing Director, for his unsurpassed support.
2 www.worldbank.org/archives
3 During the pandemic, the welcome area was switched off but the Archives continued to invest in delivery of virtual events and digital service to its users.
4 https://documents.worldbank.org/en/publication/documents-reports/documentdetail/410901468142480458/using-history-to-inform-development-policy-the-role-of-archives
5 https://documents.worldbank.org/en/publication/documents-reports/documentdetail/235751532573412101/world-bank-s-engagement-with-transport-in-cities-the-early-year
6 www.worldbank.org/en/archive/New-retrospective-on-President-McNamara-by-his-Personal-Assistants
7 the Presidential Speeches site at worldbank.org/en/archive/history/past-presidents-speeches#5
8 www.worldbank.org/en/events/2018/10/23/annual-bank-conference-on-development-economics-2019-multilateralism-past-present-and-future#1
9 https://documents.worldbank.org/en/publication/documents-reports and https://openknowledge.worldbank.org/
10 http://history-lab.org/
11 projects.worldbank.org/en/projects-operations/projects-home

Chapter 15

Evaluative Perspectives

Was It Really So?

Monika Weber-Fahr

Were Knowledge and Its Management Really the Driving Factor Behind Organizational Change?

The World Bank's Independent Evaluation Group (IEG) raised its voice loudly and clearly in 2014[1] and 2015[2] with its assessments of the organization's ability to learn and share knowledge. Despite the best efforts of many individuals, structures, incentives, and culture in the World Bank at the time were not conducive to learning. Neither staff nor clients seemed to be able to learn as much as they could from either *past* experiences or from the experiences and solutions of other actors in the international development community. As a result, opportunities for getting development solutions to World Bank clients faster and better were being lost, and innovation was limited. Strong recommendations were made to change and improve structures, incentives, and culture for learning and knowledge sharing. In doing so, the two evaluation reports built on each other, and some of their observations served as inspiration and input to specific elements of the change process. Four years later, when IEG evaluated the Bank's "knowledge flows" in 2019[3], both the setting and the evaluation's findings were entirely different: organizational change had just happened, and the report was avidly—and ultimately successfully—used to argue for a different setup by those unhappy with the horizontally oriented matrix structure established by the 2014 reorganization.

Incentives and organizational culture were at the heart of the 2014 evaluation. Both were considered in terms of the direct signals sent to individual staff as well as in terms of the broader organizational setup needed by staff to "do the right thing" and to "do things right" in sharing and using knowledge. The evaluators were facing a number of conceptual hurdles throughout the evaluations, one of them being that there is no clearly defined "benchmark" that would allow stating whether "enough" had been learned or whether excellence was or was not achieved in learning from an evolving context or past experience. Staff perceptions mattered as did the experience of competitor organizations. A competitive edge would no longer be driven by the availability of data and documents or by the functionalities of systems for retrieval and use of knowledge assets. Instead, the most relevant learning opportunities and moments for knowledge sharing rested on interpersonal exchanges. Where such exchanges were limited or nonexistent—because of gaps in opportunity, motivation, or capacity—progress would be limited, and structures, incentives, or event technology tools were not fully conducive to knowledge sharing.

The 2014 evaluation's conclusions make a strong case for a different organizational setting in which "knowledge flow and learning is mediated through interpersonal exchanges,"

DOI: 10.4324/9781003199083-24

Box 15.1 The Independent Evaluation Group: A Crown Jewel in the World Bank's Knowledge Treasure Chest

Often comparing itself to a *satellite circulating in the world's orbit*—"close enough to engage and reach but far enough to not be drawn into things"—the World Bank Group's Independent Evaluation Group (IEG) evaluates the organization's development effectiveness. IEG is looking to function both as an instrument of accountability and as an instrument of learning. It strategically and selectively assesses specific projects and programs, entire sectoral or regional portfolios, and corporate structures, functions, and ambitions, and it reviews and confirms (or disagrees with) the self-ratings that World Bank staff do of each and every World Bank project upon closure. A manifest itself to the World Bank Group's strong evaluative culture, IEG also designs and advises on the methodologies of multiple internal evaluative processes, also offering insights at broader questions, such as the Sustainable Development Goals agenda, and so on. Reporting not to the World Bank Group's President but to its Board, IEG prides itself on its independence and is led by a Director General whose contract does not allow for a further career with the World Bank Group to ensure avoiding any appearance of a potential or actual conflict of interest. With an annual budget of nearly US$40 million and 100+ full-time staff,[5] IEG is larger and more broadly operating than the evaluation teams of other international financial institutions, bilateral donors, or foundations, and it is recognized as a leader in its field. Based on its evaluation reports, IEG seeks to make its insights available to development professionals around the globe, leveraging webinars and life discussions with high-level or otherwise attention-drawing participants, as well as "bite-sized" formats such as blogs, video clips, podcasts, and other formats. In staffing its evaluations, IEG relies on a mix of its own staff and on individual consultants drawn from a pool of World Bank alumni and external subject-matter experts. In "taking its own medicine," IEG itself also operates along a *theory of change* and a *results framework*, both publicly available, and invites an external team of global evaluators to regularly offer assessments of IEG's strategy and budget and of IEG's performance in terms of the impact of its evaluations. IEG also operates a management action records database, accessible globally, for audiences to follow which of its recommendations are being taken up by the World Bank Group's management team and what progress has been made (or not) so far. IEG's public database includes some 10,000 evaluative documents, going back 20+ years, and others can be found in the World Bank Group's Archives. In their totality, IEG reports constitute the single largest treasure trove of independently documented insights about progress made by and lessons learned from World Bank projects. Nearly 50 years old, IEG's roots go back to the Operations Evaluation Department or OED that then World Bank president Robert MacNamara had set up in 1973, already then operating as a fiercely independent team.

---

suggesting that attention be paid to team dynamics and connection through social networks and communities as well as to approaches that reward learning, including through explicit and ongoing "senior management commitment, leadership, signaling and role modeling."[4] Interestingly, the 2014 report pointed to a tendency among World Bank staff to rely—for analytical information—primarily and often exclusively on their own analyses.

It also confirmed the relevance of conducive interpersonal settings as the most important source of learning and knowledge sharing, calling for more and more structured use of tools to facilitate the formation of networks and for mentoring. The evaluation arrived on the desks of the World Bank's management team and board right at the moment when the 2014 reorganization was about to be launched. It confirmed the Bank's own analysis—that enhancing "knowledge flow" would strengthen client services. Sensibly so for a report released right when an organizational change process was kicking off, it offered no specific recommendations as to the "what" for the new organizational setup: these decisions had already been taken based on months-long assessments and negotiations among various groups within the World Bank, resulting in the newly balanced matrix organization that favored horizontal connections over vertical ones (see Chapter 2). However, the evaluation did offer important insights into the "how" of making learning and knowledge sharing happen.

The 2015 evaluation arrived a year later—when the World Bank's staff and leadership found themselves at the deep end of the initial months of the organizational change process, right in the middle of shifting "boxes," reset reporting lines, and confusion about new roles and appointments. Unlike the first evaluation, this second one made very specific recommendations. Given the timing of the evaluation—it was undertaken throughout and in parallel to the first year of organizational change—the evaluators were able to directly "take the temperature" across the organization, offering a fresh and very practical set of perspectives. With its focus on staff's role in making "knowledge flow," tacit knowledge and informal learning were at the heart of the 2015 evaluation. One of the report's strongest statements—that "[World] Bank staff rely first and foremost on a process of informal learning, leading to a gradual accumulation of tacit knowledge"[6]—was the prelude to a careful review of multiple instruments deployed for encouraging staff to invest in knowledge-sharing and productive-learning behaviors. This included insights on how to consider bias and the limitations of focusing on one's own knowledge, be it tacit or explicit.

Just like for any other global organization, balancing global knowledge creation with local customization is a competency the World Bank should strive for. While the 2015 evaluation found some good evidence for getting the balance right, it also identified serious limitations. Interestingly, people-focused insights yet again dominated. The evaluation found that the stronger the World Bank's relation with a client—often driven by the number of years a staff had been assigned to a client and worked consistently on a particular project—the higher the quality of learning from results and the quality of a project.[7] At the same time, IEG's country studies showed how the World Bank can excel as a knowledge broker by facilitating exchanges between countries, a practice that was at the heart of GSURR's knowledge management approach, as highlighted in Chapters 6, 9, and 10.

In building on each other, the two evaluations formed a series and came to five main recommendations: to develop an updated strategy for learning and knowledge sharing with clearly identified accountabilities; to make optimal use of informal learning and tacit knowledge; to adjust incentives and promote learning and development outcomes; to balance global and local knowledge; and to promote adaptiveness. When reading the formal management responses included in the reports one can't help but assume that the recommendations might not have been met with a whole lot of love on the side of World Bank's management. The Independent Evaluation Group runs a *management action record* database, publicly available to anyone interested to see what actually happened after an evaluation put forward recommendations. In looking at the actions following the 2014 and the 2015 evaluations, one can see how implementation of individual actions evolved along a series of many smaller and seemingly somewhat disjointed elements. The most visible among the recommendations—to develop an updated strategy with clear accountabilities—resulted first in an *Update to the Bank's Board*, then translated into a *Learning Strategy*, separately from the subsequent *Knowledge Management Action Plan*.[8]

For knowledge management technical specialists, both evaluations are a read to be recommended. They are unusual reports in the world of knowledge management, both in terms of their thoroughness and conceptual lucidity, drawing on significant analytical work. They defined learning in projects as a combination of creating new knowledge (exploration) and the use of existing knowledge from different sources (exploitation). At their core was an extensive review of both existing literature and World Bank internal documents, adding to a broad consultation with the Bank's staff and leadership, several staff surveys, an in-depth review of 134 projects, and an analysis of documents generated by the World Bank's staff performance review mechanisms,[9] as well as on structured interviews and focus group work, on project document reviews, and on past evaluations and studies done by IEG.

Did What This Book Describes Really Happen?

When the IEG published its third report, "Knowledge Flow and Collaboration," in 2019, the evaluators were able to assess early progress made in terms of improved access to and use of knowledge in the aftermath of the World Bank's 2014 reorganization. Striking is its observation right at the beginning: only 2 of the 17 Global Practices across the World Bank had developed an approach that was both coherent and strategic in addressing "knowledge gaps by creating and organizing knowledge and then transferring it to support operations."[10] One of these two Global Practices was, indeed, the Social, Urban, Rural, and Resilience Global Practice (GSURR), whose experiences are featured throughout this book. The evaluators also noted major inconsistencies in terms of the knowledge management tools and instruments developed and deployed across all of the Global Practices. In stating that "leadership, incentives, budget arrangements and trust fund availability account for the World Bank's uneven knowledge performance,"[11] they confirm that the unevenness is neither fate nor externally driven but entirely up to managerial prowess and leadership. As a record of the evolving knowledge ecosystem, the evaluation is thorough and comprehensive, going well beyond the dimensions discussed in this book. The broad scope was a result of IEG's intent to dig deep into *all* aspects of the reorganization, including those that are more germane to the World Bank itself.

Importantly, the 2019 evaluation confirms the usefulness and relevance of many of the knowledge management approaches described in this book. In assessing the relative success (or failure) of efforts to enable global knowledge flows, the report points to mechanisms such as staff rotations across regions, online knowledge platforms, South-South Knowledge Exchanges (Chapter 9 and 10), knowledge hubs in country offices (Chapter 6), and knowledge communities like global solutions groups (Chapter 5). Most of these practices are featured in this book. The evaluation also mentions "innovative knowledge sharing practices" including those discussed here, help desks (Chapter 12), safe-space meetings (Chapter 9), and other platforms. Others included offering "flagship courses" for staff and clients alike, piloting "project handover checklists," and hosting monthly "knowledge cafes." Many of the examples used by the evaluators to illustrate particularly effective practices for encouraging knowledge flow draw on experiences made by GSURR—such as creating a dedicated land team, given that land-related interventions cut across all sectors, and creating a dedicated global solutions group on resilience and disaster risk management, able to foster several smaller knowledge communities.

Collaboration is the second major theme for the 2019 evaluation—not by chance, of course, but rather because enhancing collaboration had been one of the main objectives of the 2014 reorganization. Matrix systems are meant to stimulate collaboration but often fail to do so when those managing the "nodes" of the matrix do not mitigate the territorial or isolationist tendencies that teams in large organizations tend to develop. As it were, staff surveys undertaken by IEG found that while silo behavior across regions had significantly decreased through the reorganization, the silos between sectors had increased. In short: knowledge traveled well from one region to another but poorly between different topics. There was no debating: collaboration across sectors had become tougher. Indeed, the evaluation found the organizational structure to be at fault in inhibiting collaboration, and it pointed to incentives set by processes and structures leading to fragmentation, internal competition, and turf behaviors. It was very simple: Global Practice departments were rewarded for accumulating own-managed projects; this gave them recognition, budget certainty, and access to clients for further business development, plus more staff with a guaranteed multiyear funding.

Despite these odds, some of the Global Practices, notably those with a coherent and strategic approach, were highlighted by the evaluators for having found ways to break silos and to stimulate collaboration. To underpin its findings with data, IEG suggested an innovative metric for collaboration, considering the absolute number (or share) of collaborative projects led or supported by a particular group. GSURR emerged as a "prolific leader and contributor to joint lending projects" (see Figure 15.1; World Bank 2019), partially based on its size but also driven by the incentives and modalities set for collaborative practices within the group.

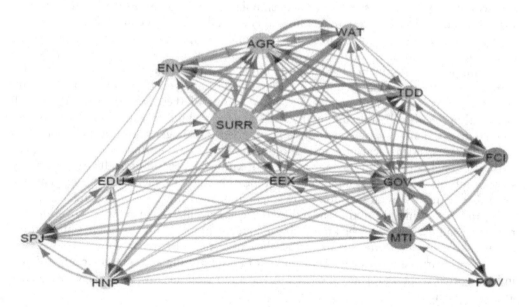

Figure 15.1 Collaboration Across Practice Groups in the World Bank's Lending Portfolio

Source: Based on a social network analysis approach (from World Bank (2019), p 38).

Evaluative Perspectives on the Role of Leadership and the Way Forward

One of the most note-worthy findings of the 2019 evaluation was that each global practice managed knowledge differently. This finding pointed to the lack of a central governance structure for knowledge and knowledge management at the World Bank, as described in Chapter 1. But how could this have happened? Or rather: how would the organization's leadership have let this happen? If knowledge had been any other costly resource needed for production—such as land, energy, cash—could one imagine any organization allowing its business units *at the same location* to all deploy different approaches for managing this resource? And to do so with practically no metrics to manage towards effectiveness and efficiency? Perhaps we are still in a space in the evolution of managerial practices in which knowledge is not uniformly appreciated as an element of performance and competitiveness that would need to be managed? After all, it was only in the 1990s that management literature picked up on the "knowledge topic"; knowledge management is not a compulsory course for MBA students and, even as an elective, is not as frequently found as finance, controlling, human resource management, or logistics. Whatever the reason, the "free for all" approach that IEG observed during the years following the 2014 reorganization gave forward-thinking units such as GSURR the freedom to introduce a lot of new and good ways to address the challenge of making knowledge flow and enhancing collaboration. Many of those were noted explicitly in the 2019 evaluation and are described in more detail in this book; approaches used for identifying knowledge gaps; creating inquiry typologies and log information; stimulating informal, bottom-up learning; promoting innovation; and fostering integration, among others.

In the end, an organizational model originally designed to stimulate better client services—by accelerating the speed and broadening the depth at which World Bank clients would be able to access knowledge accumulated by the organization and by creating space for innovation and collaboration—failed. It failed not in creating better access to global knowledge—but it failed in stimulating multidisciplinary collaboration across the organization, a critical element for World Bank clients who look to address today's ever more complex development challenges. It failed *despite* the highly effective knowledge management and learning techniques designed and deployed by many staff and management teams across the organization. Quite a few of these successful practices still exist within the World Bank, and many have transitioned into organizational habits, not consistently perhaps but wherever there is supportive management attention. The 2019 evaluation was crystal clear in pointing to the change effort's shortcomings: *inconsistency* in the approaches to and in the management of knowledge, counterproductive incentives set through the budgeting systems, unclear reporting lines for client-facing engagements, inconsistent quality assurance for knowledge embedded in advisory and financing services, and discontinuities in the leadership of the change management efforts overall. The relevance and usefulness of the knowledge management tools and approaches highlighted in this book, however, are not in doubt; they were indeed confirmed by the successive evaluations featured previously. They make for an interesting and often helpful read also in many other respects for anyone keen to learn more about how to manage knowledge and learn well.

Notes

1 World Bank. 2014. *Learning and Results in World Bank Operations: How the Bank Learns; Evaluation 1. Independent Evaluation Group*. Washington, DC: World Bank.
2 World Bank. 2015. *Learning and Results in World Bank Operations: Toward a New Learning Strategy. Evaluation 2. Independent Evaluation Group*. Washington, DC: World Bank.
3 World Bank. 2019. *Knowledge Flow and Collaboration under the World Bank's New Operating Model. Independent Evaluation Group*. Washington, DC: World Bank.
4 World Bank. 2014. *Learning and Results in World Bank Operations: How the Bank Learns; Evaluation 1. Independent Evaluation Group*. Washington, DC: World Bank.
5 Numbers are drawn from World Bank. 2021. *FY2022 Workprogram and Budget. Independent Evaluation Group*. Washington, DC: World Bank. https://ieg.worldbankgroup.org/sites/default/files/Data/reports/iegworkprogramfy22-24.pdf
6 World Bank. 2015. *Learning and Results in World Bank Operations: Toward a New Learning Strategy. Evaluation 2. Independent Evaluation Group*. Washington, DC: World Bank.
7 The notion that the length of a staff's assignment with a particular project—or rather: the less often staff managing a project were exchanged—directly and positively affects project outcomes, has been investigated previously in Denizer, Cevdet & Kaufmann, Daniel & Kraay, Aart, 2013. "Good countries or good projects? Macro and micro correlates of World Bank project performance," *Journal of Development Economics*, Elsevier, vol. 105(C), pages 288–302. This kind of research confirms the relevance of tacit knowledge for the quality of client services and the difficulties encountered by World Bank staff to effectively transfer their tacit knowledge to their successors when team compositions change.
8 IEG formally tracked progress on the 2015 report's recommendations only twice, in 2016 and 2017. The final IEG statement in regard to the strategy notes that the Bank has launched a series of knowledge and learning initiatives, including the Operational Core Curriculum. These important steps now need consolidating into a strategy that takes into account the important role of informal learning and tacit knowledge. The recent reorganization of the World Bank has not created the governance structure needed to ensure that accountability for incorporating knowledge and learning into operations is clearly delineated. https://ieg.worldbankgroup.org/mar/learning-and-results-world-bank-operations-toward-new-learning-strategy
9 The World Bank's performance review process is built around a document called Operational Performance Evaluation (OPE) and around associated guidelines and processes for how managers and staff should use the document to understand, assess, and rate performance.
10 Knowledge Flow and Collaboration (2017), p. xiv
11 World Bank. 2019. *Knowledge Flow and Collaboration under the World Bank's New Operating Model. Independent Evaluation Group*. Washington, DC: World Bank.

Chapter 16

Leadership Perspectives

Knowledge Management for Change, Innovation, and Competitiveness

Ede Ijjasz-Vasquez

The Excitement and Initial Challenges of a New World Bank Structure

In 2014, the creation of the new Global Practices brought a sense of excitement to the organization. Many of us were convinced that the core comparative advantage of the World Bank was its globality and the unique combination of services it provides to clients. While other multilateral banks provide similar financial and advisory services. Still, only the World Bank covers all developing countries and emerging economies. Other organizations—like the United Nations agencies—have the same global coverage, but they do not have the range of services—financial and advisory—that the World Bank offers.

The change was massive: it moved reporting lines, staff, and leadership from a regionally focused structure to one that brought—in its design—a balance between country-based services, on the one hand, and global technical units, on the other, enabling the latter to connect the world and bring the most relevant experiences to a particular country. The possibilities looked quite exciting for us in the Global Practices.

As it emerged from the reorganization, our Global Practice combined four diverse technical teams: urban development, disaster risk management, social development, and territorial/rural development. And unlike other practices with a single-sector focus (transport, energy, or health), our Global Practice was an amalgamation of different technical disciplines. In the beginning, we did not even have a name. We were known by our number in the nomenclature: Global Practice 13. Not much of an identity to begin with.

The organizational change process brought its own difficulties, like all organizational changes do. We had four main challenges in our Global Practice:

- *Trust:* Our four diverse technical communities did not have much experience working together. While we were all going through a major organizational change, there was little trust and lots of suspicion across the different groups.
- *Viability:* Our Global Practice was over-staffed. Even though the global challenges of urbanization, climate change, social inclusion, and war and conflict were central development challenges in basically every World Bank client country, our business lines and products were not seen as innovative by clients. Our future business prospects were not too strong. Our clients did not understand our services, given the diversity of topics we covered. Even within our own organization, many did not believe our Global Practice was viable.
- *Tools:* The reorganization had placed global knowledge flows at the center of the change process. However, many corporate knowledge management initiatives had failed in the

DOI: 10.4324/9781003199083-25

past or had lost momentum after a few years. As a result, there was quite a bit of skepticism about knowledge management tools and little, if any, corporate-level guidance on how to go about encouraging and sustaining high-quality knowledge flows.

- *Technical leadership:* Like many other organizations with a robust technical cadre providing services based on deep expertise and knowledge, there was an imbalance between the managerial track and the technical leadership track. The only way to move up in the organizational hierarchy was to shift from the technical stream to the managerial stream. This led to a continuous loss of technical leadership into the management cadre. We also had insufficient depth and diversity in our Global Practice leadership bench initially.

A Critical Choice: Knowledge and Its Management to Be Our Core Comparative Advantage

In organizations like the World Bank, knowledge and the people who hold it are core assets. In the case of our Global Practice, we knew that our staff were not only our core assets but the keys to our survival as a Practice. However, knowledge curation and sharing among our team members were not enough. As our knowledge was not seen as innovative enough or at the frontier of development challenges, we knew that simply creating mechanisms to share this existing knowledge would not be sufficient.

In response, our strategy was to combine knowledge with innovation, co-create solutions with clients, and undertake informed horizon scanning exercises to be ahead of the curve on the next generation of development challenges.

We also knew that our core comparative advantage was not knowledge in the abstract or knowledge in documents or databases. Our comparative advantage was the tacit knowledge of our team members and the written compilation and analysis of lessons learned from decades of development experience. The depth of expertise in each of the four technical disciplines in our Global Practice was a core advantage. But it was not enough.

Our differentiator—vis-à-vis competing organizations offering solutions to client countries' development challenges—was our ability to combine technical disciplines and develop insights for new solutions. We had the opportunity to bring anthropologists and urban specialists together and have them collaborate to understand the best global experiences on how to change the behavior of communities and households for a more sustainable quality of city life. We could bring together conflict specialists and infrastructure reconstruction experts to identify the most effective way to build peace by recovering government services that would reach all groups in society. Our specialists could bring nature-based solutions and innovative urban designs to reduce the risk of flooding in low-income communities. The possibilities for new business lines were immense.

We identified three essential conditions to achieve this potential. First, a strong knowledge ecosystem that would help team members across the world and from different technical disciplines connect, learn from each other, and co-create with clients new solutions to their challenges. Second, we needed to break the silos across the World Bank's internal organizational boundaries that separated staff working on different technical disciplines or in different regions. Humanity's problems—from unplanned urbanization to the exclusion of persons with disabilities—have more commonalities across countries than differences. Third, we needed to leverage the globality of the World Bank. Our ability to present to a client a menu of solutions—including failed attempts—from other countries worldwide was a unique advantage.

The initial common reaction to challenges regarding the globality of knowledge and siloed behaviors is to believe that the solutions reside in a technology-driven knowledge platform. Under this scenario, all it takes is for every staff member to write down their tacit knowledge relevant to a particular topic. Then an artificial intelligence or machine learning algorithm will help recombine that knowledge to find the best solution to common problems faced by clients worldwide. Internet search algorithms and Wikipedia-style repositories of information can give the illusion that most knowledge challenges can be solved with an app. Nothing could be further from the truth. Knowledge is created by people and resides in their minds. A knowledge ecosystem must be built around people and, most importantly, for people—in ways that entice them to use it.

A People-Centered Approach: Building an Action-Oriented Knowledge Ecosystem

We did not have time to build a new knowledge platform or technology system. Our leadership team had the intuition that knowledge flows, combination, and repurposing can only be done by people working together. We decided to build a knowledge ecosystem that would be designed to serve. It would help to support people's connections, offer the spaces—virtual or real—to create new knowledge exchanges, and set the incentives to drive the culture change that would make it all happen. We made our knowledge ecosystem work with and for our communities of practice (see Chapter 5).

The communities of practice had five key features. First, the leadership team decided to follow a bottom-up process rather than choosing the topics and community leaders. The general rules of the game given by the leadership team were simple: a preference for communities combining different disciplines, a focus on developing new solutions to real and urgent challenges faced by our clients, and a commitment to make the community work for our survival and growth. In many different forms, we also emphasized that communities of practice were not going to be a fringe activity in our Practice. Everybody was expected to join and actively participate in at least one community of practice, and the communities were expected to contribute to the core business of the Practice.

In the leadership team, we were convinced that innovation emerges from a diversity of thinking and experiences. Therefore, the most critical feature of the communities of practice was that they were supposed to break silos—across regions, across technical disciplines, across the Global South and the world. For that reason, we called them "knowledge silo breakers." The acronym—KSBs—had a nice ring to it and caught the teams' imagination.

The concept and experience with communities of practice were not new to the World Bank. What was new was the urgency, purpose, and support our leadership team gave them. This emphasis was somewhat different from the corporate approach to knowledge management at the time. Some of the corporate solutions developed involved new information technology platforms for collaboration, an organized structure around "core development challenges," a solutions catalog, and top-down communities called global solutions groups. These global solutions groups were led by Global Leads, senior staff selected for and placed into a global technical leadership role for a particular topic or business line. For example, we had Global Leads covering our major business lines in urban development and resilience, social development, and land within our Global Practice. The global solutions groups were expected to become the "knowledge holders" for a particular business line or development challenge. They were to mobilize existing expertise across the organization to respond to client requests. Our Global Practice's global knowledge ecosystem worked with, and leveraged, this corporate structure. However, we wanted to be more nimble, fast, and focused. We had no time to lose. We developed or modified knowledge tools adapted to our needs.

The global knowledge ecosystem tools—The GSURR global knowledge ecosystem and its many tools have been described in previous chapters. As a leadership team, we used three principles to base our decisions regarding the setup and operation of the ecosystem:

- *Offer knowledge management as a core service*: Most other Global Practices had, on average, one knowledge management specialist supporting groups of 200 people or more. As our Practice nurtured the newly formed communities of practice, the demand for specialized knowledge management skills was rising. We decided to create a central team to support all of these communities. This was a change from the initial arrangement whereby each community was left to find part-time support. The central unit allowed us to increase quality, improve efficiency, and strengthen learning across communities.
- *Move from knowledge sharing to co-creation with clients:* Knowledge exchange visits between clients were common in the World Bank. We decided first to enhance the quality and efficiency of these exchanges by using a structured methodology and by building staff capacity for good knowledge exchange design (see Chapter 9). But we wanted to go further. We needed to move from single retail exchanges to a whole-sale, higher capacity, higher efficiency approach. Also, the modality of unidirectional knowledge transfer (World Bank to clients, North to South) was increasingly seen as outmoded. Instead, the leadership team decided that we needed to move towards brokering knowledge sharing between clients, co-creation of solutions, and multifo-cal learning. The transformation of the Tokyo Development Learning Center was a strategic choice in that direction. Chapter 6 tells the story and results.
- *Bring the knowledge ecosystem tools to clients:* The knowledge ecosystem tools also had intrinsic value to our clients. Some wanted to develop similar ecosystems to create, curate, and share their own knowledge (Chapter 10). Others wanted to use these tools to create new networks and partnerships. Technical assistance and advice to clients on knowledge management became an unexpected business line.

The best tools, alone, are not enough to effect change. While building the knowledge eco-system, we identified the critical cultural changes needed to make the system work.

Changing the culture—As a leadership team, we had to take accountability for investing in the shift in culture necessary to make our strategies work. We did so by defining the journey ahead, communicating progress regularly, and—most importantly—leading by example. The new culture we were looking to build evolved around four crucial dimensions.

First, silos are there to be broken. We had four separate teams with very different cultures. We had teams with a regional tradition from the old structure. The intention was not to destroy the silos but to break them. We used the image of an open office to communicate the cultural change ahead. In an open office with lower walls, each team member works on a particular desk and knows it deeply and well. At the same time, with a simple movement of the eyes, team members can connect to everybody else across the floor.

We did not want individual team members' deep technical specialty and expertise to disappear nor did we want our team members' profound understanding of and focus on specific countries to be lost. Instead, we wanted everybody to develop an understanding of the fact that no one person has all the answers. The world is small, and many others are working on similar challenges simultaneously. Even though these pearls of wisdom may seem obvious, they were not displayed in people's behaviors when our Global Practice started out. Changing the inward-looking "stay-in-my-bubble" culture required the entire leadership to constantly model what it meant to laterally connect and collaborate.

Next, a single type of service is not enough. In an organization that measures and reports on its success mainly on the volume of financial services provided, being very explicit about the relevance of nonfinancial services took a big step. When we started out as the GSURR leadership team, we saw the comparative advantage of our services as not being limited to the financial resources—loans and grants—provided to countries. Instead, knowledge—and specifically global knowledge when applied to a country's specific challenge—was a distinct advantage. The change was to move from a lending culture to one where teams provided a bundle of knowledge and lending services to clients. Some of these included global lessons of experience—successes and failures— that our clients could use to select their preferred combination of solutions. It could also include platforms to co-create solutions through exchanges and workshops with other practitioners. Or it could be facilitating their connection to peers worldwide.

However, knowledge sharing was not enough. New knowledge is needed at the core of an innovative bundle of services. We identified a critical shift in culture: knowledge creation is as important as loan closure. The culture changed through two mechanisms we introduced. First, intense monitoring of delivery dates and progress made with knowledge service engagements with the same attention we paid to monitor financial services and loan closures. Second, a new performance indicator for our managers with specific quantitative targets for knowledge creation by their teams. Financial services and knowledge creation were seen to be on the same footing.

Third, the technical stream is as important as the managerial stream. There is a common tension between technical leadership and management in knowledge-based organizations—for example, engineering or information technology firms. Moving technical gurus into executive jobs can lead to losses of skills and mismatched preferences. In GSURR, we sought to promote a culture change that encouraged and celebrated both career tracks—technical and managerial. In our view, we needed both excellent technical leaders and excellent managers. So, we set out to promote an appreciation of both roles. The culture change came about through practical steps and decisions that signaled the direction of change.

For example, the Global Leads—the technical leaders in charge of the global solutions groups or formal communities of practice—became part of the GSURR leadership team. We had technical and managerial leaders at the table for the first time.

While we did encourage rotations between managers and global technical leads, we decided not to let managers have a dual role as technical leaders. This would have diluted the two tracks. Some managers decided they missed the technical leadership and wanted to refresh their skills. The GSURR team at-large saw the rotations as a positive signal that both tracks were important.

The communities of practice also gave us a unique opportunity to identify emerging leaders and help with succession planning. Leaders of these communities developed essential skills for future managerial positions, including working across boundaries, influencing without authority, creating a new business line, and defining a vision for a group.

Finally, the new culture needed a strong emphasis on upskilling and learning. A core message was that our business—present and future—required team members with the latest technical knowledge. Continuous learning was everybody's responsibility. The global solutions groups and the Global Leads were explicitly tasked with identifying their members' core technical skills and training needs (see Chapter 5). Many of the knowledge ecosystem tools served as learning opportunities. The leadership team began to monitor the time spent by each team member on learning and the core technical courses they took to upgrade their skills.

Fourth, the knowledge management and communications team were integral to the success of the Global Practice. Although every team member was expected to be a knowledge citizen and a communicator, we strengthened the standing, size, and role of the knowledge management and the communications and outreach teams. They were not seen as mere backroom support functions. The Practice's success and the objectives we set out to achieve required deep knowledge and communications expertise. The leaders of these teams joined the extended leadership team of the Global Practice. They were not silent voices in the group but had specific roles. They were responsible for pushing us to new frontiers and new services to our clients, weighing in both during upstream strategy discussions and downstream implementation.

Leadership's Role in Developing the Tools and Achieving Results

When describing the evolution of the GSURR knowledge ecosystem, we always get questions about the leadership team's role in this process. The previous section of this chapter discussed the strategic choices and the culture changes we implemented. There were four other areas where the leadership team's role was, in retrospect, quite important.

Proactive engagement of the leadership team in the development of communities of practice—Although the establishment of new communities of practice was a bottom-up voluntary process, the leadership team had an important role in many other dimensions. First, it defined the vision and objectives for these communities. Second, the leadership team nurtured the creation and growth of these groups. Chapter 5 discusses the *gardening* approach we used. It wasn't an approach that let a thousand flowers bloom unattended. Instead, it was akin to a proactive gardener that looks for new plants, cares for them, allows them to grow, and prunes them periodically to shape the garden while valuing a diverse landscape of flowers and plants. This approach required a disciplined process using an Impact Framework developed by the GSURR Knowledge Team (Chapter 5).

It may seem contradictory to have a disciplined approach to nurturing vibrant, diverse, and informal communities of practice. Balance is the key word. Too much control and you stifle creativity through bureaucratic rules. Too little control and many communities may get lost in their journey and not achieve their objectives. The communities of practice leaders appreciated the opportunity to present their progress and results to the GSURR leadership team. The feedback and attention from the leadership team gave them the visibility and recognition that encouraged them to continue volunteering their time.

Incentives—A lot of the work done by members and leaders of communities of practice is intangible and difficult to incentivize with the regular mechanisms we had at our disposal. We focused a lot on visibility and recognition. The GSURR Knowledge Fairs and town halls with senior management of the organization (president, CEO, and vice presidents) were unique opportunities for community leaders and members to showcase their work. Years later, the team members who made presentations at these events would still remember them as highlights of their work.

For recognition, we used two mechanisms. First, we recorded the significant achievements of the communities of practice in the annual performance evaluations of their leaders. The same held true for staff members who went beyond expectations in using their communities to create new business lines or deliver impactful knowledge and co-creation events with clients. Second, we encouraged communities to nominate their work for corporate awards, including the President's Innovation Awards. The creativity and innovation of most communities of practice meant that our teams received about one-quarter of all such prizes, even though we were only one out of thirteen Global Practices.

Budget allocation—As communities of practice and knowledge ecosystems, in general, tend to be *intangible* activities without a paper product or a loan delivery, it is difficult for organizations to plan and provide budgets. Even when corporate budgets allocated resources for knowledge activities, they were generally insufficient for our ambition. We used a three-pronged approach. First, to connect and aggregate diverse initiatives to leverage resources. For example, partnerships with external organizations and donor agencies provided invaluable resources. The learning budget was leveraged to support the upskilling activities led by communities. The Tokyo Development Learning Center budget was leveraged to finance activities designed by communities.

The leadership team had an important balance to achieve in budget allocation. Too much budget would reduce community leaders' incentives and entrepreneurial spirit to mobilize other resources. Too little funding and the community members would not see the initiative as serious. This balancing act translated into a limitation on the number of communities of practice that could be supported. A smaller number of communities would mean more budget for each of them. However, a larger number would lead to a higher probability of new innovations and business lines. To some extent, the budget allocation to communities of practice had to follow a venture capital approach.

Bureaucracy, turfs, and client engagement—The leadership team had a unique role in helping communities of practice in this issue. First, innovators and intrapreneurs sometimes need to find ways to achieve their objectives by working through the maze of rules that large organizations usually have. Sometimes, the support of leadership team members to find solutions with the fiduciary or legal teams was indispensable.

Second, building coalitions with other Global Practices or organizations based on proposals from communities of practice needed the leadership team's support. Same for promoting the innovations and new approaches developed by these communities. The symbiotic relationship between communities of practice and the leadership team required a good understanding of the communities' work programs and their new business lines and services for effective support.

We found that as helpful as these actions were, team members would also observe the behaviors of the Global Practice leadership very carefully to understand how serious we were about the change process and the new culture.

Leadership Behaviors to Change the Culture and Keep the Knowledge Ecosystem Active

During change processes, the behaviors of leaders are examined by teams with incredible attention. Everybody tries to read the signals from the top. Leading change processes requires careful attention to the new behaviors on the part of leaders. In our case, the change towards a people-centric knowledge ecosystem at the core of our business required several new behaviors.

Walk the talk and talk the walk on knowledge management—the leadership team engaged in numerous knowledge-sharing activities—from knowledge fairs to the GSURR Forum or the weeklong technical deep dives at the Tokyo Development Learning Center. When teams saw us actively engaged in these events, our participation sent two signals. First, knowledge management activities are essential enough for group leaders to invest their time. Second, everybody needs to learn—nobody has all the knowledge.

The campaign "We Are All Communicators" to build the external outreach of our Global Practice's knowledge assets required everybody to get out of their comfort zone. The leadership team had to take training courses on media engagement, public speaking, and blog writing. This was communicated to the entire team to show we were leading by example. Afterward, we reported on our communications—from participation in video blogs to interviews with national and international media. Teams felt more comfortable joining the communicators' cohort once they saw the new behaviors of the leadership team.

Overcommunicate for change—We launched a series of campaigns with simple messages to drive behavior change. For example:

- Knowledge is our business.
- We are all communicators.
- Everybody should join at least one community of practice.
- Knowledge is not enough—we are all about collaboration.
- We don't want collaboration collaboration's sake—we want real change.
- Communities of practice are not only about knowledge sharing, but they are also our future business.
- We are not in the business of competition but of cooperation.
- Knowledge is always about people, not information technology systems.
- Tacit knowledge is as crucial as explicit knowledge codified in reports.

- Innovation is not only about development solutions, but it is also about new ways of delivering services.
- Finance, infrastructure, and institutions are essential, but remember, it's all about people.

These campaigns, spread over five years, reinforced the change process in its different dimensions. Regular reports to all staff on progress with the change process, important milestones, and reasons to celebrate were part of our "over-communication" approach.

We also took the time to select names and icons that reinforced the change process. For example, communities of practice was a name commonly used in the World Bank. Thematic groups or beams were terms also used. We wanted to communicate the change needed in connections and collaborations, so the name we selected for the GSURR communities was knowledge silo breakers. The acronym KSB had a nice ring to it and stuck. Other Global Practices began to recognize the GSURR communities of practice as a different type with specific characteristics. The new name reinforced the change.

The new name for our Global Practice emerged out of a broad participatory process that involved everybody in the team. The four technical teams needed new spaces to build trust and see themselves represented in the Practice name. The initial name of Global Practice 13 reminded everybody that we were an amalgamation of different teams without a history of working together. The name that emerged from the participatory process included every-body—the social, urban, rural, and resilience teams. The acronym GSURR gave a common identity to the group. But it was not enough.

We also needed a short description of what the group was all about. Again, a participa-tory process developed our *motto:* Our Global Practice's work was on building sustainable *communities*. By sustainable, we meant green, resilient, inclusive, and productive communi-ties. By communities, we meant rural communities, small towns, cities, regions, and nations. The leadership team gave this motto life by using it to review proposals, new projects and knowledge assets, and for the narrative used in our offers to clients.

Recognize your failures and share them—If the new culture requires experimentation and innovation, then it also needs failure. Creating a culture that embraces failure and learns from it is difficult. Teams will not believe leaders if they only *talk* about failure. Messages and speeches are not enough. Unless teams see leaders failing, learning from those fail-ures, and moving fast to incorporate lessons, then teams will wait on the sidelines. In the GSURR leadership team, we experimented and failed sometimes. We shared the failures, lessons, and new experiments. We also shared our thinking and learning process. Only then, teams began to slowly believe in the new culture. But it was not easy.

Throughout this book, we have shared some of our failures. For example, we wanted everybody to feel the need to learn all the time. We diagnosed that only a few team members were reading enough about the latest research or good practices in their technical areas of expertise. To help change the culture, we established "Reading Fridays." Every Friday at lunchtime, we reserved some of the largest conference rooms in the World Bank and invited team members to come there and read. Every Friday. Half an hour. Members of the leader-ship team joined. The experiment started well with more than 100 staff joining. The numbers slowly went down, and after a few weeks, less than 20 people showed up. We analyzed the many reasons for failure, shared them, and modified the approach to have communities become agents of reading and learning with a more targeted audience and reading lists. This failure showed the Global Practice that even leaders fail and learn.

One of the most significant failures we could not find a solution to despite multiple attempts over the years was the documentation of failures (see Chapter 12). We found it extremely difficult to document failures, even if temporary, in a manner that was productive and did not cause resentment among the World Bank staff and clients involved.

Learn and adjust—The global knowledge ecosystem evolved over the years through a disciplined process of analysis, cost-effectiveness considerations, and systematic review of results. The culture change we wanted was one of continuous inquiry, self-assessment, and improvement. There were few models of large-scale global knowledge ecosystems from which to learn, so we had to experiment and adjust when needed. For example, after two years, and as described in Chapter 5, we decided to rationalize the formal and informal communities of practice (the *global solutions groups* and the *knowledge silo breakers*). We put groups of informal communities under the umbrella of larger formal ones. We adjusted the knowledge ecosystem in line with the small, corporate-led reorganizations that took place every 18–24 months. The leadership behavior was of continuous improvement. We created an environment of open dialogue for anybody to develop practical suggestions and a disciplined analysis of these new ideas. The annual review based on a self-assessment of communities of practice was designed to deepen that culture.

Top-down rarely works in knowledge—the final behavior we want to highlight in this chapter is humility. Knowledge is democratic. There is no monopoly of knowledge in an organization's headquarters. The best knowledge emerges from diversity and inclusion. Our leadership team tried to live by these principles in an attempt to trickle down this change of culture.

Knowledge and its management can be the source of comparative advantage of organizations. It can be at the core of efficiency, innovation, and growth. It can motivate a culture change for more inclusive, diverse, and creative teams. This can only happen if leaders embrace knowledge and its management as a central tool of their strategic toolkit. And if leaders lead by example, changing their own behavior to become knowledge citizens and communicators. This book tells our story of change. We believe it can work for you. We wish you luck in your journey.

Index

Printed in the United States
by Baker & Taylor Publisher Services